ADDITIONAL PRAISE FOR *The Peer Effect*

"With an engaging mix of biography and research expertise, Ali and Chin present strong arguments for the connections between inequality, communities, and individual well-being. Peers matter. This is a really witty and compelling read!"
—Prudence L. Carter, author of *Stubborn Roots: Race, Culture, and Inequality in U.S. and South African Schools*

"Ali and Chin write with passion about the influence of peers in a variety of domains—education, policing, and the workplace. They bring a wide range of sociological insights and a good dose of humor into this wide-ranging book."
—Natasha Warikoo, author of *Race at the Top: Asian Americans and Whites in Pursuit of the American Dream in Suburban Schools*

"*The Peer Effect* is a refreshingly honest evaluation of political and family dynamics that have driven personal and systemic educational decisions in NYC and around the country. This is a must-read for anyone interested in better understanding the educational landscape."
—Akil Bello, *Senior Director of Advocacy and Advancement at FairTest*

"There's a certain allure to agency—to the idea that we make our own destinies or, in the case of parents and educators, that we can dictate how our kids' lives will turn out. The reality, however, as *The Peer Effect*, with its propulsive style and its engaging blend of personal anecdotes and research-based evidence makes clear, is that our agency is both created and constrained by the groups to which we belong."
—Jessica McCrory Calarco, author of *Negotiating Opportunities: How the Middle Class Secures Advantages in School*

"Whether you're an educator, policymaker, or organizational leader, this book will challenge you to account for the social dynamics that shape our lives and transform the places where we learn and work."
—Sam M. Intrator, coauthor of *The Quest for Mastery: Positive Youth Development Through Out-of-School Programs*

THE PEER EFFECT

The Peer Effect

*How Your Peers Shape
Who You Are and
Who You Will Become*

Syed Ali and Margaret M. Chin

NEW YORK UNIVERSITY PRESS

New York

NEW YORK UNIVERSITY PRESS
New York
www.nyupress.org

Library of Congress Cataloging-in-Publication Data
Names: Ali, Syed, 1968–   author. | Chin, Margaret May, 1962–   author.
Title: The peer effect : how your peers shape who you are and who you will become /
Syed Ali and Margaret M. Chin.
Description: New York : New York University Press, [2023] |
Includes bibliographical references and index.
Identifiers: LCCN 2023003744 | ISBN 9781479805044 (hardback ; alk. paper) |
ISBN 9781479805051 (ebook) | ISBN 9781479805068 (ebook other)
Subjects: LCSH: Peer pressure. | Youth development. | Organizational behavior.
Classification: LCC HQ784.P43 A45 2024 | DDC 303.3/27—dc23/eng/20230130
LC record available at https://lccn.loc.gov/2023003744

This book is printed on acid-free paper, and its binding materials are chosen for strength and durability. We strive to use environmentally responsible suppliers and materials to the greatest extent possible in publishing our books.

Manufactured in the United States of America

10 9 8 7 6 5 4 3 2 1

Also available as an ebook

To our Stuyvesant High School peers

CONTENTS

When I was in graduate school, I (Syed) read a book on immigrant assimilation by two of the foremost scholars in the field. They were interested in the educational outcomes of the kids of immigrants. They found that whether the kids did better or worse in school, and then later in life, was a function of factors like parents' education, income, immigration status, and race/ethnic group. Even a study of whether kids of immigrants joined gangs put the onus on parents and the ethnic community.

I was kind of annoyed by this. Top scholars in the field were arguing that kids of immigrants had things happen to them, but they were not seen as independently making choices that affected their outcomes. But I was a child of Indian Muslim immigrants, and I did things independently of my immigrant parents' wishes. I was not an automaton! I was an active agent in charge of my own life, making my own choices. Like the choice to not be religious even though I came from a religious family. If you make the case that parents have a huge effect on kids' outcomes, well, how do you explain this?

Hardly any scholars in this field of immigration studies seemed to understand that kids sometimes just do stuff that has nothing to do with their parents, nor could these scholars incorporate the idea into their worldviews that sometimes kids rebel and it's something they *choose* to do. Sometimes it's young Muslim women choosing to wear the hijab in spite of their parents, and sometimes it's kids choosing to be delinquents. But, again, these choices are independent of their parents. It sounds as though I'm caricaturing these unnamed scholars (this is a preface, so I don't feel the need for a deep literature review here), but trust me, I'm not. (You can read the articles cited in footnote 1.)[1]

Were academics like these authors ever kids, I wondered? Did they not have friends when they were young? If they did, they should know that friends steer us to do some incredibly stupid shit, things that we most decidedly *do not* tell our parents. They also steer us to do some interestingly smart things.

The importance of parents—how they raise us, the values they instill in us—is greatly overblown.[2] Sure, we listen to our folks, but we only act on their advice or directives if they jibe with what we are already thinking or already "know," which, from a very young age, is a function of our peers. If our peers are thinking or doing things differently from our parents, who is going to win? Parents across the United States have said to their kids, "If your friends jumped off a bridge, would you?" They say this in exasperation, and they mean this as a rhetorical question. But, the answer is, of course, duh, yes. We love our parents, but we live our own lives and ultimately make our own choices. Do those choices often accord with our parents' wishes? Yup. But not because they said to do those things. (Correlation is not causation.) We looked around at what our peers were doing and that informed our choices.

* * *

I (Margaret) was also irritated at some of the literature on immigration as well as on race and class. Scholars assumed I must have gone to Stuyvesant and was a student at Harvard because my Chinese immigrant parents insisted. Their understanding was that my parents' concept of learning and success was traced from their home country of China.[3] On the contrary, my father immigrated when he was twelve years old, and lived in the back of the family Chinese hand laundry in New Rochelle, New York. He hadn't finished his education at New Rochelle High School before his father passed away and instead worked full-time, as a teenager, in the laundry supporting his family. My mother only had a grade school education in China because that was all her family could afford. She worked on the family farm. By the time she arrived in the United States, she was already a mom to my older sister. My parents settled in New York City, with my father becoming a waiter and my mother a garment and assembly line worker. Both of them were proud union members for their whole lives. They would have been very content and happy if I had gone to a college in the City University of New York (CUNY), as my older sister did. It was I who wanted to follow my peers to more prestigious schools.

Scholars also wrote about the effects of class and race. They noted that poorer and nonwhite parents had more difficulty sending their kids to college. As I mentioned, my working-class parents thought a local New York education was best for me because they could afford it. I could live at home if it were close. If not, I could come home on the weekends, and even have a home-cooked Chinese dinner with them on occasion. But, I really wanted to leave New York City and took out a loan and got a Pell grant to get myself out. That is what my Stuyvesant High School peers of all different class and racial backgrounds were doing, and so did I.

Race is often treated as static, but affirmative action programs, holistic admissions policies, and diversity initiatives did not see it this way. They recognize that each individual may have inextricable factors, such as their family histories or immigration stories that are tied to their race but have different meanings for each person. Likewise, affirmative action is also used for class and gender.[4] I moved between the worlds of rich and poor, of women and men, of Whites, Blacks, Latinos, and Asians at Harvard. Well, of course, if I lived, ate, and learned with diverse people, I could learn to be with people from all backgrounds—at play and at work. That is what my peers did, so I did too. When I see first-generation college students with parents who are little informed about entrée into private higher education, I know that these students, too, have peers who know how to gain admission to private colleges.

How much durability do these experiences have? I can guess that they matter a lot, because we can all do as we want, so long as our peers behave like us. If there are no peer sanctions and there is encouragement to be among a diverse crowd, we are more likely to hang with a diverse crowd.[5]

Thus, our choice of where we live, whom we marry, where we attend school may be so different from our parents' wishes, not because we are rebelling but because our peers are living life in a way that allows us to select differently.

* * *

We met at a lecture in Manhattan five years ago, and did the thing that people who find out they grew up in the same place do, quizzing each other on our local bona fides. Where exactly did you grow up, where did you eat, where did you hang out, where did you go to school? It turns out, we both went to the same high school five years apart, Syed graduating in 1985, Margaret in 1980. This high school, Stuyvesant High School, is the best public high school in the country. (This is a fact, not opinion. We will fight you on this.) And it's also important that Stuyvesant is in New York City, specifically Manhattan, the physical and metaphysical epicenter of the universe. (Again, fact.) The city has a lot to teach us about culture, people, and power, as it's the cultural center of this country, the immigration hub for this country, and the seat of economic power of this country. You can feel all this just being in the city.

So we talked all things Stuyvesant for a long time. One thing in particular that we talked about was how Stuyvesant shaped us, and how we still feel this today. Stuyvesant, more so than other high schools, is an intense crucible. It has a longstanding, well-developed student culture that pushes everyone to achieve more than they otherwise might. Being a small fish in this big pond is a good thing. Even the stoners turn out exceedingly well.

We're not privileged kids: Syed grew up sheltered and middle-class in the hinterland that is Staten Island (though technically one of the five boroughs that makes up New York City, it is the blind spot of the universe), and Margaret grew up working poor in public housing on the Upper West Side of Manhattan. We didn't know how the world worked. But we went to school with people who had "cultural capital," that is, knowledge of the unwritten rules of the game. This storied school has been a haven for smarty-smart kids throughout its one-hundred-plus-year history. The school concentrated great minds in its halls. We were not great minds. But being around people smarter than you ups your intellectual game. Being around people with cultural capital means you can learn those unwritten rules, too. And you reach further than you otherwise would without even realizing it. You don't feel tethered to your class/ethnic/neighborhood background. Margaret went to Harvard because she saw others going there, was told by peers that this was doable, and thought, "Why not? I'll go to Harvard." Syed wasn't as good academically, but still saw SUNY-Binghamton (the top public university in New York State) as his due. These are elite institutions that, had we not gone to Stuyvesant, we likely would not have even considered. But *hundreds* of students from Stuyvesant go to these, and other elite schools, every year. And this is a school with a poverty rate higher than 40 percent. Stuyvesant's students are not elites, like kids at rich suburban schools, or private schools, and yet we end up at these places—and in the professions—in droves. But that's part of our school's peer culture—it gives us the arrogance to *know* that we're as good as, and usually better than, the truly privileged kids. Hillary Anger Elfenbein, who graduated from Stuyvesant in 1989, went to Harvard, and is now a very well-known business professor at Washington University in St. Louis, said, "You should write this: I got into Harvard and couldn't believe how many stupid people I met. I had never met stupid people at Stuyvesant."

* * *

Our initial plan for this book was that it was going to be about peer effects at Stuyvesant. While we were in the beginning stages of writing, Mayor Bill de Blasio, out of the blue, announced in June 2018 that he wanted to scrap the Specialized High School Admissions Test, which is the single criterion for admission to Stuyvesant and seven other New York City high schools, and which many people see as the reason why there are so few Black and Latino students at these schools. Our research was timely! In quick succession, we wrote two articles for the *Atlantic* and the *New York Daily News* about peer effects.[6]

The idea that this would be a book about peer effects was always there, but it took us a while to realize that the story was not about Stuyvesant. Once we figured that out, and that we had to look at peer effects in different places, then the book took shape. Where do peer effects happen? In somewhat bounded groups. So we looked at schools and workplaces, among kids and among adults. Whatever behaviors you see there, good or bad, peers and peer cultures have a hand in them.

Introduction

Why Peers and Peer Culture Matter

We are told on a near-daily basis that the American public school system is in turmoil. Kids these days, they are just not learning. They need to learn more and learn better. We need parents to do more. We need teachers to do *way* more.

Oy! These poor parents and teachers—so many reports and studies, so many think pieces and hot takes about homework, screen time, experiential learning, about what constitutes good parenting, great schools, and gold-standard educators. Studies affirm a link between school performance and more experienced teachers, for instance, and emotional anecdotes make it clear that phenomenal teachers *can* make a profound difference in a kid's school life.[1] We vividly remember our favorite—and our least favorite—teachers and gobble up articles on outcomes-based learning.

Mountains of research also attest to the power of parents in preparing kids for adulthood and managing their education accordingly. In one prominent sociology text, Annette Lareau's *Unequal Childhoods*, we learn about the unequal outcomes caused by working-class parents' tendency to allow for "natural growth" and middle-class parents' "concerted cultivation" of their kids via after-school and weekend programs. Lareau notes that, in her study, middle-class children became middle-class adults, and working-class children became working-class adults.[2]

Other accounts are more prescriptive, claiming to tell parents *how* to raise children and make the education system work for them. The biggest title here is perhaps Amy Chua's best-selling memoir, *Battle Hymn of the Tiger Mother*, which extolled the virtues of overbearing parenting, basically claiming that Chua's kids turned out success stories because of her, her, her.[3]

On the surface, it seems obvious that what parents and teachers do is going to affect the learning and social outcomes of children. But what else affects whether kids do drugs, get straight As, or go on to change the world? As we will argue throughout this book, the single most important factor in why kids—and adults!—do the things they do and achieve the things they achieve is *peer effects* (hence the title). One of the reasons why most people think parents and teachers are so crucial in kids' lives is that, in thought-shaping studies throughout the years, writers and researchers have largely ignored the peers that surround our kids day by day, year by year. Judith Harris makes this point in her groundbreaking book *The Nurture Assumption*, which argues that a century of Freud and psychotherapy and research in the field of developmental psychology has shifted the onus of kids' outcomes squarely onto parents when, instead, *peers* shape who kids are and what they do. In other words, we should lay off blaming parents if their kids are screw-ups—they don't deserve that agita. But we also cannot take full credit should our kids become successful lawyers (we are looking at you, Tiger Mom).

Peer effects, we should point out, are separate from parents' effects—each has an independent effect on kids' outcomes. That is the case because parents may shape the pool of potential peers for their kids, whether by giving their children their skin color, race, ethnicity, and religion or through their education and wealth, which affect the neighborhoods their children live in and the types of schools they attend. But parents do not determine which of those possible peers end up being consequential in their kids' lives.

Our argument, to put it simply, is that your peers affect who you are and who you become, and that peer effects last beyond childhood and adolescence. To be more social science-y, we explore youth outcomes by starting with the aforementioned Judith Harris's group socialization theory, the idea that "children are socialized, and their personalities shaped, by the experiences they have outside the home, in the environment they share with peers."[4]

We also draw on the work of Murray Milner Jr., who argues that peer groups are status groups, or groups that share a "lifestyle."[5] Within those groups, status is gained through conforming to group norms and making intimate associations (especially around eating, dating, and marrying) with group members of equal or greater status. Everyone competes for status (or honor or prestige—these all roughly mean the same thing), and adopting group norms and making the right kinds of intimate associations are critical for maintaining or improving status. Milner strikingly shows how, in American schools, teenagers can confer status on each other, or take it away. They—not parents and not teachers—have the ability to define their cultural worlds and control each other's social standing within those worlds. Parents and teachers have no say in this. Their desperate striving for status affects the way teenagers behave and has been profitably exploited in Hollywood films on teens trying to be popular, such as *Heathers*, *Jawbreaker*, and *Mean Girls*, and TV shows like *Gossip Girl* and *90210*. This is not unlike the workings of status at the society level; as Milner points out, India's caste system and American high school cliques are not so very different, because norms and proper associations are central to establishing personal and group status in both.

Whatever the social group, when we become part of it, we learn its ways and act accordingly. Thus, when we talk about peer effects in the book, we are talking about two things. One is how our peers, at any age in the life cycle, *directly* affect our behavior—we do what they do because we want to be like them. The other is *indirect*, or the ways peer culture defines group membership, values, and acceptable behaviors, as well as their opposites—who and what does not fit in.

* * *

The study of peer effects has largely been of children and students, and we will examine the dynamic of peer effects among them. But what about adults? Much less research has been conducted on how peers affect the way adults behave. We are going to examine peer effects among adults in a few ways. First, we are going to discuss graduates of an elite public high school in New York City—Stuyvesant High School. This school has a well-developed culture of achievement among its students, and there are direct and indirect peer effects that shape students' behavior. The question we have is, How long-lasting are these effects? (Pretty long-lasting it turns out, according to the people we interviewed.) While Stuyvesant is a unique institution, an outlier if you will, the lessons learned there about peers and peer culture have direct bearing for "regular" schools, since every school will have peers and peer cultures that affect the way students behave and turn out.

We are also going to use the idea of peer effects to explain why misconduct happens in the office, and why workplace cultures are so hard to change. And lastly, we are going to look at a highly insular peer culture that has dramatic ramifications for the rest of us: that of cops.

Basically, we will be looking at the peer effect in a set of institutional spaces—inside high schools, offices, and police departments in the United States—and considering how this knowledge might be leveraged to reduce persistent problems created and sustained by peer cultures within these spaces. By the end, we will be audacious enough to offer up some advice for organizations trying to effect change, whether it is desegregating schools, increasing graduation rates, and amplifying schools as tools of social mobility; diversifying workplaces, reducing on-the-job misconduct, and reaping the economic rewards; or reimagining policing through radical reorganizations. Cultural change is hard, and it often takes a long time, a lot of resources, many simultaneous efforts, and indefatigable champions, but it can absolutely happen. We have seen it before.

Let us take a little space here to discuss how we are conceptualizing culture in a bit more detail.[6] First, culture is a blueprint of what we as "a people" are, and what we do. That includes language, dress, food, sport, religion, art, music, traditions, and other things that distinguish "us" from "them." But the most important part of culture, arguably, is its rules or norms, its dos and don'ts. Norms tell us what a people finds important enough that they have something to say about regulating the behaviors supporting the norm. Norms are paired with sanctions. These are rewards and punishments—follow the norms and you get rewarded; violate them and you are punished. The sanctions tell us just how important and central those rules are to what it means to be of that group; the more stringent the sanction, the more important the norm. Also, the more tight-knit a people are, the more the boundaries between us and them are going to be strongly defined.

Boundaries around "a people" tell us *who* they are; culture tells us *what* they are. There is an interaction between boundaries and culture; the more boundaries are defined (us versus them), the deeper culture runs. The more closed off the social situation of a group is, the stronger the boundaries are and the deeper the culture is—as with religious groups, or castes in India. And think about cliques in American high schools. Why are they so strongly developed? Because of the broader structure of schools, which keeps students in physical proximity for hours every day (and then many more hours at night and on weekends). Generally, kids spend more time with peers than with any adults, including parents. So, who would we expect should be more of an influence? Whom would we expect them to identify with? Their "people" are their high school peers, more specifically their cliques. And because they are very tight-knit, their culture and norms are very developed. But once they leave this social situation (i.e., graduate), those are no longer their "people" and the culture and norms they obsessed over cease to hold sway. At the same time, the cliques are constantly recruiting new members, so they can survive long after their members join other cliques or graduate.

We usually think of culture as "stuff" that defines us—language, food, music, dress, etc. That is true to an extent, but these things change over time. For instance, we New Yorkers closely identify pizza and bagels as part of our culture (and disdain others for their attempts at pizza and bagels), yet there was already a New York culture before Italians and Eastern European Jews brought these tasty items to the fore. It was just defined differently. That is why it is more useful to think of culture as a blueprint that tells us how to act, that informs the boundaries of our identity, that defines the difference between us and them. Culture ultimately is not the stuff. It is how (and by what rules) we live our lives.

When we are part of a group, there is pressure to conform; we tend to follow the norms to gain and maintain acceptance and status. If the norm is to marry your "own kind," well, that is easy. Do it and you get rewarded. Break a norm, especially a central norm, however, and you will get punished. In some cultures, marrying outside your own kind can get you chastised, shunned by your family and friends, even beaten or killed.

So, when people ask why teens behave the way they do, culture is the answer. Their behavior is not about age or hormones, but about how teens are organized within peer groups and the norms those groups uphold. Peer culture varies from school to school and peer group to peer group, and it varies by context. So, when a senior in high school behaves very differently from someone who just graduated high school, that happens because the graduate is no longer in the same peer culture in the same context that compelled their behaviors just months before.

The basic premise of this book, in other words, is that who you hang out with affects who you are and who you will become. The peer culture we are part of becomes our blueprint for behavior with those particular people in those particular circumstances. We know it is true of small children—we see it in the playgrounds and primary schools. It is also true of teens and young adults—think of cliques in high schools, conformist hazing rituals of fraternities and sororities, and the military, for that matter. But it is also true, perhaps surprisingly so, for adults. Anyone who is part of a "bounded" community—whether that is a playground, a college sorority, a workplace, a members-only Internet chatroom, or a retirement community—is affected by their peers. Individuals who are members of relatively closed groups—who are insiders rather than outsiders—will want to be like the other in-group members. They will seek their peers' approval and respect and try to differentiate themselves from those regarded as "others."

* * *

Let's get down to specifics—what is in the book? We start by looking at how in the United States we define "good" schools and "bad" schools, and why these designations matter. Here, we are looking at segregation, both past and present, and how the ostensibly "objective" criteria we use to separate the good from the bad are *really* about race and class. We discuss school choice and tracking, and how the determinations of parents and school officials result in a highly segregated, highly unequal and inegalitarian school system that, from the outset, rewards middle-class and wealthy White and Asian American students and punishes Black and Latino students. By way of comparison, we take a look at Finland, which everyone agrees has the world's best educational system, noting that the Finns have little in the way of school choice (even tracking does not begin until late in high school), as well as little in the way of segregation. At the root of our schools' problems and Finland's successes, we argue, is peer effects.

We then take a deeper look at the ways peers affect kids' outcomes in high school and college, both directly and indirectly, and how the peer cultures that define norms of behavior are specific to certain spaces. Along the way, we consider why some kids devalue academic achievement and how peers can influence school performance, hookup culture, school bullying, and youth suicide.

We know that our peers and peer culture have immediate effects upon our behavior, but just how long-lasting are these effects? Researchers have studied peer effects in schools and, to a lesser degree, peer effects among adults in somewhat narrow, and immediate, time frames. But there is not much research at all on how peers affect each other over the long run. To do that research, we conducted interviews with adult graduates of Manhattan's Stuyvesant High School, an elite, public school for which admission is competitive and dependent on high-stakes testing. Not to give it away, but most people we interviewed felt that, yes, the peer effects of Stuyvesant, a bounded, insular school context, affected them well into adulthood. To them, the effect of their Stuyvesant peers loomed larger than that of any other peer group, even from their college years and even many years later.

We are also interested in the degree to which we can say that peers affect outcomes of adults. We examine this question by focusing our attention on explaining various types of workplace misconduct, and analyzing what types of diversity programs do and do not work. And we consider some problematic aspects of peer effects in adulthood by studying a particular organizational/occupational peer culture: the culture of policing. Structural forces reinforce and strengthen the boundaries around cops, reifying a strong sense of "cops versus everyone else." Inside and across police departments, it matters little what top police officials say or do; cop culture is horizontal, created and defined by the rank and file, who impose famously stringent sanctions should one of them step out of line. Peer effects have enormous implications for police reform, suggesting that real change cannot happen without a radical reorganization of the institution. That is, at a minimum, you need a huge infusion of non-White and otherwise nontraditional personnel at all ranks if you are to have even a remote chance at lasting change.

It is fine and dandy to examine the "how" of peer effects and peer culture, but we feel that is not enough. We close by stepping back and saying, "Okay, we've learned some lessons about why things are the way they are—now what?" In conclusion, we think through what we have learned about peer effects and how we (and you!) can use these insights to change the world around us. Bullying, grades, workplace tensions, bad-apple cops—we've got thoughts on all these and more.

1

Good Schools, Bad Schools

Sami was born in Brooklyn in 2005. His parents, Syed and Eli, lived in the gentrifying Clinton Hill neighborhood that for decades was largely poor and Black but had recently become Whiter and richer. Right around the time Sami was ready for school, in 2009, Mayor Mike Bloomberg instituted a system of school choice. This meant that Sami would not *have* to go to the family's local, zoned K–5 school. His parents could now opt to send him to another school within their district, outside it even, so long as that school had space. New York City had undertaken a massive experiment in education, and Sami would be participating.

The family's local, zoned primary school had a bad reputation. Only 27 percent of eligible students from that school's zone actually attended the school, and the student population that did was largely poor and Black. The year before Sami was to start pre-K, the school's principal was arrested for "knocking a kindergarten teacher off a chair, kicking him in the head, and stomping on him."[1] After school choice went into effect, both the richer gentrifiers and a meaningful number of Black longtime residents avoided sending their children to this school.

Very few of Sami's parents' neighborhood friends (three of thirteen), almost all mixed race or Black, would end up sending their kids to the local, zoned school for kindergarten—but that number was on par with what happened in other gentrifying neighborhoods.[2] Bloomberg's "reform" made it pretty easy to avoid the "bad" schools in the neighborhood and still access free, public alternatives—including gifted and talented programs, "good" local schools in other zones and districts, and charter schools.

Five years before Sami was born, before Bloomberg's reform, when almost every child had to go to their neighborhood or screened school,

Margaret was looking at public schools for her son. She lived by Columbia University in the Upper West Side of Manhattan, and was part of a community of graduate students and new faculty parents—a group in which four out of five children attended the same private preschool on 113th Street.

Margaret's friends with young preschool children at that time included one junior professor (White) and three other graduate-student couples (Latino, White, and interracial Black/White—diverse peers are a theme in her life!). They all agreed that they wanted their children to attend school relatively close to where they lived. Neighborhood mattered even though they all knew how segregated communities were. Two within the friend group remained in New York City. One sent their child to a dual-language school in the district, two moved north to Westchester and the Bronx, another moved to Pittsburgh. In the end, Margaret moved away from Columbia and sent her child to a local neighborhood public school in Manhattan.

In New York City, Margaret encountered problems that her friends did not have, especially if she wanted to send her child to a smaller, special dual-language or "gifted and talented" curriculum program. At the time, most of these special programs, while higher performing, were Whiter, were wealthier, and had testing or "screens" to get in.

Moreover, these higher-performing screened programs were shockingly located inside of larger school buildings that had more Black and Latino students than the special programs did. These programs were segregated into an island of their own within the school. One Upper East Side school, the Lower Lab school, even had separate entrances for students in these programs—White and Asian American students entered in the front, Black and Latino students in the back. Even the teachers and staff had to use separate entrances.[3] The whole kindergarten search made Margaret queasy. Choosing schools for a five-year-old child is an awful experience!

School Gentrification

These early periods of school gentrification can be a bumpy ride—sometimes because of the kids, quite often because of the parents. (Let's not forget the violence of White parents during desegregation and busing from the 1950s to the 1990s.) "Native" Black parents see their friends and families displaced from apartments and houses they can no longer afford. Richer, Whiter newcomers take their places. It happens for years. When the White people's kids show up in the school, well, that must surely feel to some longtime residents like insult heaped upon injury.

Including Black families' feelings here is intended not to evoke pity but to make it clear that, according to some urban studies scholars, it does not actually matter whether gentrifiers and landlords are pushing out long-term residents in "significant" numbers.[4] (It could just be that as poorer people move—which they do frequently—landlords upgrade the amenities and raise the rent for their apartments. In pre-gentrifying times, in poor, ghetto neighborhoods, you could leave one cheap apartment and find another nearby. But in gentrifying neighborhoods today, that is not possible.) It matters that poorer Black people see it this way, and that affects how they feel and behave toward people they see as colonizers.

A great podcast from 2019, called *School Colors*, about schools and segregation and gentrification in the historically Black neighborhood of Bedford-Stuyvesant, or Bed-Stuy, in Brooklyn (where Syed now lives), describes this process well.[5] Unlike Syed and most of his friends in Clinton Hill, a group of White parents in Bed-Stuy wanted to send their kids to their zoned neighborhood schools. Before their kids were of school age, they formed what they called the Bed-Stuy Parents Committee. This was a mistake because, well, they were White, gentrifying newcomers and some Black parents who had been in the neighborhood for much longer thought that name was just a bit too cheeky, since, after all, *they* were Bed-Stuy parents, and *they* were there first, and who are these people anyway to come in here like that?

As the group reached out to local stakeholders, they were met with cold shoulders and hostility. Meanwhile, their kids were getting old enough for school. So these parents started a "two-tour pledge"—a pledge to tour at least two schools in Bed-Stuy as they made their choice. When one parent called a school to ask about a school tour, the secretary hung up on her. These schools were not used to, or ready to host, parent tours. People did not want to send their kids there, and these schools were already well under capacity. But the White parents had an answer to this, too: they offered to help schools market themselves and organize tours to help recruit more families to attend. What may sound at first like a nice idea was not received well by the schools' administrations. It was unsolicited and a bit condescending.

Things got worse once the Bed-Stuy Parents Committee's kids actually enrolled in the local schools. Some of these moms tried to get involved with the PTA (parent-teacher association). At one school, a pair of newcomer moms got elected as co-PTA presidents, but were fervently resisted by the former PTA president, now the secretary, as well as the school's office staff, janitors, and security. The conflict got so intense that the White moms stopped going to their own meetings in December. In January, they pulled their kids out of the school.

After almost two decades of gentrification, there are still few White faces in Bed-Stuy's neighborhood schools. Many newcomers had already decided to send their kids to out-of-district schools before word got around that White families were being treated like unwanted outsiders in "their" local schools. After the Bed-Stuy Parents Committee's interventions, the school the PTA moms left was just 7 percent White in 2020–2021—that is, fifteen White students, up from two students five years prior.[6] What hope do other gentrifying neighborhoods have for integrated schools at this point?

A question then arises: Can segregated schools integrate in gentrifying neighborhoods where parents have a choice of public schools to send their kids to? That is, can neighborhoods that are getting richer and Whiter have schools that become integrated? The answer is yes, but there will be a significant time lag between neighborhoods' demographics changing and school demographics changing. The Clinton Hill school that Sami attended for pre-K (out of zone but within district) had its own PTA issues with racial tension. White parents would send their kids for pre-K and kindergarten, but increasingly take them out before they reached higher grades—something you could clearly see when the kids lined up in the schoolyard before going into the building each morning (and was common in schools in gentrifying neighborhoods throughout New York City). But today, about a decade later, that school is highly desired among Whites in the neighborhood, and the antagonisms seem like distant history. Instead, the number of Black students has decreased dramatically. It turns out that integration was but a quick stop on the path to "White-ification." The demographic shift in this school was swift: in 2008–2009, it had 83.7 percent Black students and 6.7 percent White students. The next year, when Sami started pre-K, it was 77.2 percent Black and 10.3 percent White. A decade later, it was 58 percent Black and 15 percent White. The total enrollment at the school has actually gone up, and so, from 2016 to 2020, there was a net gain of forty-four White students but a loss of thirty-five Black students.[7] It seems entirely possible that Black students could become the minority in this school, losing out as the school becomes "good."

To call school gentrification and the resulting resegregation of public schools an unintended consequence or even a natural outcome of economic forces is entirely, even willfully, naïve, though. To understand why requires a (necessarily short) primer on American school and neighborhood segregation and how we got to this point of calling entire schools "good" and "bad."

School Segregation in the United States

Education for Black children only required government-level consideration after Emancipation, in the late nineteenth century. Pretty much wherever Black children were schooled, they were schooled separately.

Nationwide, schools would remain segregated until pretty late in the twentieth century. In the more urban North, this was the case largely because children were assigned schools by neighborhood, and the neighborhoods were racially segregated. In the more rural South, Jim Crow laws kneecapped many of the possibilities Emancipation opened up for Black residents and dictated separate schools.

Mandated Desegregation in Southern Schools

In the South, Jim Crow laws mandated separate schools for Black and White children. That is, until the 1954 *Brown v. Board of Education* case. In this case, the Supreme Court found that separate educational facilities are inherently unequal, and it ordered states to desegregate schools, but it did not specify *how*. Thurgood Marshall, the famed Black lawyer (and, later, Supreme Court justice) who argued the case, threw a big party after they won. But late into the night, he told people there, "I don't want any of you to fool yourselves. The fight has just begun." By 1964, in the Deep South, just one in eighty-five southern Black children attended an integrated school. Justice Hugo Black wrote for the Court that "there has been entirely too much deliberation and not enough speed in enforcing" the *Brown* decision.[8]

In 1964, the Civil Rights Act was passed. This was a wide-ranging law, but with respect to our discussion here, it essentially forced southern public schools to desegregate by empowering the federal Department of Justice to sue and withhold funding from school districts that refused to integrate. Because northern schools did not segregate by law, the law did not apply to them. This was no oversight; northern congressmen did not oppose segregation per se, just in the South. They were perfectly happy for school segregation to continue in their back yard, something Malcolm X trenchantly observed in a 1964 interview when he said, "You don't have to go to Mississippi to find a segregated school system. We have it right here in New York City."[9] Southern schools that did not comply found themselves under court directives to desegregate. And it worked. By 1973, about 90 percent of southern Black children attended integrated schools—southern schools were far more integrated than northern schools.[10]

The main way that these court directives were enforced was through busing. Kids in the United States have been bused for as long as we have had buses. But that is not what people mean by "busing." The term took on a pejorative meaning after these court orders. Busing to integrate schools started to happen in some parts of the country soon after the *Brown* decision, and accelerated in the 1960s and 1970s. And just as soon as the court orders came down, White protest began. And in San Francisco, the Chinese community, in the protests against busing, argued that desegregation court orders disregarded their concern for language differences.[11] What happens to a new immigrant kid who cannot speak English when there are no translation services at a school outside of Chinatown? Some of the loudest protests in San Francisco were from the Chinese community.[12]

This resistance—mostly White resistance—killed busing, but not all at once. Throughout the 1960s, 1970s, and into the 1990s, there were street protests, sometimes violent. There were angry voices shouting at school board meetings. There were lawsuits. Busing presented segregationists with a great political opportunity: *opposing busing*, in the words of historian Matthew Delmont, became a "palatable way" for Whites (especially, over time, northern Whites) "to oppose desegregation without appealing to the explicitly racist sentiments they preferred to associate with Southerners."[13]

"I have probably talked before 500 or 600 groups over the last years about busing," Los Angeles Assemblyman Floyd Wakefield said in 1970. "Almost every time, someone has gotten up and called me a 'racist' or a 'bigot.' But now, all of the sudden, I am no longer a 'bigot.' Now I am called 'the leader of the antibusing effort.'" White parents and politicians framed their resistance to school desegregation in terms like "busing" and "neighborhood schools," and this rhetorical shift allowed them to support white schools and neighborhoods without using explicitly racist language.[14]

Court-ordered desegregation was effective in the South, though it had no teeth in the North; there, White parents found proxy issues to stave off local notions about integration, should they arise in the public schools. And today, as court decisions have started to find racial integration measures unconstitutional, school districts across the country are rolling back desegregation measures. Politically dominant Whites have proved unwilling to accept school integration at every possible opportunity.

Segregating the Chinese in California Schools

Many people do not know that Asian American students in the West and South also attended segregated schools from the 1850s until the 1950s. The West, in particular California, was different because it was not a slave state, but there was xenophobia wherein the Chinese and other Asian groups were treated as outsiders and were not considered White.[15] The very first public school for Black children was a "Colored School" established in 1854, on Jackson Street and Virginia Place (between Stockton and Powell Streets) in the basement of the St. Cyprian African Methodist Episcopal Church in what is now San Francisco's Chinatown.[16] A few years later, between 1857 and 1859, the "Chinese School" (a nonpublic school) was established only a few blocks away in a Presbyterian chapel.[17] In 1865, California legislated that children of "African or Mongolian descent and Indian children not living under the care of White persons" must attend separate schools. By 1875, "Colored students" were, however, allowed to attend public schools in San Francisco, by law. And by 1880, Sacramento followed by requiring all California districts to allow "Colored students" to attend public schools.[18] On the other hand, the Chinese and, later, all Asians, even the US-born, were not considered full Americans, nor White, and were still victims of school segregation as there was still de facto segregation for all "Colored" students.[19]

The Chinese fought for the right to be in public schools. Seventy years before *Brown v. Board of Education*, in 1884, the Chinese parents of Mamie Tape, a US-born child, took their case, *Tape v. Hurley*, to the California Supreme Court. American-born children, by 1880, had the right to attend public schools, but because she was regarded as a "foreigner," as her parents were not allowed to naturalize because of the 1882 Chinese Exclusion Law, she attended the Chinese missionary school. The judge in her case argued that barring her from attending local public schools violated the Fourteenth Amendment since "Colored" children were allowed to attend public schools. However, Mamie was barred from attending public schools as the San Francisco school board quickly authorized separate schools for Chinese students.[20] By 1906, with increasing immigration of Japanese and Korean students to San Francisco, children of Chinese and Mongolian descent were ordered to attend the "Oriental Public School."[21] This separation was reinforced again in 1927 with the *Lum v. Rice* decision in Mississippi, where Chinese were considered "not-White." In both cases, Chinese parents fought to have their children attend public schools but lost; separate but equal remained the rule until the 1954 *Brown* decision.[22]

San Francisco was not unlike the North. There was also residential segregation, which worked to create segregated public schools. The Chinese children, like the students from Mexican American and Black communities, attended segregated schools because they were redlined into specific neighborhoods.[23] According to the 1970 census, the Asian population of 3.5 percent Filipino, 1.6 percent Japanese, and 8.2 percent Chinese summed up to a total Asian population of 13.3 percent, which was as large as the Black population at 13.4 percent, and persons of Spanish surname made up 9.7 percent.[24] The Asian American communities were ignored in the racial schema and were not included in the original San Francisco discussions during the 1960s, even though they had fought for integrated public schools almost a hundred years earlier.

San Francisco instituted court-mandated desegregation in September of 1971, seventeen years after the *Brown v. Board of Education* decision.[25] In 1971 San Francisco, Margaret's husband, Perry, was bused from Spring Valley Elementary School, which was over 90 percent Chinese, to the racially mixed Starr King Elementary School in Potrero Hill. As a child, he was swept up in huge desegregation mandates that oftentimes neglected or omitted the wishes of the Chinese community, which was 8.2 percent of the population. At Starr King Elementary School, he was placed in a racially diverse gifted classroom. This was the first time in his life when he was in a classroom with Black and Mexican American children. His class at Spring Valley had only two White students, and the rest were Chinese. Mandatory integration had lasting effects. His San Francisco middle school and high school experiences in racially diverse environments certainly affected his tastes in music and pop culture (peers!), which in turn helped him be more trusted among his racially diverse colleagues at the public municipal hospitals or community health centers where he works.

Legislated desegregation worked in San Francisco through the 1970s. With changes in demographics, especially with the increase of the Asian American population, the original criteria that limited the number of years that children could be bused could not be enforced. Black children bore the burden of being bused for more than half of their elementary school career. A new educational design was adopted in 1983 with a consent decree, in which an integrated school was defined as a school with no fewer than four of the nine racial/ethnic groups and with no one group constituting more than 45 percent of the school population.[26]

This racial/ethnic grouping policy was contentious because it was a policy that did not reflect the sweeping demographic changes in the student population after the consent decree took effect. In 1983, Black and

White students accounted for just under 40 percent of the San Francisco school district, while Asian and Latino students accounted for just under 37 percent. By 1992, Black and White students fell in numbers to 33 percent, and Asian and Latino students grew to 44 percent. The demographic transformations meant that the school attendance boundaries were no longer compatible and were much more difficult to accommodate without more busing. Moreover, this policy did not allow predictability from year to year. Parents could not plan which schools they were allowed to apply to since racial/ethnic demographics could change the allocation. This policy was removed by 2005, and segregation in the schools increased shortly after.[27]

Residential Segregation in the North

Until the early 1900s, there was very little residential segregation in American cities; Blacks lived in close proximity to Whites, physically integrated, though not really socially integrated. Of course, not many people lived in cities; in the early 1900s we were still largely an agricultural country that was transitioning to a manufacturing base. After Emancipation, Black people largely stayed put in the rural South. The small number of Blacks in northern (and southern) cities tended to cluster in certain neighborhoods, but there just were not enough of them to form their own neighborhoods, for the most part.

Then World War I happened. There was an increased demand for industrial labor, as White workers went off to war, and would-be immigrants were not able to come to the United States. Thus began the Great Migration, wherein hundreds of thousands of Black people migrated to northern cities in just a few years. (This was repeated during World War II and lasted until about 1970; around six million Blacks migrated northward in total.)[28] As they moved north, they found housing options limited in cities, and were forced into what would become ghettos, which the urban scholars Douglas Massey and Nancy Denton, in their book

American Apartheid, define as areas of hyperconcentration of the Black population.[29] Harlem, for instance, was 10 percent Black in 1910, but by 1930 was 70 percent Black.[30] By 1950, it was 98 percent Black.[31]

By the time the *Brown* case was decided in 1954, Black ghettos were a permanent part of city landscapes throughout the country. The GI Bill gave servicemen returning from World War II free college educations and housing loans. But nearly all of these benefits went to Whites.[32] Similarly, housing loans through the Federal Housing Administration (FHA) and the Veterans Administration went to Whites. The FHA in 1938 instigated a policy of "redlining." Color-coded maps of cities (created by the federal Home Owners' Loan Corporation) were made to indicate where loans could and could not be made. Areas that were outlined in red were not to be given loans.[33] These were mostly Black neighborhoods, but sometimes were areas populated with poor Italians and Jews.

In the 1950s, interstate highways were being constructed at a rapid pace. These highways allowed for people (White people) to commute into cities for work from further out, which helped to spur on the construction of the suburbs. Between 1950 and 1990, metropolitan areas grew by 72 percent, but central city populations declined by 17 percent. One economist found that when highways pass through central cities, they reduce the city population by 18 percent. Had the interstate highway system not been built, central city populations would have grown by 8 percent![34]

So by the 1970s, Black ghettos had become widespread, Black and White neighborhoods were highly segregated within cities, city populations had decreased dramatically from their peaks in the 1940s, and suburban populations, that is, the White population in the suburbs, had increased significantly nationwide. The school systems mirrored these demographics: Black neighborhoods had Black schools; White neighborhoods had White schools.

In the past couple of decades, cities across the country have seen demographic changes in ghetto neighborhoods, as the process of gentrification has led to poor Black neighborhoods in many cities becoming wealthier and Whiter. For instance, in Harlem. By 2019, Central Harlem's Black population was at 54 percent, and falling fast, as property values and rents were through the roof. Even still, in gentrifying neighborhoods like Harlem and Bed-Stuy, the schools tend to be segregated long after neighborhoods Whiten, as the gentrifiers will do almost anything to keep from sending their kids to these schools, a point we will come back to a little later in the chapter.

Bad Reputations

In the United States, as in many countries, there are good public schools and bad public schools. Where parents can, they avoid the bad schools and opt for the good schools. But what is a "good" school? It is one where kids have resources to learn in a safe environment. In practice, though, "good" schools are those largely populated by middle- and upper-middle-class Whites, with a smaller percentage of Asian kids, and an even smaller percentage of Black and Latino kids. This is key because, in the United States, as in many other countries, the kids in "good" schools get good grades, do well on standardized exams, and go to good colleges. The "bad" schools are usually largely populated by Black and/or Latino students, who are disproportionately poor, and the schools are relatively underfunded. Students in these schools do not do as well on standardized exams, and the rate of college going is far lower. This racial divide of good/bad schools is not anything most people would own up to. So how do parents learn good schools from bad?

What is a good or bad school, who decides, and how does everyone seem to know the difference? "Reputation" is an almost circular answer, being something that is dependent on word of mouth. For instance, if you ask New York City parents to name their best public high school, the clear answer is Stuyvesant High School. They will not offer objective criteria, because there are not really any objective criteria by which you can make this assessment. It is just something that is "known," just as it is "known" that Harvard is the best university in the country. Saying that a school is "good," then, is basically saying that it is desired. And with the density of parent information networks in schools and neighborhoods, word gets around through the grapevine.

Syed's wife, Eli, first learned about the out-of-district grade school that their children eventually attended from a Black father at a playground who said he would never send his son to their local, zoned school (the one where the principal beat up a kindergarten teacher). He said he was sending his son to this other school because he liked its culture, it was very diverse, and the (Black) principal was very good. What sealed the deal was when Syed's high school friend sent her son, who was one year ahead of Sami, to that grade school—at that point, there was no longer any question about whether this school was good or not. To Syed and Eli, this school was "good" because many parents, especially richer, Whiter parents than they, repeated these vague but convincing things about the school, and the school always had a waitlist of kids trying to get in.

But while word of mouth has always been important, today we get a lot of our information about schools online. The biggest online rater is GreatSchools; forty-three million visitors went to its site in 2018, and it is prominently featured on the real estate sites Zillow, Realtor.com, and Redfin. GreatSchools aims to provide an objective assessment of every school in the United States to help parents make their school choices.

These ratings systems use state-level data, the collection of which was mandated by the federal 2001 No Child Left Behind Act. Great-Schools uses proficiency scores—tests on the topics states deem students should know in certain grades—as the biggest factor in their ratings. These proficiency scores are correlated with race and income. So, in cities across the country, nearly all the schools that GreatSchools rates at seven or higher (out of ten) are White-majority or White- and Asian American–majority, and the parents of students in those schools have higher incomes.[35] If you look at growth—how much better a student is doing compared to where they started—you see that a lot of schools with higher percentages of lower-income and Black and Latino students do really well. It is just that few states report this measure, and it only matters half as much as proficiency in the GreatSchools rating, so schools that do well on growth are rarely rated highly.[36]

The out-of-district school where Syed and his wife ended up sending their kids for grade school in 2010 was, at the time, 31 percent Black, 26 percent Latino, 35 percent White, and 5 percent Asian American. Great-Schools only gave it a four out of ten, but its long waitlist and word of mouth indicated desirability, and the local InsideSchools.org rating site gave it a "staff pick" designation. The principal was beloved, and the parents and kids were happy. Few New York City schools are so diverse—to the degree that, with a large number of Yemenis included in the "White" category, the school's voicemail was recorded in English, Spanish, and Arabic. More often, we find many schools in New York City with a Black or Black/Latino supermajority (i.e., very few Whites and Asians) and a smaller number with White or White/Asian majority. (A 2014 report on New York State found that its schools were the most segregated in the country, that New York City schools were especially segregated, and that three-quarters of the charter schools in the city were "apartheid schools," with less than 1 percent White students.)[37] So Syed's kids' school stood out in terms of ethnic/racial integration, and it was richer than most. Where 73 percent of New York City public school kids qualified for free/reduced-price lunch (a proxy measure for poverty rate), just 40 percent at this school did. By 2021, though, the school had gotten much Whiter (and richer still, with the free/reduced-lunch rate dropping to 35 percent): it was 48 percent White, 10 percent Black, 18 percent Latino, and 6 percent Asian American. This is still highly integrated in terms of the city's schools, but the Whitening over time is clear.

Elsewhere in the United States, it is difficult to achieve integration like this, especially without an active intervention like busing. The places that are already integrated are moving away from integration as demographic, social, and political forces aside from gentrification work in concert to undo the diversity. The court-mandated desegregation of the latter part of the twentieth century is faltering, to the point that American schools are now more segregated than they were in the 1960s. Localities, especially in the South, are carving out richer, White-majority districts from the larger, integrated districts.[38] Today, roughly 15 percent of Black and 14 percent of Latino children attend "apartheid schools," in which the student population is less than 1 percent White.[39] Another way to think about this is to imagine a spectrum of integration, on which the midpoint is an even non-White/White student split. That spectrum is heavily weighted at the ends: 20 percent of schools are more than 90 percent White, and another 20 percent are more than 90 percent non-White.[40] And this school segregation is increasing across the country.[41]

In the past, White flight described a physical movement—White families fleeing schools and neighborhoods in the city to move to the suburbs, away from Black and Latino families. Today, White flight comes in the form of carveouts to create smaller, White districts out of larger, integrated ones, and can also be seen in policy changes, like the implementation of school choice, which can have the effect of turning particular schools White. A different sort of White flight happens if you have too many Asian Americans. For instance, in Cupertino, California (Apple's headquarters), the White kids in a local, high-achieving public high school were seen as academically inferior to Asian American kids. Some gave up on trying to excel academically, "opting out of what they characterize as an achievement rat-race that places them as slow runners because of their Whiteness."[42] Even the higher-achieving White kids could not keep up. Many White parents soon pulled their kids from the local high school, in favor of less competitive public high schools and expensive private schools that were less academically rigorous and that, not coincidentally, had fewer Asian Americans. Asked why they left, White parents said they believed such schools would provide "a more balanced environment, allowing their children a better chance to thrive."[43]

In New York City, admissions testing has served as another mechanism of school segregation.[44] Nine public high schools are collectively called "specialized high schools," the most prestigious among them being Stuyvesant High School; in eight of them you gain admission *solely* by doing well on a two-and-a-half-hour standardized entrance exam. (The ninth school, LaGuardia, bases admission on an audition or portfolio.) Until the early 2000s, White kids tended to try to get into Stuyvesant because their local, zoned schools were perceived as "bad schools" and dangerous places for nerdy White kids. In Jonathan Lethem's novel, *The Fortress of Solitude*, set in pre-gentrification 1970s Brooklyn, one White kid says to the other, "Just pass the test. Your life depends on it. If you don't get into Stuyvesant, or at least Bronx Science, you're dead. . . . Brooklyn Tech's a last resort. Sarah J. Hale or John Jay"— two neighborhood schools—"those places are practically like prison."[45] But throughout the 1980s, the number of Asian American students increased steadily and the ranks of White students thinned dramatically. The "tipping point" for when White people run away will vary, but too many of these non-White kids and White flight is nearly inevitable.[46]

Around 2003, when Michael Bloomberg became mayor, the number of White kids dropped at all these specialized schools. Partially, this was due to a doubling in the total number of New York City schools that began screening for academic criteria like grades or exams and requiring an audition or interview. Effectively, this exclusivity increased the pool of schools considered "good," which attracted White students away from the specialized schools. The prestige self-replicated as the schools gained large enough White student populations that other White parents began trying to get their kids in, too.

It is a rare school that has a reputation among parents as "good" and *doesn't* have a critical mass of middle- and upper-middle-class White kids. And there are two simple reasons: money follows the White kids, and White (and, increasingly, Asian American) parents do not want their kids to have too many Black and Latino peers. They usually won't say it that bluntly, but their actions make it plain.

Mechanisms of Modern Segregation

Integration is good for all students, despite White parents' rejection of it. Rucker Johnson, an economist, says, for instance, that integration has benefited and continues to benefit Blacks in terms of education, earnings, and decreased incarceration rates. Society, he adds, benefits from a decrease in prejudice, and Whites lose nothing.[47] In fact, they gain.

Alie Stumpf, a White teacher in Manhattan, wrote, for instance,

> I also witnessed the powerful benefits classroom diversity had on my white, middle-class students. One boy learned through his interactions with a Latinx classmate who lived in public housing that the phrase "all lives matter" was offensive, and a girl found inspiration in a black peer who boldly shared her critical insights with peers but who privately struggled with writing mechanics. In his final evaluation of the class, a white student, who flaunted his wealth and openly ridiculed his less affluent peers, reflected that his experience that year taught him how to listen more to people and be kinder. "You never know what someone is going through," he wrote.[48]

Again, the problem with integration is not the kids, really; the problem is parents. The argument that Whites do not lose out with integration is true, as Rucker Johnson and others point out, in the sense that White kids become less prejudiced, and at the same time do not lose any ground academically. But they lose their racial exclusivity and distance from Blacks, something the kids' parents do not really care for. If you do not understand that integration is a perceived loss for White *parents*, then you cannot understand their resistance to integration and desire to create new segregated school districts like those we have seen in the South recently, and you cannot understand otherwise liberal White and some Asian American parents in the North fighting to keep largely segregated gifted and talented programs even though they do not really provide much in the way of advanced education.[49]

Rucker Johnson also points out that White kids who did not attend integrated schools are less likely to have racial diversity among their friends in adulthood, are more likely to live in segregated neighborhoods as adults, have a stronger preference for same-race partners, are less likely to have been in an interracial relationship, and have significantly more conservative political views. He summarizes this by saying, "Segregation may *appear* to be good for the individual, but it is not good for society as a whole. In fact, it is a type of market failure."[50]

Okay, this is a rather liberal view, and a value-laden conclusion. But if we were Republican politicians reading Johnson's book, we would actually come to the conclusion that we need to ensure that *more* White kids go to segregated schools so that, as Johnson points out, they would have more conservative views and they would vote Republican! If we were White Republican politicians, we would be terrified of another of his statements: that "integration has the power to transform communities, and society, in ways we have only begun to realize."[51] And historically in this country, White politicians in all branches of government of all parties and White parents did everything they could to thwart the possibility of such societal transformation after *Brown* and civil rights legislation. The 1973 Supreme Court decision *Milliken v. Bradley* drove a truck through busing programs, when it disallowed a Detroit program of busing that traversed the boundary between Detroit and adjoining suburbs. After that, as the historian Matthew Lassiter observed, "White parents in most cities knew that if they moved to the suburbs, their children would be beyond the reach of any busing plan."[52] That is, White parents would be safe from the transformative power of integration.

School Choice

For decades, "school choice" has been a mantra in education policy circles. This is the idea that parents should not be tied to just their local public school; they should be able to choose between different public schools. The historian Nancy MacLean points out that the history of school choice really got its start as a reaction to the 1954 *Brown v. Board of Education* decision. White parents did not want to send their kids to school with Black kids. In Virginia, the state Department of Education provided $250 vouchers for parents who did not want to send their kids to integrated schools. The vouchers, combined with private donations, made it possible for even the poorest Whites to send their kids to private schools, called "segregation academies."[53] Libertarians, like the Nobel Prize–winning economist Milton Friedman, loved this idea of school choice, even though the vouchers were clearly designed to fund the segregation academies. (Friedman's ultimate goal was the abolition of public schools altogether, part of the fever dream of libertarians to dismantle public investments.) These libertarians and conservatives hit upon a new tactic they taught to segregationists—to talk in code about "liberty, competition and market choice while embracing an anti-government stance."

The more current usage of the school-choice mantra has coincided in the past few decades with the rise of charter schools, magnet schools, gifted and talented programs, and, in some places, government-funded vouchers to help parents send their children to private schools. A generous take is that parents acting as education "consumers" will force public schools to get their act together in order to compete for students (and the funding that comes with enrollment). More critically, we can see that school choice is, essentially, a rebranding of parents' preferences for and "rights" to segregated schools and a politically expedient way to weaken local, public education and the power of teachers' unions.

School choice looks different for different people in different places: for Blacks and Latinos in cities, it means avoiding the "bad" local school and sending your kid to a charter school. On average, charter schools do not perform any better or worse than public schools, and they tend to cost more because of higher administrative costs, including salaries, which are not regulated in the same way public school salaries are.[54] They cream resources and students from local, public, zoned schools.[55] Charters are also mostly segregated, and their presence actually increases segregation across entire school districts.[56] In short, charters are a costly "solution" to the problem of poor-performing public schools. Still, they offer the promise of hope (often unfulfilled) to parents who are desperate.

For White parents, school choice means avoiding the exact same "bad" local school and sending your kid to a "good," or at least a less "bad" (i.e., less Black and Latino) school. In the suburbs, sometimes it is Whites sending their kids to charter schools—if they do not opt completely out of the public school system—with Blacks and Latinos consigned to the local public school. In many cities, magnet schools and gifted and talented programs are preferred. While the choices look different according to race, place, and the availability and affordability of private schools, the effects of school choice are similar most everywhere: increased school segregation.

The Ultimate Experiment in School Choice

In many ways, twenty-first-century New York City has proven to be the ultimate experiment in school choice. There, you can apply to pretty much any public school regardless of location within the five boroughs for schools of all levels. The assignments for K–5 and middle school follow a preference ranking, so that students who live in-zone for the school are prioritized, followed by kids who live in-district, then kids who live out-of-district.[57] High schools are generally open to any student regardless of district residence. That is, there are hardly any local, zoned high schools or high school programs in New York City anymore.

A team of researchers at the Center for New York City Affairs set out to detail which parents exercise school choice and how.[58] They narrowed their inquiry to kindergarten enrollments, because families must report their current addresses at the time of enrollment—which means that the researchers could tell which kids were attending in-zone schools. This also reduced potential confusion in the data, since families may move out-of-zone, but once their kids have started school, they can remain in their same school regardless. Kindergarten is the only moment we can get a clear look at student movement across zones.

To assess movement, the researchers looked at who stayed in, and who opted out of, their local, zoned school in the 2016–2017 school year. Of 75,634 kindergarten students, 16 percent were Asian American; 24 percent, Black; 40 percent, Latino; and 17 percent, White. Only 8 percent were born outside the United States (85 percent were born in New York City), though 19 percent spoke Spanish at home and 6 percent spoke "Chinese" at home. (The city's forms elide Mandarin, Cantonese, and other Chinese dialects into one language category.) Astoundingly, a full 40 percent of kindergarten students went to a school *other* than their local, zoned school. In some gentrifying neighborhoods, that number rose to over 70 percent. Sixty percent of Black students "moved," as did 39 percent of Latino students, 29 percent of White students, and 28 percent of Asian students. "Even when controlling for socioeconomic and other characteristics," the study reported, "Black students are 1.6 times more likely to opt out of their zoned schools than non-Black students."[59]

These choices cannot be overemphasized. *Lots* of kids are moving. Barely over a decade ago, few kids went out of zone because, well, you couldn't, really. Further, a huge majority of Black parents are basically saying that their local school is not good enough. Nearly three-quarters of all parents in some gentrifying neighborhoods are abandoning the local school. Whites and Asian Americans are far less likely to opt out, perhaps because the schools where they live are perfectly "good," and however coincidentally, those schools have relatively lower percentages of Black and Latino students. This contrasts with research in other parts of the country, where White students are the most likely to opt out. The researchers also found that in New York City, poorer families are less likely to go out-of-zone, a result that actually fits with research elsewhere in the country.[60] This makes sense—richer families, irrespective of race, are more likely to have cultural capital, or knowledge of the unwritten rules of how the system works, to know that they have better choices, and to have the time and energy to research their choices, visit prospective schools, and figure out how to get their kids there each day. Poorer families are less *able* to move schools.

Now, we know who is opting out, but where did they opt out *to*? Charter schools are a big draw in New York City, but mainly for Black parents—30 percent of Black kindergarteners go to charter schools. Whites and Asian Americans are more likely to send their kids to gifted and talented programs (in schools usually outside their zone and often outside the district)—8 percent of Whites and Asian Americans are in these programs, but only 2 percent of Latino children and 3 percent of Black children. The study also notes that 12 percent of children who do not go to their own zoned school go to another zoned school, as Sami did. This type of movement is huge but largely flies under the radar. These kids, of all backgrounds, are typically moving to "less bad" schools with fewer poor students and smaller populations of Black and Latino students.

Stay or Go

Where is choice more or less prevalent? It should not be surprising that the Center for New York City Affairs found that wealthier and Whiter neighborhoods had less movement out of the local, zoned schools (and they had fewer charter schools). Poorer and gentrifying neighborhoods had more movement and more charter schools. In the gentrifying neighborhood of Bed-Stuy, fewer than a third of eligible students attended their local school. The authors wrote, "Families of students living in gentrifying neighborhoods are 1.7 times more likely to choose a school [to move] than families of students in high-income or non-gentrifying [lower-income] neighborhoods. Consequently, living in a gentrifying neighborhood is the largest predictor of [exercising school] choice we found over all the other student characteristics."[61]

This is a critical point: it is extremely possible that school choice is accelerating gentrification in New York City. That is likely because, when gentrifiers (especially White ones) know that they do not have to send their kids to the local public school, they are more likely to decide that they can "afford" to move into a gentrifying neighborhood.

As for the non-White gentrifiers, it is instructive to consider what Saratu Ghartey, a Black lawyer gentrifier in Bed-Stuy, chose.[62] Her child was coming of school age around the time the Bed-Stuy Parents Committee came together. Ghartey was wary, writing,

> I paid attention to the little movement, marveling at these mostly white parents who would send their kids to schools with dreadful scores in the middle of what was not so long ago a rough neighborhood, schools where their kid would likely be the only "other" in the room. Most of the middle-class black parents I knew were not willing to take that risk. It is all well and good to say that you will send your kid to a majority low-income, low-scoring school because you believe in public schools, and you are not a snob, but the stakes are higher for black kids.

She continued:

> And then there is the slippery issue of school culture, which begins to matter around the third grade, when kids start to decide what their values are, who they want to be like, what is "cool." Many middle-class black parents are concerned that their children will fall into the wrong crowd, lose focus on academics, and begin to veer off the path their parents followed to success. This is a terrifying proposition for these parents, who may have seen firsthand the results when promising cousins failed to graduate high school, or dropped out of college, or made a wrong turn into the criminal justice system.

It is important to consider Ghartey's fears. Middle-class Blacks in this country have a far more tenuous hold on that economic standing than middle-class Whites, as they have far less family wealth than Whites, and a lot more can go wrong for them.[63] Ghartey's emphasis on school culture, which is basically kids' peer culture, really lays bare this fear. A

White kid who screws up gets multiple chances to get it right. A Black kid? Not so much. In this sense, White gentrifiers can "risk" choosing a progressive educational model for their child; non-White gentrifiers cannot. Ghartey noticed that on school tours, "the majority-black schools were focused on 'college readiness' and literacy 'basics,' while 'whiter' schools were heavy on progressive elements—project-based learning and child-led inquiries." Her child was accepted to an in-district school that had an energetic, young principal, but "the school had a long way to go academically," so she opted not to send her child there. In the end, her son was accepted to a pre-K program in lower Manhattan, near her work. She ended by saying, "I guess we chickened out on the neighborhood school experiment."

Alie Stumpf, the White schoolteacher who wrote about the benefits of classroom diversity, chose to send her daughter to the kind of school Ghartey felt she could not. Stumpf wrote an op-ed, a sympathetic reply to Ghartey, acknowledging the existence of a penalty for Blackness: "But let's get real: my daughter will carry her whiteness and its privileges into this setting and will be just fine; the rocks for her are never going to be as sharp as they are for Ghartey's family. Throughout most of history, we've left it to black families to be the pioneers of integration. It's long past time for white families to step up in New York City."[64]

Now, what happens to the kids whose families do not exercise school choice? In poorer, segregated, and gentrifying neighborhoods, they attend schools with an even higher concentration of poor Black and Latino kids, and a higher concentration of poverty. Since enrollments in these neighborhood schools have plummeted as other families opt out, enrollment-based funding dries up. Today, the struggle of poor, segregated, local schools is only getting harder.

All the movement captured in the New York City study underscores our point: however much we think parents and teachers are the biggest influence on kids' school success, parents know that peers are critical to their kids' outcomes. If peers did not matter, it would not make sense for so many families to shift away from their local, zoned schools. Where given the chance, too many White and Asian American parents are making certain that poor Black and Latino kids will not be their kids' peers.

Tracking

The journalist Amanda Ripley, in *The Smartest Kids in the World*, set out to understand why some kids do better in school. More specifically, she investigated why some countries do better than others on the Programme for International Student Assessment (PISA) exam, given to fifteen-year-old students across the world to measure performance in math, science, and reading.

A big part of the story turned out to be what is known as tracking, the practice of sorting kids into different classes for remedial, "normal," advanced, gifted and talented, academic versus vocational, and other curricular types. The countries that tracked their students saw learning for many students diminish. The earlier the age at which the countries started tracking kids, the worse the country did on the PISA exam.[65]

Ripley gives as an example Poland. Between 2000 and 2009, Poland's PISA scores jumped massively, but not uniformly. That is, the biggest gains were made by kids in "regular" schools who were, *after* they took the test, tracked into vocational schools. This was pretty incredible, and it happened because Poland delayed tracking for a year. In the past, these fifteen-year-old students would already have been shuffled off to vocational school, taking the test surrounded by other less-than-stellar academic performers. With delayed tracking, they were still in academic high schools with higher expectations and academically higher-performing peers when they took the PISA.

To test whether the gains were "real," Poland gave the PISA test to a sample of sixteen- and seventeen-year-olds who had gone off to vocational school in 2006 and 2009. The gains disappeared; the vocational students performed worse than students on the academic track. An adviser in the education ministry who had lobbied for Poland to join the countries administering the PISA test, seemed flummoxed: "It might be motivation," he said. "It needs more research. But the peer effects are somehow very influential."[66]

Indeed. Ripley hypothesized that *something* happened to the kids once they got to the vocational schools; they seemed to lose abilities or drive almost overnight. Our take? The drive was likely a product of being around more academically inclined and driven peers on the academic track. When you are in an academic environment where the peer culture defines learning as normative and expected, you have more incentive to rise to the challenge. But once you are in a situation where you are surrounded by peers deemed ill suited for academic tracks, the norms are different. Without peer norms actively promoting academic achievement, well, your academic motivation may disappear as well.

By the early twenty-first century, Ripley found, many countries had begun delaying tracking. Those countries that delayed tracking, like Poland, had better educational outcomes across students than those countries that did not, like the United States.[67]

The United States Embraces Tracking

In the United States, we have an entrenched apartheid school system that is, in many places, becoming even more racially segregated. With the expansion of charter schools, magnet schools, and, especially in urban areas, gifted and talented programs, our tracking of students is also on the rise. For high-achieving students in elite programs and schools, tracking is just fine. (This is largely the story of chapter 3.) But for those in the apartheid schools, not so much. So as a number of districts in the country drop within-school tracking, the proliferation of alternative public schools and programs has led to between-school tracking.

Tracking in the United States often starts in grade school, where many students who test well are sent off to gifted and talented programs. In New York City, for two decades four-year-olds were tested for giftedness and talentedness for the program that begins in kindergarten. A 2021 study on students in gifted and talented programs throughout the

United States found that most students in these programs are neither gifted nor talented, and in fact are only slightly above average. The average gifted student scored between the 75th and the 80th percentile on tests used to gauge them.[68]

The programs are highly desirable, though it is arguable whether they confer any academic benefit. Nationally, enrollees hardly see any boost in math scores and test only slightly higher in reading when compared to kids not included in gifted and talented programs. Black students did not even get those modest gains.

Potentially, the lack of significant learning gains is attributable to teachers' tendency, revealed in a 2019 survey, to focus on "enrichment activities" in their work with gifted and talented students. They instituted fun projects and critical thinking exercises, while keeping students' learning at grade level, rather than pushing the students toward advanced content.[69]

So why would a parent put their kid in a gifted and talented program if learning gains are nominal? Well, they are pretty exclusive. Nationwide, about 3.3 million kids—7 percent of grade school students—are in gifted and talented programs. Broken down by race, that is 13 percent of Asian American kids, 8 percent of White kids, 5 percent of Latino kids, and only 4 percent of Black kids. In New York City in 2021, the gifted and talented enrollment population consisted of 43 percent Asian American, 36 percent White, 14 percent Black, and 14 percent Latino students; only a quarter were low income.[70] For perspective, the full pool of New York City school kids is 73 percent low income, 41 percent Latino, 25 percent Black, 16.5 percent Asian American, and 15 percent White.[71]

Parents—not children, *parents*—are loath to give up these programs. White and Asian American parents, in particular, cry "meritocracy" and protest in favor of gifted and talented programs, magnet schools, and "specialized" high schools with test-in requirements. And district and city-level administrators are terrified of these parents. They are terrified of their visibility and political clout and terrified that they will leave the school system altogether. Where they are not terrified of these parents, politicians quickly find that they should be.

The Politics of New York City's Specialized High School Exam

In June 2018, New York City's Mayor de Blasio proposed axing the required entrance exam for the city's eight specialized high schools that use it. (This test is called the Specialized High Schools Admissions Test, or SHSAT.) The majority of students in these schools are Asian American, mainly of modest means; Blacks and Latinos, who are more than 70 percent of students in the public school system, take up few seats in these schools. (In 2018, their number ranged from 4 percent at Stuyvesant, the most difficult to get into, to 24 percent at Brooklyn Latin.) From the outside, the move looks like a cheap ploy to make de Blasio look like a champion of diversity (which, in this context, it was clear that Asian Americans did not contribute to).

Why do we think it was a cheap ploy?[72] Because school advocates had been calling for a system-wide approach to desegregating for the first five years of de Blasio's administration. At one point, he ignored a comprehensive proposal from a task force he himself created.[73] Rather than address all schools, de Blasio homed in on the prominent specialized high schools, which account for just 6 percent of high school seats citywide. And, most damning, these tests are enshrined in state law (the Hecht-Calandra Act, passed in 1971); to get rid of it, de Blasio would have had to sway legislators in the capital. This was barely a proposal, and it had barely a chance of coming to fruition. But it looked good—as if de Blasio was fighting for school diversity.

Moreover, let us be clear that about 80 percent of all Asian American New York City high school students do not attend the SHSAT public schools. For example, the latest data from spring 2022 show that there were 71,349 high school freshmen. Of those there were 12,082 Asian

Americans, 45,069 Black and Latinos, 9,767 Whites, and 4,431 multi-racial students.[74] For that year, 2,638 Asian American, 1,188 White, 635 Black and Latino, 162 multiracial, and 255 unknown-race students were admitted to the SHSAT schools. That is only 4,908 students, which is 7 percent of New York City public high school freshmen.[75]

If de Blasio actually wanted to increase diversity in the high schools, he could have easily eliminated the selective admissions requirements ("screens" like attendance, grades, portfolios, etc.) that a third of the city's high schools and high school programs have. But that would have required the resolve to stand up to the richer, typically White parents of kids in the more popular screened schools. He also could have exempted five of the eight schools from having to use the exam as their admission requirement—as only Stuyvesant, Bronx Science, and Brooklyn Tech are written into the 1971 law. It could be that his proposal, which only affected schools with a disproportionately high number of Asian American students, demonstrated that he thought it was easier, politically, to fight state lawmakers and immigrant Asian parents than to fight rich White parents. Indeed, after months of public wrangling and protests by Asian Americans (including Chinese hotel workers, who got Eric Adams, when he was fundraising in 2018 for his future mayoral run, to go from opposing the test to supporting it), the move to change the law died in Albany.[76] The chair of the New York State Senate education committee—John Liu, a graduate of Bronx Science, the second most prestigious public high school in New York City—killed de Blasio's proposal.[77]

There is nothing new about this kind of wrangling. Thirty years ago, Jeannie Oakes, the preeminent scholar of tracking, said, "I think it's a political issue having to do with people who have precocious children and who have, over the last 40 years in particular, won special programs and special advantages for their children. White and wealthier families, in particular, have fought to maintain a system that guarantees that their children will have a rich curriculum, extraordinarily well-qualified teachers, a peer group who is very much like them in terms of background and values and interests. The political pressure from those groups to maintain that system is extraordinarily great—the counter-vailing forces that make educators feel so insecure."[78]

She is right: the reason why the exam for the specialized high schools in New York City is codified in state law is that White parents demanded it. In the late 1960s, it seemed that then-mayor Lindsay was going to do away with the do-or-die admissions exams at the specialized high schools (at the time, Stuyvesant, Bronx Science, and Brooklyn Tech had 90 percent White student populations).[79] Without the test, it was expected that there would be a huge rise in the number of Black and Puerto Rican students at these schools. Parents lobbied two Bronx State Assembly and Senate representatives in particular, and thus the Hecht-Calendra Act of 1971 came into being. Legally, the exam was now the sole entrance metric for these three schools (a group that expanded to eight under Bloomberg). Now, to get rid of the exams or to change the admissions criteria, you would have to change the law.

And let us be clear: tracking hurts Black and Latino students, a lot. Jeannie Oakes, reflecting on more than two decades of research, con-cluded, "Tracked systems provided African American and Latino stu-dents with disproportionately less access to a whole range of resources and opportunities, including highly qualified teachers, classroom en-vironments conducive to learning, opportunities to earn extra 'grade points' that would raise their grade point averages, and courses that would qualify them for college entrance and, in turn, to high-status adult careers." In her research, Black and Latino students who had the same test scores as White and Asian American students were more likely to be placed in low tracks. She also found, in a study on tracking in San Jose high schools, that 93 percent of White and 97 percent of Asian American students were in accelerated classes compared to 56 percent of high-scoring Latino students. In other words, education specialist Oakes confirmed that discrimination is occurring at all levels of tracking—at the higher end, it is used to push White and Asian American students in and keep Black and Latino students out, and at the bottom end, to funnel Black and Latino students in and keep White and Asian American students out.[80]

Integrating Schools

The busing movement was the right idea—remember, mandates *worked* to desegregate southern schools—but in the end, it was undone by protesting White parents, the courts, and politicians with too little incentive to fight for desegregation. Today, a new form of an integrative measure has adopted the language of school choice.

In Wake County, North Carolina, Dallas, Texas, Stamford, Connecticut, Cambridge, Massachusetts, and other places around the United States, parents can (or, for a time, could) choose their kids' schools.[81] The catch is that the district makes the final "school choice." (In a comprehensive study of school districts nationwide, the Century Foundation found that out of 13,452 public school districts nationwide, 185 districts had some kind of integrative measure, and of those, twenty-two had this kind of school choice where parents rank schools in order of their preference and districts eventually choose.)[82] If it is made clear to parents that their choices are somewhat circumscribed and the government will not budge, the parents fall in line. While integration starts pretty much everywhere with a great degree of opposition, in these cities that have stuck with it, Whites came to support the integration of their schools, even if it meant their kids had to travel a long way to school.

Take, for example, the Louisville metro area of Jefferson County, Kentucky.[83] It has a county-wide integrated urban-suburban district, and is one of the few areas that still buses between urban and suburban areas. The school district is 42 percent White, 37 percent Black, and 12 percent Latino. While more than half the population in the county lives below the poverty line, there are few struggling inner-city schools. The county ordered schools to desegregate in 1974 in response to a court order, and started busing in 1975. At first it was not popular, and thousands of

White protestors rallied against busing. After Whites vandalized police cars, the governor called in the National Guard to supervise buses.

Eventually, White people's fears of integration dissipated, and after a few years, protests ceased. Schools were integrated. After decades of relatively successful integration, the Supreme Court in 2006 struck down Jefferson County's integration plan, which was based on race. So the county devised a new plan to get around the Court's decision. Why? Because residents, including White suburban residents, largely liked it. (In 2012, seven candidates ran for the county school board on a platform of ending busing and letting students attend their neighborhood schools. All seven were defeated.)[84] The integrated schools were also a factor in mitigating White flight out of Louisville, and out of the county. And because where your kid goes to school is not tied to where you live, it had a calming effect on prices in the housing market, and housing segregation declined more than 20 percent from 1990 to 2010.[85]

There are, of course, problems. Many White parents, for instance, have opted for Catholic schools, or move to different counties to avoid long commutes for their kids. And many Black parents in Black neighborhoods chafe at the idea that their children are being bused more than White children. After nearly five decades of busing to integrate schools, it looks as though Jefferson County's busing plan's days may be numbered, as politicians consider a proposal to give students in the poor and Black West End neighborhood the choice to go to schools closer to home, which would likely make schools there even poorer and more segregated.[86]

This type of busing program in Louisville (and elsewhere) could be replicated. While the plan was imperfect and inconvenient for many children and parents, it was at least an honest attempt to better the schools and to integrate them, and overall seemed to work. But such a plan is a heavy political undertaking, and, given the current political climate, seems unlikely to be adopted. Indeed, Louisville, with the blessing of some Black parents, is in the process of abandoning it.

District 15

Integration can happen voluntarily, but it is rare. Let us look at one very recent example where it did—District 15 (D15) in Brooklyn, which, as it happens, is where Sami did nearly all of his schooling. And it was a pioneer in another experiment in New York City education. Around 2015, the city was entertaining the idea of letting individual districts take up the question of desegregating their schools. D15 is where it happened first.

The district covers a large geographical swath, including Brooklyn Chinatown, Sunset Park (largely poor, Chinese, and Latino), Red Hook (largely poor and Black), and the wealthy, White brownstone neighborhoods of Park Slope, Boerum Hill, Cobble Hill, and Carroll Gardens. Its demographics, relative to the rest of the city, are unique. In 2020, it had 13 percent Black students, 16.5 percent Asian American, 35 percent Latino, and 31 percent White students. The White parents in the district are far more liberal and richer than Whites in the outer, more suburban parts of the city (like south Brooklyn, eastern and northern Queens, and Staten Island).

D15 has eleven middle schools and, in 2021, had thirty-one thousand enrolled students. Until a couple of years ago, it was also very segregated. There were three highly desired (by White, wealthier parents) middle schools that were majority White in a district that had 31 percent White students. Every year, parents were angry because there just were not enough seats at these good schools. By 2015, a fourth school emerged as an alternative for the White kids—Boerum Hill School for International Studies (BHS), which was featured on the popular 2020 podcast *Nice White Parents*. (As BHS became attractive to White parents, the number of White students nearly tripled from 2016 to 2020.)

So, by 2016, you have the "Big Three" schools and one viable alternative that most White parents preferred for their kids. In 2016, the Big Three were more than 50 percent White; the other eight middle schools in the district were about 10 percent White and more than 80 percent poor.[87]

Then in 2017, the city's Department of Education (DOE) instituted the new effort to allow individual districts to come up with their own diversity plans. In D15, the effort was kickstarted by some White moms—the titular "Nice White Parents" who met resistance from the DOE, as documented in the podcast series.[88] But soon the DOE was working with a private firm, holding a year-long series of community meetings to gain support for a D15 diversity plan.[89]

The plan, which was approved in fall 2018 and adopted in fall 2019, was to integrate middle schools in D15 by dropping admissions screening criteria (the Bloomberg-era devices we suggested de Blasio could have simply eradicated) like grades, attendance, test scores, and "niceness." Instead, middle school admissions would be based on lotteries that gave extra weight to poor students, homeless students, and English-language learners.[90] As soon as it was in place, the plan immediately led to substantial shifts in the district's demographics. The four Whitest schools saw an overall uptick in Black and Latino student enrollment, as well as an increase in the number of poorer students and English-language learners, and a decrease in the number of White students. The schools that had very few White students in 2018–2019 gained a small number of White students. In the first year, it looked as though the plan was headed in all the right directions. (Note that because this is a lottery plan that depends upon who applies where, the demographics will take some time to even out.)

Naysayers had been certain that the plan would send White parents fleeing the district. That did not happen. The percentage of White students in the district remained at 31 percent, and the number of White students who left the district between fifth and sixth grade (to go to private school, to attend charters or public school outside the district, or to go to school in other cities) did not increase substantially (just 4 percent).[91] Why aren't we surprised? The neighborhoods that comprise D15 are some of the most desired in the city—once in, these people are not moving.

The fear that White people will run away if you challenge their advantages in the schools is a long-standing one. And it was true once upon a time, when Whites fled to the suburbs. But gentrification is dramatically changing the pattern. In New York City, the gifted and talented program was specifically designed to keep White families with money in the city and in the school system in the early 2000s at the start of Michael Bloomberg's mayoralty. But by the early 2000s, White families were no longer leaving the city for the suburbs once they had children the way they did through the 1990s. Since they were staying, there was no more need to coddle them. But the mayor did it anyway.

Other New Yorkers had a great deal of hope that the success of the D15 experiment would lead to further from-the-ground-up integration. They, too, were wrong. In fact, after D15 announced its desegregation measures, officials in districts in Queens (D32) and southern Brooklyn (D21) announced that they would *not* be participating. White and Asian American parents in racially divided D28 in Queens fought tooth and nail against a desegregation plan, even though there actually was no official DOE desegregation plan proposed or under consideration.[92] The grassroots movement came to a grinding halt, even before the pandemic hit in early 2020.

Desegregating *within* most districts in New York City would not do much, as many are completely segregated, like Bed-Stuy (D16), which has only 4 percent White students, or the Bronx's D07, at less than 2 percent. Even if a few districts desegregated, the impact would be limited. If desegregation is to happen in New York City, it will need to be imposed: top-down, citywide, and crossing district and even borough boundaries.

Finland

To this point we have mostly talked about the United States, and mostly about New York City. To be fair, this is not entirely attributable to our personal biases as New Yorkers who went to the city's public schools. No, New York City's school system is by far the biggest in the country, with over a million students—they would be the tenth-largest city in the country!—and its scope of school choice and size of its charter school population make it a unique and interesting case study.

In this last section, though, we want to dip our toes in international-schooling waters and talk about Finland. Today, the Finnish school system is the envy of the world. Finns do not bellyache about how bad the public schools are, they do not have huge problems of inequality between schools, and they do not have individual "bad" schools, so the discourse of good schools/bad schools is completely foreign to them. What is going on?

In the 1980s, the Finnish school system was pretty mediocre. Change had been underway, in fits and starts, for more than a decade, but a jarring recession in the early 1990s that brought it to the brink of economic disaster was the real jolt the country needed. Finns resolved at the highest levels of government, through various regime changes, that building a great educational system was going to be the country's path to development.

They set out to transform, and they did. The transformation was no miracle, though. It was highly thought out and planned. Leaders borrowed best practices from abroad and committed to making their schools great by—and this is key—providing equal learning opportunities for all children. Almost every year, Finland's students score near the top of the pack on international exams like the PISA—and this while they take near to zero standardized exams in their educational careers and decline to prep for international exams. Everyone wants to know, What are they doing right?

Pasi Sahlberg, a former mathematics and science teacher and the former director general of Finland's Ministry of Education, lays out the history of Finland's schools in *Finnish Lessons 3.0: What Can the World Learn from Educational Change in Finland?* (This is the third edition of the book. Apparently, the world has a lot to learn from Finland!) Sahlberg is humble, like other Finns, and points out that they do not see their school system as the world's best. But since the world seems to—whole delegations of educators make pilgrimages to Finland—he is willing to poke around and share what he finds.

He reports that one of the most important things they did in Finland concerned teachers. By making their teacher training programs highly selective and paying teachers well, they built a profession that is highly respected. Further, Finland gives these highly trained and skilled teachers lots of autonomy when it comes to their teaching content and methods. Another important factor is that Finnish students' basic economic needs are taken care of. In addition to national policies providing three years of maternity leave, subsidized daycare, preschool for all five- and six-year-olds (formal schooling starts at seven years old), and a monthly family stipend of 150 euros a month for each child until age seventeen, student health care is free, and schools provide kids with food, counseling, and even taxi service, if needed.[93]

It is also crucial to look at what Finland is *not* doing. They do not track or have gifted programs in the lower grades, and every school is essentially a good school. There is no patchwork of magnet schools, charter schools, or exam schools that let families get out of going to local, public schools. There are not even many private schools. Tracking starts at age sixteen, when kids are sent into academic or vocational tracks. But unlike in the United States, Finland's education spending is tied to need rather than enrollment; vocational schools sometimes get more money, and in some places are more prestigious than academic schools.[94] Finland has a largely racially homogenous population, though it boasts a significant immigrant population, especially in the capital, Helsinki. But their schools are not segregated by economic class, immigrants are not overwhelmingly segregated by schools, and there is no White flight.

Finally, Finns place great emphasis on being relaxed about children's learning. Kids start school later in the day and there is lots of play in the early years. Teachers teach fewer hours. Students study less than in other countries, and they are not subject to standardized testing. No child gets left behind—nearly 30 percent of students get some additional academic assistance during their first nine years of school.[95] And their students learn *a lot*.

Obviously, reader, you know by now what we, the authors, think is the most important variable: peers. We have not studied peer effects in

Finland, but Amanda Ripley, author of *The Smartest Kids in the World*, has. With her focus on teachers and curriculum, Ripley attributes the academic successes in the countries she studied—South Korea, Poland, and Finland—to respect for teachers and rigorous learning. Everyone in these countries—parents, students, teachers—is serious about learning. If students *aren't* learning, all kinds of resources are mobilized to make sure they do. When she lets the students and their stories take center stage, though, the peer effect draws the spotlight. The kids, she wrote, "didn't want to talk about tenure policies or Tiger Moms; unburdened by the nag-ups of adults, they talked a lot about other kids, the most powerful influences in teenager's lives."[96]

In Finland, Ripley followed Kim, a female exchange student from Oklahoma. Kim pointed out some glaring differences between schooling in Oklahoma and schooling in Finland, such as with teaching (no interactive white boards in Finland) and policing (no cops in schools in Finland). But there was another, more subtle difference that Kim noted: students' cultural attitudes. In Finland, all the kids took school seriously. For instance, though Kim did not expect that there would be Finnish stoner kids, it turned out that they are pretty universal. The stoner kid often showed up to class looking hungover. But unlike Oklahoma's stoners, the Finn was a proper student, attentive in class, a keen note taker who always turned in his essays—just like all his classmates. There was something, Kim and Ripley agreed, going on in this Finnish school that "made everyone more serious about learning, even the kids who had not bought into other adult dictates."[97]

We believe the "something" is peer culture. If learning and doing your work is a normative part of the student peer culture, then students—including the stoners—learn and do their work. Teacher training and curriculum, funding, equality between schools, and a whole host of other factors are important, but kids will not learn unless they want to learn (as parents know, they will not work unless they want to work, either). And their desire to learn is in large part a function of their peer culture.

2

How the Peer Effect Works in Schools and Universities

Can't Buy Me Love is a run-of-the-mill 1980s American teen comedy. Our protagonist is a nerd who games the system of high school cliques: he pays a popular cheerleader a thousand dollars to *pretend* to date him for a month. Her apparent attention gets him accepted by the cool kids. But now he has to prove his cool-kid bona fides. Mostly, this means being a jerk. He joins the jocks in hurling dog poop at his former best friend's house (because: nerd). Soon, his behavior is so mean (just like that of the other cool boys) that the cheerleader girl who had begun to genuinely like him reveals to everyone at a party that he paid her to help him become cool. (That was not cool of her.) His peers at the party are repulsed, and he immediately loses his social standing. Worse, actually—even the nerds don't want anything to do with him. Of course, it gets unrealistically resolved by the end, when the nerd—again a nerd—makes up with his old best friend and rides off into the sunset, the cheerleader perched on the back of his riding lawnmower.

The reason we bring up this early entry in Patrick Dempsey's film oeuvre is that, however far-fetched the plot, *Can't Buy Me Love* pretty effectively illustrates how peer effects and status work. School-aged kids move within relatively closed social circuits with strongly defined social boundaries. Almost everywhere, there is a well-defined boundary between students and adults. In many places, there are also group boundaries between student cliques. These can be hierarchical—in the classic American high school movies, this usually looks like a ranking of jocks, cheerleaders, and other cool kids at the top, followed by drama and band kids, various middle-level cliques, then nerds or geeks at the bottom. The number and types of cliques vary from school to school and time to time (and movie to movie). Yet the tension between the poles of jocks and nerds is enough to sustain a movie (or a franchise—*Revenge of the Nerds* made it to four sequels, after all). In real life, as is the case in lots of massive suburban schools that have staggered start times, you may not really be able to see a ranking, or even defined student groups.

The social bubbles in which students in middle school, high school, and college (at least, colleges that are not primarily "commuter" schools) are pretty untouchable for parents, teachers, and other adults. Parents, teachers, and other adults do not really have much say in or control over or impact upon how these kids lead their lives, even if they delude themselves into thinking they do. The decline in adult control over children starts as soon as they have other kids around them (daycare, the playground, preschool, kindergarten) and accelerates from there. Adults can affect certain parameters, as when parents choose neighborhoods, and, often, schools. But they cannot choose their kids' peers, even if they think they can. (They can't.) And parents do not *directly* shape kids' behavior through their methods of raising their children—their effects are largely indirect, as with choosing schools, or through such characteristics as levels of education, income and wealth, race, religion, etc., all of which impact choice of peers.

To put it a little differently, kids in school get to define their cultural world—their peer culture—and they create the norms of behavior expected of members of various groups. In *Can't Buy Me Love*, the peer culture of the jocks dictates that they *should* throw poop at the nerds' houses. Such behavior is context specific, of course: it is highly unlikely that these jocks will continue to throw poop at people's houses after high school or college. Then again, if you look at the behavior of many horrible adults, you will see that the norms of their peer groups may have only slightly changed as they entered adulthood.

Our peers have a significant impact on who we are, how we behave, and how we turn out down the road. Because their opinions of us really matter to us, from childhood into young adulthood (and beyond), their opinions are more likely than our parents' to shape our behaviors. There are direct effects—we want to be like our peers, so we do things like them. If drinking alcohol is a thing they do, we are more likely to drink. If wearing chastity rings and taking virginity pledges is a popular thing among peers at a school, well, we will do that, too. (Jocks throwing dog poop at the nerds' houses? In some places and times, sure.) There are also indirect peer effects that operate through a student-driven peer culture, which defines what is acceptable and what is not (that is, norms of behavior), without students expressly being told. These norms are something they pick up and learn, then become something they "just know." Parents, teachers, and administrators have no say in this culture.

When talking about peer effects, we are talking about how people, in certain situations, behave in certain ways in order to build their status, honor, and prestige in the eyes of others whom they respect in relatively closed settings. You may be a doctor who commands the respect of others in your hospital and your community, where you are known, but on the subway, you are just another body.

In the high school context, there are a multitude of group identities at play. The broadest category is "student," but other salient identities are categories like "female student," "sophomore," and "female sophomore." Then we have cliques like "cool kids" and "drama kids" and "burnouts," and of course racial and ethnic groups, which are varyingly prominent in different schools. Any identity that is stable over time (e.g., "drama kids," as opposed to "me and my friends who sit at that table") will have developed a culture—basically, things that are important to this group, as well as dos and don'ts (norms) that will be learned by new members as older members graduate. To gain status, kids need to do two things, as Murray Milner Jr. pointed out in *Freaks, Geeks, and Cool Kids*: do the things other kids do (i.e., follow the norms) and associate with people of equal or higher status (if they will let us!).[1] Add some distance from those considered "beneath" the cool kids, and it is better still.

A Word on American Exceptionalism

The classic American teen movies do not get made in other countries because the way their schools operate is very different from ours, and the ways schools are structured affect the way student social life will be structured. In the United States, we have sports and clubs and after-school activities in our schools. Other countries also have sports and clubs and after-school activities—it is just that these don't happen at school. School in the United States is intimately tied to and constructive of students' identities in a way that it is not for students in other parts of the world, in large part because we spend so much time there, and so many of the activities we engage in happen there. And that is where our most important friends and enemies and frenemies are.

That is not true in the same way for kids in, say, India or China or South Korea or Jamaica or many, many other countries. Take, for instance, cliques in schools. Murray Milner Jr. studied a private school in Delhi, finding that it was hard to discern whether there was a popular crowd at all. Weirder yet, there did not seem to be any students who were openly shunned or socially isolated. Where were the popular kids and the loser kids? The few high-status individuals he could locate had achieved their status by earning good grades. In another school, in northeast India, Milner found a bit more cliquishness in terms of drawing of boundaries between friendship groups and labeling of them, but still nowhere close to the way cliquishness looked in the United States.[2]

Yi-Lin Chiang found something similar in China, where she studied socioeconomically elite students in six Beijing schools.[3] Among these students, like those Milner studied in Delhi, status was solely based on academic achievement, specifically, test scores. The students sorted themselves into four status categories—intellectuals, studyholics, underachievers, and losers—but these were only individual distinctions. They did not lead to group formations. Students ate and dated and generally socialized across these porous status boundaries.[4]

In much of the world, educational life is organized similarly, and that affects the social life of students *in the school*. School is for school. Your performance in school is defined by how you do on exams—course exams, year-end exams, and admissions exams for high school and college. Because, in countries including India and China, college admissions are in no way dependent on extracurricular activities, student culture revolves solely around academic achievement, not sporting prowess or socioeconomic class or pot-smoking or show choir.

The hierarchy and cliques we find in the US context are only an extreme example of the way peer effects work. What we need to keep in mind, not just for the discussion here but when we talk about workplaces and police in later chapters, is that we are interested in how people behave in settings where group identities are defined, a culture has developed, and there is cultural pressure to adhere to group norms.

What Sociology Says about Peer Effects

Peers have an important place in the academic study of adolescence and young adulthood, including in studies of educational achievement, dating, delinquency and criminal behavior, substance abuse, and mental health.[5] But not all subfields that consider youth attend to peer effects. (There is hardly any attention to peer effects, for example, in the subfield the two of us primarily engage with, immigrant assimilation.)[6]

In the abovementioned subfields, youth peers are treated as having an effect independent of parents. Our argument, following Judith Harris's groundbreaking work, takes this further.[7] She argues—and we agree—that peers are *more* important than parents in accounting for kids' outcomes. As we noted, parents do not directly affect choices of peers.[8] Parents' education and income affect economic class, the neighborhoods their children live in, and the types of schools they go to, and parents give their children their color of skin, ethnicity, and religion. So parents shape the pool of their children's possible peers. But who children, teenagers, and young adults take up as peers is ultimately a question of whom they choose and who chooses them.

Rather than bore or exhaust you with a full review of everything sociology already has to say about youth peer effects, we will concentrate on a set of examples that illustrate the peer effects' key conceptual mechanisms: countercultural attitudes to school; hookup culture; peer effects on academic and social performance; how to end bullying; and suicide.

Slackers and Brothers

You have probably heard the term "acting White." Cultural conservatives love to bring it up to explain why Black kids at school perform worse academically than the White kids.[9] They say that this lag is the result of a cultural attitude among Black kids that if you do well at school you are "acting White."[10] Heck, even Barack Obama, in his 2004 Senate run, claimed, "Children can't achieve unless we raise their expectations and turn off the television sets and eradicate the slander that says a black youth with a book is acting white."[11]

Turns out this idea of "acting White" is more racist wishful thinking than reality. It has been convincingly debunked by many sociologists.[12] There is no evidence that Black kids generally devalue academic achievement, nor that Black students who perform well academically face backlash for "acting White."

The term *does* exist, though, and some Black kids (and adults) do actually use it to describe other Black kids and adults. But "acting White" is not about academics—it is about cultural stuff. The writer Jamelle Bouie knows this well:

> As a nerdy black kid who was accused of "acting white" on a fairly regular basis, I feel confident saying that the charge had everything to do with cultural capital, and little to do with academics. If you dressed like other black kids, had the same interests as other black kids, and lived in the

same neighborhoods as the other black kids, then you were accepted into the tribe. If you didn't, you weren't. In my experience, the "acting white" charge was reserved for black kids, academically successful or otherwise, who didn't fit in with the main crowd. In other words, this wasn't some unique black pathology against academic achievement; it was your standard bullying and exclusion, but with a racial tinge.[13]

Let us rephrase this in the conceptual terms we have been using. Black kids who conformed to the norms of other Black kids in the neighborhood in terms of dress and having "the same interests" were accepted. The kids "who didn't fit in with the main crowd," that is, did not conform to the norms, were sanctioned, or punished. And the punishment was that the other Black kids would tease them by saying they were "acting White." It was, as Bouie says, "your standard bullying and exclusion, but with a racial tinge." That is, the kids who did not conform to the norms were punished. Here, the punishment for violating the norms of this particular group's culture (and by "group" we mean these particular Black kids in these particular neighborhoods who self-identify as belonging to this particular "tribe," not Black people in general) is to have the behavioral deviance pointed out and labeled as "acting White." It is easy to imagine a different punishment being substituted in—any number of hurtful insults that have nothing to do with race could have been used, or even physical beatings. If those other punishments became linked to those norms, we would have nothing to talk about in this section.

The sociologist Prudence Carter takes this idea that the insult "acting White" is a response to cultural violations a bit further in ethnographic work she did among Black and Latino youth in Yonkers, a small city just north of New York City.[14] Through in-depth interviews, she found that students did sometimes accuse classmates of "acting White," but they did so for nonacademic reasons. She found that the most frequent reason to be called out for "acting White" was "language and speech styles." Dress styles and taste were another way to mark boundaries between Black and Latino students and Whites. And Black and Latino kids who primarily hung out with White kids often were labeled as "acting White." We should note here that in her study, where kids went to mixed schools, these Black and Latino kids who were labeled as "acting White" were mainly in the honors tracks, which mostly had White students, with much smaller numbers of Black and Latino students. It was not the academic achievement that got them the label of "acting White"; it was that they were hanging out with White kids.

Charges of "acting White" are all about *boundary maintenance*. Where the boundaries are strong, group identity is strong. The group's cultural aspects and norms are well defined and help maintain the integrity of the group. For some Black students in some places, their *group* identity is culturally defined in a way that requires sanctioning members (and those who would otherwise seem to be natural members) for violating norms and therefore weakening the group boundaries. Teasing others for "acting White" is an effectively hurtful way to promote adherence to norms where groups are at least partially characterized by racial homogeneity.

Now, if we take the racist layering and essentializing off, we are left with a plausible idea—that there are certain kids in certain schools and certain neighborhoods who have decided that academic achievement is conformist and they want nothing to do with it. And this is a theme across lots of ethnographies focused on teens.[15]

Ain't No Makin' It, by Jay MacLeod, was originally published in 1987. Set in "Clarendon Heights," a pseudonymous public housing project in an unnamed, northeastern US city, it is about two groups of teenage boys. There are the "Hallway Hangers," a mostly White group that clusters by doorway #13, and the "Brothers," the predominantly Black teens. This housing project, when MacLeod first started his study in the early 1980s, was 65 percent White and 25 percent Black.[16] Very few adult males lived there—85 percent of households were female headed. Everyone was poor (there was an income ceiling to qualify for this housing).[17]

The Hallway Hangers were tough and streetwise, and they drank and fought a lot. Among roughly eighteen boys, the eight core members were Irish or Italian, except for one Black kid and one with mixed Black-White parents. Five were dropouts, two graduated, and one was still in high school. All but two had been arrested. These core members were very concerned with being "bad," one clarifying, "If you're to be bad, you hafta be arrested. You hafta at least know what bein' in a cell is like."[18]

All but one of the Hallway Hangers were pretty racist. The Black and half-Black members, who still suffered racial abuse within the group, had become Hallway Hangers because they were the first Black kids in the projects. Joining with the Hallway Hangers was "natural." This being the 1980s, racist jokes very easily rolled off the tongues of most White kids, and the non-White kids in the Hallway Hangers did what they did anywhere else: they played it off, made a joke of it, or ignored the insults. Sometimes, the Black kid agreed with their racist statements. The half-Black kid told MacLeod, "I take it as a joke. They're just fooling around. It doesn't bother me at all. If they hit me or something, that's a different story."[19] All this can sound awful to adult ears in the twenty-first century, but it makes sense—if these are the only other kids around, you need them. Readers who were once minority kids surrounded by White kids will read this as a familiar story—in retrospect, a sad and embarrassing one.

The Brothers counted about a dozen members, and all but one of the seven main members were Black. They went to school regularly, did not smoke or do drugs, drank infrequently, and kept their noses clean. None had been arrested. One of the Brothers graduated, but was unemployed, while another was an academic high achiever; both were admired by their fellow Brothers. Unlike with the Hallway Hangers, going to jail was not a badge of honor in this group; on the contrary, a night in jail would lower a member's esteem in the eyes of the other Brothers.[20]

Both groups were poor, though they differed significantly in their aspirations. The Hallway Hangers did not have any. They did not believe that school would do anything for them, only that the future held jail or death. The Brothers, on the other hand, believed wholeheartedly in the American Dream—work hard and you *will* get ahead. Where the

Hallway Hangers were clearly countercultural, the Brothers bought into and exhibited middle-class respectability. When they got together, they did not just hang out by a door; often, they played basketball (most were athletes). And they did not like or want to be associated with the Hallway Hangers. One of the Brothers, incidentally, the younger half-brother of the Hangers' half-Black member, told McLeod, "I would never hang with them. I'm not interested in drinking, getting high, or making trouble. That's about all they do. . . . I don't like to just sit around." (How did half-brothers who lived in the same house end up in such different peer groups? The one in the Brothers got a scholarship to go to a prestigious private school in the third grade.)[21] Another Brother was more succinct: the Hallway Hangers, he said, were "just a bunch of fuckups."[22] Still, the Brothers tended to walk away before confrontations with the Hallway Hangers could explode into fights. There were fewer of them, and the housing project was majority White. The odds were not on their side.

While the Brothers bought into the achievement ideology, for the most part they did not do particularly well in school. They were in low educational tracks, and got bad grades. But where the Hallway Hangers put the blame for poor performance on everyone else, the Brothers blamed themselves—if they did poorly in school, it was the fault of their own laziness, stupidity, or lack of self-discipline.[23] Again, they demonstrated their allegiance to the American Dream. If you are not thriving, it is your own damn fault.

The culture of the Hallway Hangers was marked by an aversion to school. They valued "physical toughness, emotional resiliency, quick-wittedness, masculinity, loyalty, and group solidarity." So if and when they went to school, these boys were frequently drunk or high and always disrespectful. "Yeah, if you're a straight-A student, you get razzed," the current leader told MacLeod. Another kid chimed in, "Then you're a fucking weirdo, and you shouldn't be living here in the first place."[24] By the time of MacLeod's study, the group had been around for years; the current members had older siblings who were Hallway Hangers first, who taught them the well-defined culture of doorway #13. And they came by their disillusionment honestly: "What we gonna do when all we seen is fuckin' drugs, fighting, this and that, no one going to school?"[25]

The second edition of the book (1995) followed these teens into young adulthood, and a third edition (2009) found them approaching middle age. By the second edition, MacLeod found that some of the Hallway Hangers had gone to jail, and some of the Brothers to college. But in spite of their middle-class aspirations, the Brothers and Hallway Hangers ended up in the same socioeconomic boat—in low-paid, insecure jobs. A big part of the story for the Brothers was, of course, racism in the job market. The Hallway Hangers, on the other hand, blamed not their low aspirations but Black people.[26] In 2006, most of the now thirty- and forty-something men were still at the lower end of the economic scale, though a couple had broken into the middle class.

In a research appendix, MacLeod talked about a breakthrough moment early in his study. He was an undergraduate himself, back then, and when he played kind of well in a pickup basketball game with both groups, he gained their respect. That night on his bus ride home to the university, the leader of the Hallway Hangers unexpectedly sat down next to him. On the long ride, he opened up to MacLeod, speaking of his brothers in prison. Then he said, "I gotta get away. I gotta do somethin'. If I don't, I'm gonna be fucked; I know it. I ain't ready for fucking prison, man."[27] This young man, on the verge of graduating high school, the leader of a peer group and definer of its norms, was fully cognizant of what being in that peer group and adhering to its norms could possibly do to him and his future.

The point of all this is that, if you want to understand how peers affect kids' outcomes (grades, drugs, cutting school, dropping out, etc.), you have to look closely at what happens *within* their peer groups. These could be smallish cliques like the Hangers and the Brothers, or groups as large as their entire school body, but you have to actually dig into the culture, as Jamelle Bouie, Prudence Carter, and Jay MacLeod did. Surveys are not going to capture the interplay of how people affect each other's behavior in the group context, and how they create their own culture and norms. To explain how the kids from these two groups, who are so similar in many respects, have such different outlooks, though they live in the same place and come from the same socioeconomic background (let alone to explain the brothers from rival gangs living in the same apartment), you have to look at the microdynamics.

At Stuyvesant High School in Manhattan (where both of us went), there is a generalized peer culture of achievement, the flip side of the Hallway Hangers' attitudes. In both cases, individuals conform to the norms that are important for their peer culture. At Stuyvesant, academic achievement is paramount, and kids who drink and smoke weed during school days still know they need to get their schoolwork done—not to make teachers and parents happy, but because they do not want to look like schmucks in front of their peers. For the Hallway Hangers, drinking and smoking weed during the day were an important part of their peer culture; so was *not* doing their schoolwork, so they didn't do it. They were always on the verge of dropping out, and some did, while others transferred to a program for kids who were on the verge of dropping out. But for the kids at Stuyvesant who were drinking and smoking and cutting class, dropping out was not even a question. They were going to graduate and go on to college and on to the professions. Period.

Hookup Culture

Kids today . . . you know the refrain. According to the olds, the kids are practically devil children, what with their "rainbow" oral sex parties and their sexting and their drugs and stuff.[28] (For the record, the rainbow parties are an urban legend, and sexting, while real, is way overblown as commentators ignore that teens are sending sexts largely to partners, not strangers—though, yes, there are certainly issues with that.)[29] The thing is, the "kids today" discourse is dead wrong. The kids are far, far tamer than previous generations of American teens. They have less sex, and start having it at an older age. They drink less and smoke cigarettes way less. They rarely use "hard" drugs. In fact, let's just pick some actual statistics on twelfth graders from the national Youth Risk Behavior Surveillance System survey, conducted every other year from 1991 to 2019 by the Centers for Disease Control and Prevention.[30] They may not account for rock 'n roll, but in terms of sex and drugs, the news is far from dire: twelfth graders were 10 percent less likely to have had sex in 2019 than in 1991 (57 percent versus 67 percent); only 42 percent in 2019 reported that they were sexually active at the time of the survey, down from a high of 53 percent in 1993; and the proportion of students with four or more lifetime sexual partners dropped from 27 percent in 1993 to 16 percent in 2019. Though twelfth graders have consistently used marijuana at a rate of roughly 25 percent in the month prior to the survey since the outset, most types of drug use have plummeted. Ecstasy (MDMA, or molly), was used by 14 percent of twelfth graders in 2001, and just 5 percent by 2019, and twelfth graders' drinking dropped from 62 percent in 1999 to 40 percent in 2019. Vaping has only been measured since 2015. Though frequent vaping (twenty days out of the preceding month) increased from 3 percent in 2015 to 17 percent in 2019 in this national survey, data from New York State show a drop in vaping (any amount) from 27.5 to 22.5 percent from 2018 to 2020, then another huge drop to 11.3 percent in 2021.[31] (This could be pandemic related—it is tough to hide stuff from your parents when you are around them all day every day!)

Pretty much any way you measure it, kids today are "better behaved" than kids of their parents' or grandparents' cohorts. A big reason why we do not recognize how good kids are these days is that we fall prey to "moral panics." That is, we hear that the rate of, say, teen pregnancy, is up (it isn't; it is actually way down) and it *feels* true, so we believe it without looking into the sketchy evidence.[32] Plus, we get to feel a bit of superiority when we pass on the news about these people doing supposedly awful things.

Which brings us to this section's topic: hookups. Like teens, college students are actually more conservative than yesterday's regarding sex and drugs. The Online College Social Life Survey, conducted between 2005 and 2011, found that about 20 percent of college seniors surveyed had never had sex, and 30 percent had never "hooked up."[33] But look to the headlines, and it is hand wringing about the harms of hookup culture everywhere you turn.

What is the disconnect? To some degree, it is the lack of a real definition for a hookup. The hookup is in the eye of the beholder! Results from the abovementioned survey tell us that about a third of hookups involve intercourse, another third, oral sex, and the other third, kissing and "non-genital touching."[34] Even when college seniors responded that they had hooked up, they were not doing it often: 40 percent had three or fewer hookups; 40 percent had four to nine hookups; and just 20 percent had ten or more over the course of their college careers. Another way to phrase the chasteness of college students is to point out that 80 percent of seniors who have hooked up in college have had on average one or fewer hookups per semester.

Lisa Wade, one of the most astute analysts in this area, wrote *American Hookup: The New Culture of Sex on Campus*.[35] Her study focused on hookup culture at "traditional" colleges where students mainly live in dorms and social life revolves around the college. This is opposed to "commuter" colleges, where students commute to campus for their classes, then head to work or home, where they often have spouses, children, or parents to take care of; for "commuter" students, college is just one part of their lives. For their peers attending colleges with dorm life and fraternities and sororities, hookup culture *is* all-encompassing. "Even if you aren't hooking up," one Black woman wrote about her first year on campus, "there is no escaping hookup culture."[36]

This last quotation is key. It is not that many students are actually hooking up, as the numbers from the survey indicate. Wade closely studied 101 college students through the course of a semester in their first year. It was typical for students to have mixed feelings about the opportunity to have casual sex: thirty-six were simultaneously attracted to and repelled by hookup culture when they got to college; thirty-four opted out; twenty-three enthusiastically opted in; and eight kept their monogamous relationships. The culture—in this case, hookup culture—just sets the norm that hooking up is socially acceptable (especially in the context of parties and drinking) and that the hookup partner's status is key to determining whether to be proud of or slightly chagrined by the hookup.

The culture, in other words, is heavily infused with status concerns. First, for both men and women, the hookup partner should be hot. Women are also attuned to whether their male hookups are athletes or "fraternity stars." If you are potentially too drunk to pay proper attention to the "quality" of your hookup partner, do not fret: your friends are watching out, making sure you don't hook up with someone ugly or otherwise low-status. Ideally you want to hook up with someone above your status level, or at least at your own level, and avoid a downward hookup, which is cause for social embarrassment. Second, while hookups are about pleasure (mostly men's), their more important function is their value for your social standing. They are not to be kept to yourself; you have to tell people about them. You have to impress them. And you must post pictures to your social medias—or it didn't happen. One of Wade's female college student informants told her, "The whole point of hookups is get some and then be able to point the person out to your friends and be like, 'Yeah, that guy. That's right. The hot one over there. I got that.'" Another woman said, "It's almost bragging rights if you hook up with a guy with a higher social status."[37] More sociologically, a third explained, "Average guys just don't cut it. Sure, it's not a social tragedy to hook up with an average-looking guy. But hooking up with someone attractive is a social asset for sure. It raises your standing in the hierarchy of potential partners. It makes you more attractive."[38]

The key indicators for hookup-worthiness on college campuses are attributes like hotness, blondness, fraternity membership, and athletic status. In hookup culture, "beauty"—really hookup-worthiness—is socially determined.[39] If you think he or she is hot, but your peers don't, sorry—culturally speaking, they are not hot or hookup-worthy.

Here we need to reiterate the point that most people are not enthusiastic participants in hookup culture. Some refrain because they feel a bit "prudish" about casual sexual activity, others have religious reasons, and others still are kept out due to discrimination. The latter group includes Black women and Asian American men, who even if they want to participate in the culture are disproportionately shunned. But students of color generally (including Black men and Asian American women and Hispanic men and women) are less inclined to hook up to begin with.[40] Overall, participants in hookup culture are pretty White, disproportionately wealthy, cisgender, and heterosexual. And while women, especially White women, are willing participants, it is very much a game stacked in White men's favor.

Hooking up, at the same time infrequent and common, has not killed off dating. By senior year, 69 percent of heterosexual students had been in a relationship of at least six months. Hookups, usually one-off encounters, sometimes become committed relationships, and committed relationships sometimes become hookups.[41]

Alright then, so why does it *seem* like everyone is hooking up? Wade points out that the college students who are involved in casual hookups take up a lot of physical and psychic space: the primping and prepping and predrinking in the dorms before parties; the loud return after the parties; sex in the dorms chasing roommates out (being "sexiled"); the postparty morning recaps; and, of course, the social media posts. Those who are not part of it *feel* like they are in a tiny minority, not realizing that there are lots of other people, right there in their dorms, declining to hook up, too. It is also true that the gung-ho participants in hookup culture are, again, mostly White, pretty, athletic, well-dressed, and moneyed. They are hypervisible on campus, lounging on the quad, front and center in the student sections of football stadiums and basketball arenas, ubiquitous at the bars in the college towns. And, as one Latina student said, "For some reason, they exude dominance."[42] In the case of hooking up, the culture is broad, but the boundaries between subgroups' behaviors are ill defined and often invisible—one of the crucial norms may, in fact, be that "everyone's doing it," regardless of individuals' participation. So those not "doing it" may feel further exclusion as they are violating the central norm of the culture.

How Do Peers Affect School Performance?

There is a fair amount of support for the idea that peers affect grades at all levels of school. Most of these kinds of studies are quantitative, and their notion of peers is usually straightforward: they look to see how race and gender of peers, economic class of peers, different types of behaviors of peers, and randomly assigned roommates and class sections affect academic and social outcomes of individuals. These studies tell us a lot about how peers affect behavior and outcomes, including the ways variations in the structures of peer groups affect academic and social performance in college.[43] For example, one such study of Dartmouth students found that randomly selected roommates have an effect on their peers' GPA and decisions on joining social/fraternity groups.[44]

While quantitative studies are relatively plentiful, we also want to talk about a couple of qualitative studies that look at how variations in structures of peer groups affect academic and social performance in college.

Friends or Flunk

Janice McCabe, a sociologist, studied peer effects by looking at friendship patterns among students at a large, midwestern university that she calls "Midwestern University." She was particularly interested in two things: first, what do friendship patterns of college students actually look like, and second, how does that affect academic outcomes?[45]

The friendship networks of McCabe's sixty-seven-student sample fell into three distinct types: tight-knitters, compartmentalizers, and samplers. The tight-knitters had one large friendship group, where everyone was friends with everyone else. Compartmentalizers had between two and four distinct and independent friendship groups; friends knew each other within groups, but not between groups. And the samplers had one or two independent friends in several different social areas. Each network type supported academics and social success/failure in different ways.

Most of the Black and Latino students in the study were tight-knitters; these students were so close with their friend groups that they often called them their "family" or their "home." That could be a function of being a minority on a White-majority campus, but without data from colleges with large or majority Black and/or Latino populations, it is hard to tell. We would also be interested to learn whether there is a difference in friendship structures at "traditional" versus commuter colleges. Regardless of race, though, the tight-knitter students had only one group of friends. If the group was more supportive of academic work, they did better academically. If the students in the group lacked academic skills or motivation, the group could pull an individual down. Half of the tight-knitters in McCabe's study had friends who pulled them away from academics, and of these, only half graduated. But the ones who were in a group that was more supportive of academics all graduated. The tight bonds in these types of friendships often helped minority students navigate college life, but they could prove counterproductive to academic life when the friend group was more about partying.

Most of the White students at MU were compartmentalizers who got social support and academic support from different groups. One of the women McCabe interviewed said she had her "fun" group to go to parties and watch movies with, then a separate group for study sessions. The woman felt that these two clusters helped her balance partying and work, and she graduated in four years. McCabe found, though, that students with *additional* compartmentalized clusters of friends had a harder time maintaining these ties—it was very time intensive! There were some Black and Latino compartmentalizers, and many had support systems within one of their Black/Latino clusters. Those who did not have such a cluster to help them deal with racism and classism at the school had lower GPAs.

Samplers came from a wide variety of backgrounds and had many separate friends. They might have had the same number of friends as tight-knitters or compartmentalizers, but the quality of their interactions differed. The samplers' friends tended to not be close, or particularly socially supportive—samplers reported feeling lonely and lacking social support. One student described her friendships as "disappointing." Many samplers also yearned for deeper intellectual friendships. Samplers were academically successful *in spite of* not having an academic support network—possibly because they didn't have a friendship network that could negatively affect their academic work, either.

Privileged Poor and Doubly Disadvantaged

A second qualitative study we are interested in is by the sociologist Anthony Jack, who wanted to know what happens to Black, Latino, and White students (and a few Asian Americans who volunteered for his project) from poor, urban backgrounds who end up at elite universities. He looked at two such groups—one from local, public high schools, and one from fancy private high schools. Jack referred to these groups as the "doubly disadvantaged" and the "privileged poor," respectively. While these kids were from similar backgrounds, the kind of schooling they got in high school made their college experiences vastly divergent.[46] Jack counted himself among the privileged poor, having gone to a prep school his senior year, then on to Amherst College and Harvard University for graduate school. (Now he is a professor at Harvard. You go, Anthony Jack!) He found that half of lower-income Black students at elite universities came from private schools, though few very poor Black kids go to such high schools overall. Only one-third of lower-income Latinos attended private high schools. By recruiting the "privileged poor," he wrote, "Elite colleges effectively hedge their bets: They recruit those already familiar with the social and cultural norms that pervade their own campuses."[47] So these students add diversity, without the "trouble" of diversity.

When they entered elite colleges, Jack tells us, the doubly disadvantaged were fish out of water; they had trouble with classes, and in figuring out which peer groups they fit. College was a culture shock. The privileged poor, though, found an easier transition. Because of their prep-school backgrounds, they already knew how to pick classes and knew about that mundane, yet critical phenomenon of professors' office hours. Where the doubly disadvantaged did not know what to make of the "my door is always open" offer—the privileged poor took it literally and walked right in through those open doors and gained the advantage of rapport with professors. This seemingly small thing can have huge ramifications—it can be the difference between an A and a B, or between passing and failing a class. Too much trouble in classes, which can often easily be addressed by talking with professors, can even lead to failing out of school.

The privileged poor, having been exposed to them in high school or earlier, were also at ease with wealth, with White peers, and with "White" cultural activities. While the family backgrounds and home situations of both groups of poor students were similar, the private school kids had very different peers, whom they socialized with, learned their aspirations from, and from whom they got a lot of cultural capital. That is, they learned the unwritten rules of various social "games." For instance, as Jack put it in an interview, "The privileged poor know that summer can be both a noun and a verb. They've been conditioned to be around rich people for the last four years of their life. They know about the vacation spots, the second homes, the private jets, the private islands. They sometimes have been on those private jets and private islands."[48] (Shamus Khan, in his groundbreaking book, *Privilege*, calls this knowledge that students learn at elite private schools the "ease of privilege.")[49] The doubly disadvantaged kids coming from public schools did not come to college with such cultural capital, nor did they hang around with kids in college who could pass it along. Many of the doubly disadvantaged withdrew from campus life feeling somewhat isolated and like an outsider.[50] Others made the best of it, learning as the privileged poor did, but years later.

This point about cultural capital is critical in all sorts of domains. In the school system, from K–12 up through college and graduate programs, there is a hidden curriculum—the stuff that does not go on your transcript but is far more important than your grades. Kids with cultural capital already know this; kids without it cannot know it unless they interact with peers who already have it. It can take years for doubly disadvantaged kids, Jack says, to catch up on the hidden curriculum, and by then, it is late in the game. The privileged poor have already learned these life lessons about school, about professors, about broadening their social networks, and about interacting with adults as equals—and they find college and life beyond a much easier go.

How to End Bullying

Ask any grade-school or middle-school student about the anti-bullying assemblies they have been forced to sit through, and they will laugh. Do they have any effect? Any self-respecting kid will snort-laugh at this one and answer no. That is because most approaches to bullying are top-down, adult-designed, and adult-driven. It should be no surprise that they are ineffective. But you do not have to believe children. There is not any research-based evidence that anti-bullying programs reduce student conflict or improve school climate.[51] And yet, they are well funded and repeated to the point that kids laugh them off.

What kind of anti-bullying strategy *does* work? One promising approach centers on—what else?—peer effects. Elizabeth Paluck and her colleagues wanted to see if they could use peers to reduce bullying in schools. So, they took fifty-six New Jersey middle schools and divided them into two groups of twenty-eight: an experimental group of schools in which kids would be given anti-bullying training to help them implement anti-bullying measures, and a control group where nothing was done to address bullying. At the experimental group schools, Paluck and her research team randomly selected students to participate in the conflict-intervention program, dubbing them "seeds." On average, each school had twenty-six seeds. Among the seeds were "social referent seeds," kids who were in the top 10 percent of their school in connectivity—that is, they were the kids that all the other kids knew and spent time with, in person or online (note, they did not just go with who students said was "popular," but measured interactions).

After seeds were selected, they were trained. A research assistant met with the seed groups every other week to help them identify common conflict problems *at their schools*, so that the interventions would be tailored. (To state the obvious, each school is different, and the prevailing conflicts will be different. Race may be important here, economic class over there, and the bad blood between the chess club and the band may have riled that other school.) Then they encouraged their seed students to become the public face of opposition to these types of conflict. The seed groups created hashtag slogans about conflict behaviors, then made the slogans into online and physical posters. Their photos were posted next to the slogan to associate the anticonflict statement with them personally, and the seeds rewarded students observed engaging in friendly or conflict-mitigating behaviors with an orange wristband with the intervention logo (a tree). Over twenty-five hundred wristbands were distributed and tracked. The researchers write, "This intervention model can be likened to a grassroots campaign in which the seed students took the lead and customized the intervention to address the problems they noted at their school."[52]

The brilliance of this study is the way the researchers let the kids drive everything. The kids figured out what the problems were. The kids crafted the interventions. The kids worked on the other kids. The seeds understood the peer culture and norms, then figured out what it would take to change the norms. Where were the researchers? Behind the scenes, and, crucially, unseen by other students. After a year, the experimental schools saw a 25 percent reduction in disciplinary reports of student conflict.[53] No school administrator or nonprofit organization, no effort that tried to make adults agents of change, had ever achieved anything like it.

Another important finding the researchers had was that the highly connected students, the social referent seeds, that is, the popular kids, were the most effective at influencing social norms and behavior among their network connections and at the school-climate level. The researchers concluded by saying, "Our empirical results suggest that future interventions would do well to use as many social referents in their intervention group as possible."[54] This makes complete sense as the more connected (popular) kids are already influential as they are the ones who get to define group norms; this is just one more way they are exercising their influence. And their influence has a far reach among their peers.

Suicide

We generally think of suicide as a private and hidden thing, and likely a result of mental illness. Is it, though? Anna Mueller and Seth Abrutyn, the most prominent sociologists studying youth suicide today, want us to understand that suicide is social. It may be rooted in social isolation, in some cases, or in social settings that are *too* tight-knit. And there is definitely a peer-effect component in the incidence of what are known as "suicide clusters." In one particularly insightful finding, Mueller and Abrutyn report that, just as one can observe so-called suicide contagion, with proper interventions one can also amplify what they have dubbed the "social inoculation" effect and reduce the likelihood of additional suicides.

In one study, Mueller and Abrutyn showed that when a person knows about their friend's suicide attempt, they report significantly higher levels of emotional distress and are more likely to report suicidal intent; however, if the friend's suicide attempts and thoughts are hidden, that has no significant effect on the first person's mental health.[55] Contrary to what most people think, however, *discussing* suicide with friends may actually discourage suicidal intent or prevent its escalation to a serious attempt. How? The authors suggest that this effect may possibly be due to "deepening bonds of trust between friends and generating opportunities for social support and integration."[56] One thing Mueller and Abrutyn make clear is that, because they are using longitudinal data in this study, they can see how a first suicide attempt can lead to a second suicide attempt. The survey they are using is school-based, so we do not know about friends outside of school. And while the survey lets us know who are friends, we do not know how close these friends are. Still, using the longitudinal data makes clear that there is a peer effect going on with suicide attempts and thoughts between friends.

Wanting to get more specific, and to consider peer effects in a real-world case study, Mueller and Abrutyn spent years working in and studying a small, tight-knit, wealthy, White community they call "Poplar Grove." The population is under fifty thousand people, and yet one two-thousand-student public high school in Poplar Grove had sixteen suicides of current students and recent graduates in a ten-year period. (Nationally, we find eleven suicides yearly per one hundred thousand fifteen- to twenty-four-year-olds.)[57] By studying the town in depth, Mueller and Abrutyn found that the suicides were linked to kids' perceived need to achieve (really, to overachieve) in school, sports, and social life in order to feel that they lived up to a community standard as a "good Poplar Grove kid." We often think of a tight-knit community as a good thing, providing a welcome emotional and social safety net. But the flip side of a tight-knit community is that everyone knows everyone else's business; it can be suffocating to be watched for deviation, sanctioned with gossip, and otherwise live with your life on public display. And there is no way out of the unrealistic expectations.

Mueller and Abrutyn write that "high levels of integration and regulation resulted in Poplar Grove feeling like a pressure cooker and a fishbowl: success and failure were clearly defined, highly visible, and often publicly sanctioned or rewarded. In this context, youths who are struggling to make it sometimes see suicide as their only escape. Mental health problems, like diagnosed depression, certainly matter to suicide in Poplar Grove, but our study demonstrates that structural-cultural conditions also play a significant role, both by increasing adolescents' emotional distress and by decreasing youths' and parents' willingness to seek help."[58] In this study, they make it clear that there is a peer culture of achievement, so defined that even the highest achievers feel they are falling short. Suicide becomes a means of expressing their inner, subjective pain in collectively understood ways.[59] The small number who complete suicide are essentially sanctioning themselves in the most extreme way.

Mueller and Abrutyn's research is not definitive, but it highlights the role of social context and culture in the incidence of suicide and offers, in tandem with other work, fascinating possibilities for the use of peers in the prevention of youth suicide.

* * *

Peers, as we have seen, are going to be most influential when we find ourselves in bounded groups that develop norms of behavior. For instance, students at dorm-based colleges act an awful lot like high school students (kind of immature) while their same-age peers who may live at home and go to commuter colleges often act far more mature. The kids living in the dorm acting immature has nothing to do with hormones and everything to do with social context. That is, dorm living in college is very similar to being in high school—it is an all-encompassing, bounded, social environment, filled primarily with other kids, and so students will conform to the norms of the dorm culture. The kids who go to the commuter colleges often seem more mature, as they look at school as "a job." They are not in the same kind of social situation where they feel compelled to act like their peers.

3

Stuyvesant High School, Where Iron Sharpens Iron

Stuyvesant High School in New York City is the best public high school in the country. Its alumni include four Nobel Prize winners, pathbreaking artists (from actors James Cagney, Tim Robbins, and Lucy Liu to musicians like Walter Becker—cofounder of Steely Dan—and rapper Heems, of Das Racist and the Swet Shop Boys); political power players (New York congressperson Grace Meng, eighty-second US attorney general Eric H. Holder); business titans like Home Depot founder Arthur Blank; education reformers, from teachers' union leader Albert Shanker to charter school empire builder Eva Moskowitz; many doctors and medical researchers such as the twins Uché and Oni Blackstock; and, heck, even a couple of Olympic fencers. Even the kids who did not graduate have gone on to prominence—jazz legend Thelonious Monk among them.

Syed ('85) and Margaret ('80) both had the good fortune and privilege of going there. The building was pretty decrepit, even more so than other public-school buildings at the time, and while it featured a few superstar teachers, the instructional staff was nothing to write home about. Still, it consistently sends droves of graduates on to elite universities and distinguished careers. Needless to say, along with eight other "specialized" New York City high schools, it was highly desirable to families betting on its ability to provide their kids with the opportunity for social mobility—a chance to move up, class-wise, and secure a successful adulthood. A two-and-a-half-hour standardized exam, despite political attempts to do away with it, remains the *only* way to get into eight out of nine of these schools. (The ninth, LaGuardia, the school on which the movie and TV show *Fame* is based, requires portfolios or auditions for admission.) The students who are accepted tend to already be academic overachievers, like Margaret, who was a dedicated student who earned excellent grades while participating in a myriad of activities in high school. But there is room in this school for deviants like Syed, who was, to put it generously, a slacker. He regularly cut school and got weak grades. True to the schools' reputation, however, your coauthors both ended up success stories, getting PhDs in sociology and establishing rewarding academic careers.

Why didn't our academic performance in high school set us on different paths? Because students' individual talents and predilections were less important to Stuyvesant's lauded outcomes than the culture shared by the entire student body, class after class, year after year. The durable peer culture at this school is based on achievement, a culture each incoming class of kids learns upon their arrival. Quickly, they acculturate, trying to impress their peers. Good grades are just a baseline, college a minimal expectation. Students learn that they are rarely the smartest ones in the room, but that only spurs them toward greater and more diverse achievements. The slackers at other schools might be labeled "at risk" to drop out, but slackers from Stuyvesant go on to good colleges and professional careers, right alongside the academic worker bees and nerdy superstars. This is the profound, direct, and long-lasting effect of a peer-driven culture of achievement.

There are many studies about student outcomes at specialized, elite, and/or magnet schools like Stuyvesant. So, how do these kids do in terms of grades, graduation, and college attendance, compared to kids at other schools?[1] The evidence is mixed—it turns out that it is hard to tell whether the students or the school is responsible for positive outcomes, let alone whether such schools "improve" their students. But what about the long term? Do the effects of peers and peer culture in high school last beyond graduation? Here, we catch up with a wide swath of Stuyvesant graduates, finding one consistent theme: the school's strong peer culture, fellow students told us, was directly responsible for a range of long-term wins. Apparently, you *can* believe the hype.

Why Stuy

From its founding in 1904, the school has been a haven for academically high-performing students, often from the bullying and low expectations of neighborhood schools. In early decades, this was especially true for working-class Jewish boys (girls were not admitted until 1971), then for a significant number of Black and Latino students in the 1970s and '80s (whose numbers dropped precipitously in the 1990s), and, from the 1980s on, for the children of working- and middle-class Asian immigrants.

Across race and class boundaries, successive cohorts of students developed and maintain a generalized culture of achievement through informal peer interactions. That is, the culture of achievement at Stuyvesant is created and sustained from the ground up, by kids rather than parents, teachers, and administrators. And, without being defined, measured, or even explained, it raises everyone's game. You simply sense the dos and don'ts, you sense when you have violated the norms of the peer culture by the reaction from other students, and you endeavor to avoid doing so again. (Repeat offenders do not last at the school.) The strivers adapt well and strive even further—but so do the slackers. In the long run, all students reap the benefits of the shared culture, the exchange of cultural capital (more on that in a bit), and accrual of social capital saturating the Stuyvesant experience.

Of course, there are plenty of kids who perform well academically in K–12. What is it about the population of Stuyvesant students that sets them apart? By looking closely at how peer effects at a world-class public high school affect long-term outcomes—looking for what it is that makes this school produce especially successful adults at especially significant rates—we aim to provide invaluable information and analysis for parents, educators, and social scientists.

To understand whether there are long-term peer effects that go beyond the context of high school, we conducted more than seventy in-depth, open-ended interviews with Black, Latino, White, and Asian

American alumni who graduated from Stuyvesant between 1970 and 2013.[2] We used our personal networks as well as Stuyvesant alumni Facebook pages, Twitter, and LinkedIn profiles to reach out to our fellow alums. Many of the people we interviewed grew up poor, and many were first- or second-generation immigrants. Right away, we confirmed the school's reputation for success: nearly all went to college, quite often to elite schools, and even the first-generation college students graduated and tended to have accomplished professional careers.

This story—and our choice to study it—is also personal. Neither of us is sure we would be where we are today without having gone to this specific public school. In the 1980s, New York was not the shiny, clean, safe city it is today—it had a high crime rate and the local public schools were often physically dangerous places for nerdy kids like us. Our neighborhoods were not particularly great, either: Margaret grew up poor, in public housing projects in Manhattan's Upper West Side (well before it became a wealthy neighborhood), while Syed's middle-class upbringing was taking place in the cultural and physical hinterland of Staten Island. These were not glamorous places or necessarily promising starts. Stuyvesant, though, was an infinitely fascinating place, accessible to (and transformative for) kids who were not rich.

That last bit is key to Stuyvesant's allure. Students flock to Stuyvesant in part because it is a mobility machine. A 2015 Pew Charitable Trust study found that children of poor and wealthy parents "inherit" to a large degree their income earning later in life.[3] That is, in this country, if a person is born poor (or rich), there is a good chance they will stay that way—they are economically immobile. The experiences of Stuyvesant graduates upset that correlation. There is a substantial poor population at Stuyvesant (today about 40 percent receive free or reduced-price lunch—a proxy measure for poverty), but almost everyone graduates and goes to college, mostly selective or elite ones, and go on to have, as most people we have interviewed have subjectively described, successful careers in their chosen fields. This has not really changed even though the demographic profile of Stuyvesant has gone from approximately 52 percent White, 12 percent Black and Latino, and 37 percent Asian American in the 1986 class to 18 percent White, 72 percent Asian American, and 5.4 percent Black and Latino in the 2022 class.[4]

So, what is it about Stuyvesant that aids such mobility? It must be the teachers and administrators, the resources, and highly driven parents, right? Nope. Our data show that what is most important is the peer effect. Put three thousand relatively "smart" kids, rich or poor, boys or girls, Black or White or Latino or Asian American, into this school (whether the aging hulk we attended or the stunning building that opened in lower Manhattan in 1992), and magical things happen. They push each other, they strive to be like each other, and they learn from each other. A former principal, Abraham Baumel, says as much: "The fact is, if the teacher is not delivering at a place like Stuyvesant, the kids will find the answers from one another, from books, and from other classes. They will find a way to learn the material, and the teacher thinks he is responsible for that marvelous achievement."[5]

The peer effect, as we have mentioned, operates both directly and indirectly. Wanting to be like their peers can nudge kids toward higher academic achievement as well as "negative" behaviors, like cutting class, and drug and alcohol consumption (the degree to which these are truly detrimental is placed in doubt by our interviewees). And the student-driven culture of achievement indirectly raises everyone's expectations and transforms their worldviews. High achievers and "slackers" and everyone in between simply "know" that college and career are nonnegotiables.

Culture: Work Hard

In the halls of Stuyvesant High School, the common response to "How are you?" is simply, "I'm tired." That tiredness is because of an old—but still current—truism among the students: you can, they say, have two of three things: "sleep, social life, or grades." Doing your work is central to what it means to be a Stuyvesant student. You could not coast on just "being smart," as you were surrounded by smart kids. Alex Outhred ('92), a very successful White professional poker player, said his thinking was, "Holy shit, I'm smart but that guy's a genius." He took that as a challenge. Smart was not enough; you had to work.

Rudi-Ann Miller, a Black graduate ('10) remembered that she and her classmates were always "coming into school every day, complaining" about the sleep they had lost "because they were up working so hard on whatever project or extracurricular activity." She had "always been very driven and disciplined," but the competition was invigorating for her: "I guess it's just the added pressure or feeling that literally everyone else around you is doing so well . . . kind of . . . 'I have to step up my game a bit.'"

And you did not just work begrudgingly. Tania Khan ('99), an Asian American graduate told us how she would throw herself into it: "I was not one of the kids that just naturally got everything. I definitely had to work hard and put in the hours and elbow grease to get good grades. . . . My stamina for studying was just never tiring."

Work, real school work, means putting in the time, anywhere, anytime. For instance, Manisha Shah-Balagong (Asian American, '90 graduate) told us, "It's like of course you have to go home to study. I have to go home and study. I can't hang out with you. Like, we all have to go home and study. . . . And if you weren't going home and standing on the train, you were doing it on the train. Like, you're studying all the time."

Again, being smart is not enough when everyone else is smart. It is about the grind. But if you are efficient, there is still time for a bit of other stuff. Yin Chan (Asian American, '85 graduate) told us,

> Like many Stuy students, I was the top student in elementary through middle school, but I knew it didn't mean I was supersmart, just the one with the best grades. My parents did not really push us hard to do well in school, so any pressure was just due to myself. I graduated with a ninety-seven-plus average, which probably put me among the top Stuy students based on GPA. Stuy was a lot of work but I had enough free time for clubs

and got a reasonable amount of sleep. But I did not have any social life outside of Stuy and its clubs. I was very studious but compared to others I knew who read ahead of the lessons, and knew more than the teachers, I was probably just a bit above average in my studies. I was always doing homework or reading for English class during homeroom and lunch time so I would have time after school for clubs. I think I spent about five hours a day on weekdays doing homework and studying and another ten hours a day on weekends. I spent one to two hours a day on club activities.

This sounds like a lot (and it is!), but we were told about these kinds of schedules over and over. At most schools you have kids like these, but they are smallish in number. At other schools, students like Yin would be exceptional; at Stuyvesant, working hard and getting top grades and doing all the extracurricular stuff was fairly common.

We do not want to romanticize this idea of hard work—it needed to be done, but not everyone loved it—though in the end, you are a Stuyvesant graduate, and you *know* that is a meaningful feat. Take Emily Mollenkopf (White, '01 graduate): "I can't say I look back on Stuyvesant all that fondly with that much work." Then she qualified this, saying, "I think it's the hardest thing I ever have done and probably proudest of getting through that. . . . You know graduating from Stuyvesant is probably the most difficult accomplishment that I'll be able to claim."

Even people who downplayed the amount of work they did probably did a lot more than they admitted to us, or even themselves—like Steve Berczuk (White, '83 graduate), who said, "I did well at Stuyvesant, but I wasn't the best student and I think my SAT scores weren't the best, but Stuy . . . helped me get into MIT . . . and gave me the confidence that I could do it." He also said that one thing he learned at Stuyvesant, something we heard many times, was that you are not the best in the room. And when you are not the best or smartest in the room, you have to consistently prove yourself, something Stuyvesant graduates were very comfortable doing then, and are still comfortable doing in their professional lives.

The peer-defined need to work (again, this is not coming from parents or teachers) spurred students on, and it could be competitive. Odetta Macleish-White ('89), a Black graduate, said the friendship dynamic among her classmates was, "I love hanging out with you, but I totally want to get a higher grade than you." She, too, rose to the occasion. "The phrase I've learned here in the South is 'iron sharpens iron.' That's how I feel about the kids I went to school with at Stuyvesant," the lawyer mused.

Jenny Che, an Asian American graduate ('10), recalling her time, nearly twenty years after Macleish-White's, said, "It was competitive, and we were all looking over our shoulder and looking over each other's report cards. I think that competitiveness . . . it made us all want to be the best that we could." In fact, when Jenny got to Dartmouth College, she "felt like it was more relaxed, chilled—expectations were slightly lowered, I would say." In fact, lots of graduates said the same: going to the country's most vaunted colleges and universities seemed, after Stuyvesant, relatively easy and laid back. Margaret's class alone ('80) saw the friendly competition between future physicists Brian Greene and Lisa Randall (both White) spur them toward science stardom. If one got an award, the other was never far behind. Iron sharpened iron.

Counterculture: Slacking

Like any public high school, Stuyvesant had its "slackers," the "marginal" students who got mediocre grades. But because of the internalized norms imparted by their school's peer culture, mediocre for them was actually in the range of Bs and A minuses. Syed was in the bottom half of his class with an 87 average, and Carlos Moya ('93) boasted just an 85. A Puerto Rican graduate who grew up in pre-gentrification Hell's Kitchen with a mom who was a cleaning lady, Carlos was a good student in junior high and, like everyone else, tested his way into Stuyvesant. There was a long stretch where Carlos cut class almost every day (until buckling down in his senior year). His "bad grades" might have spelled disaster, but Carlos turned out alright, too. He attended Hunter College and SUNY-Binghamton, and he became an upper-middle-class computer programmer. It was not about "grit," Carlos told us, but peers. "You just feel sort of uplifted, like, having these people around you. I guess it's really *inspiration*, is the word." He said you realize, at this school, not that you are special "but that you're in a group with a lot of special people and you don't want to fall under. . . . There's sort of this feeling where 'there's no way I'm going to be the loser in this crew,' you know what I mean?"

Like other kids, "slacker" Karin Trujillo (White, '89 graduate) made social life a priority. She had a "B+" average—middling by Stuyvesant standards—as well as a habit of cutting class to hang out in the park on Fifteenth Street and Second Avenue, smoking cigarettes and drinking the occasional forty-ounce bottle of malt liquor with her friends.[6] At most schools, those habits are for underachieving "bad" kids, the ones labeled "dropout risks." But at Stuyvesant, Karin's behavior was *also* normal. Students like Karin and Syed (who cut class to hang out in that same park!) learned early on that failing out or not going to college were *not options*. No matter what, the work needed to be done. And the work got done. It should not be surprising, then, that Karin eventually became a thoracic surgeon.

What we are saying is that the peer culture of achievement affected *all* the kids at Stuyvesant. Even the slackers, like Asian American Andrew Wong ('85), who said homeroom was his favorite high school class, were concerned with maintaining "good enough" grades to graduate and go to college. "I tried to keep up, but I wasn't studying all night, and I would just sort of get what I had to do done," Andrew admitted. The rest of the time he helped out at his parents' drugstore in Chinatown or, if he had a spare moment, hung out with friends. Today, the Cornell graduate is a well-regarded lawyer.

Slacking is not something most start off doing; it comes to them later. A number of our interviewees worked hard during their freshman and sophomore years, but figured out that they could ease up on the number of hours spent studying starting their junior or senior years, either because they became more efficient or, more commonly, because they figured there was more to life. For instance, Bucky (White '80 graduate) was studying four to five hours a day—"pretty much just to keep my head out of water because algebra was a shock to my system"—until his junior year, when he discovered sex, drugs, rock 'n roll, and football. Soon the hours of studying went down as he spent more time on the football team and other "extracurriculars." In spite of this slacking, he got a PhD and is now a professor. Syed, too, was a studious sort initially—get to school, go to class, then go straight home on the 3:30 p.m. Staten Island Ferry. But by junior year, he too found the pleasures of the park and extracurriculars. But again, as with Karin and Carlos and most of the other slackers, so as not to incur the disapproval of his peers, he got the work done and eventually got into a reputable college.

Cultural Capital

The peer effect shows up pretty clearly in these stories of academic achievement. Arguably, though, the more important function of the peer culture at Stuyvesant is its transfer of cultural capital—all the "stuff" that makes one understanding of and able to navigate the implicit cultural rules that determine who gets ahead in life. Examples of hard-to-measure but critically important forms of cultural capital include having the confidence to speak to adults as equals, knowing when to ask for advice, appreciating travel, the theater, museums, and the arts, and being comfortable around wealth. Dianne Morales ('85), who is Afro-Boricua and grew up in pre-gentrification Bed-Stuy, said in a *New York Times* interview that she went to loft parties in SoHo and friends' luxurious apartments by Washington Square Park. She said that "all of New York City was new to me," and going to Stuyvesant and being in Manhattan, she "learned there was so much more out there for me."[7] (Dianne ran for mayor in 2020; her upstart campaign started strong, but eventually money and ties to the political machine won out, and we ended up with former police captain Eric Adams as our mayor.)

Students at Stuyvesant develop a sense of how the world really works from each other, and they begin to learn to navigate it as they spend time together in Manhattan, in Stuyvesant's halls, and, yes, in the park. For other schools, it is a simple lesson: if there is a critical mass of achievement-oriented kids (it does not have to be the majority!), and— let's be frank—kids who already have a degree of social and cultural capital, the rest of the student body benefits.[8]

This effect was especially strong for poor and minority kids. Margaret, for instance, grew up working-class. Her father was a waiter and her mother a garment worker. The family lived in a public housing project in Manhattan's Upper West Side on Sixty-Third Street and Amsterdam Avenue. Her housing project faced the back wall of the Lincoln Center complex, which was built to block access to project residents. Those who did not wake to the wall every morning saw a welcoming fountain when they visited Lincoln Center, and never understood the extra physical and psychological work it took for her to get to the same location. Margaret went to a middle school in a gentrifying (though at the time, still dangerous) neighborhood where a rumored reputation for low academic achievement was topped only by the reputation for violence. Getting into an advanced track with many White students helped her test into Stuyvesant, where her new peers had access to all kinds of different information about the world—cultural capital that helped her make life-changing decisions. Not only did her peers teach her about eating in restaurants by asking her to join in on meals with their parents; they showed her the appropriate topics of conversation among the upper classes and imparted knowledge of internships over dessert.

Parents like Margaret's and Syed's were no help when it came to choosing colleges—so much for the many academic studies emphasizing parents' importance in this regard—but fellow students filled that role. They took her to a Chinatown college fair, for instance, where she met Harvard undergrads who encouraged her to apply to their school. She did. And she got in. (Syed applied to SUNY-Binghamton because, well, everyone else at Stuyvesant did. He got in.) Such examples of peers trading and transferring social and cultural capital are common at richer schools, where they are key to the whole "rich kids become rich adults" truism, but it turns out they can happen at any school where at least some kids have this capital and see other kids as their legitimate peers.

College Admissions

Getting into college was critical for Stuyvesant students. Throughout the years, most students mentioned that they could not rely solely on the Stuyvesant college counselors, because like all New York City public schools, Stuyvesant was underresourced. Many could not remember meeting with the counselors, and if they did have a meeting, it was only to review grades and such and did not really address the college application process. Thus, the students were left to their own devices. This was felt more acutely by the Black, Latino, and Asian American students, as quite a few of them told us about the peer effect working among them.

"These [college] names were almost nothing to me, because I had no [point] of reference—what these schools were, where they were, or anything," recalled Maria Acevedo* ('79), a Puerto Rican Stuyvesant alum of her college search. For many of our interviewees, often first-generation college attendees from working-class families, the biggest factor in their college application process was "where is everybody else applying to," in Maria's words. (She went to Cornell.) These students' parents worried about financial aid and colleges' locations (preferably near their homes in New York City—just like Margaret's parents!). This is common, especially with working-class students who often choose colleges closer to home, rather than "better" colleges that may be further from home, something education scholars call "undermatching."[9] These Stuyvesant students, however, relied on information gleaned from other, more connected students whose parents and older siblings attended the schools to learn more about specific colleges. Mark Eng* ('95), for example, was typical of the Asian American, Black, and Latino students who needed more financial aid for college. In homeroom, he learned from other Stuyvesant students that SUNY schools provided reduced in-state tuition and that Cornell had Ivy League credentials *and* SUNY colleges (he went to Cornell's College of Agriculture and Life Sciences). He did not apply to any schools outside the SUNY system.

Maria, from above, later worked as an Ivy League college admissions professional, and she affirmed that many of Stuyvesant's minority students effectively used the high school as "a pipeline . . . to the Ivies." She noted that this pipeline especially worked for Black and Latino kids. Some kids might have gotten there no matter what high schools they attended, but the peer culture of Stuyvesant was transformative for Asian American and especially for Black and Latino peers. Maria told Margaret that as an admissions officer she counted on Stuyvesant, and schools like it, to be feeder schools, to have a strong pool of Black, Latino, and Asian American student applicants.

Black and Latino Stuyvesant students formed close friendships, frequently calling or treating each other as fictive kin. Those relationships buoyed them as teens, raised their game, and lasted well beyond high school. Ivy League graduate Carla Powell* was at the school in the 1970s and 1980s and remembered that Black kids like her did not always get great advice from school counselors when it came to college applications. Their peers, however, were instrumental. "We considered our community a family," Carla said, noting that she had, among her classmates, a "mother" and a "grandmother." "My 'grandmother' went to Princeton, and I think my 'mother' ended up at Cornell. But the point is . . . if you spoke to most Black kids from our era, most of us . . . relied very heavily on the advice we got from other students like ourselves. So, there were people who were just a year or two ahead of me, who did well and applied and were admitted to Ivy League schools. I used them as kind of my guide when it came time for me to apply to colleges." Looking back, she said, "It was a very supportive environment. That peer group meant everything. I got more from that peer group than I got from any staff or faculty member at Stuyvesant. My community was a source of support and encouragement regarding what was possible."

The peer group of Stuyvesant students clearly extended into the realm of graduates, in that alums shared information about their experiences at highly acclaimed colleges and universities. That helped the younger group know about which schools might be good fits, where they could apply, be accepted, and succeed. Carla went on to explain, "But after talking to other Black students who were ahead of me and getting a sense of what their grades were like and what their scores were like and what their activities were like, I felt pretty confident that I'd get into the school of my choice."

Manhattan as Cultural Capital

At fourteen, Stuyvesant students are commuting to school. Riding the subway into Manhattan for school each day, said many of our interviewees, it felt as though the world opened up to them. After all, Manhattan is the physical and metaphysical epicenter of the universe—it's "the city," and the other four boroughs are, well, the *outer boroughs*. To Steve Marchese (White, '82 graduate), it was "the Emerald City": "You knew that this is where the opportunity and the access and the power were in New York. If you wanted to be able to tap into that, you needed to go there. And it wasn't where I lived every day; it was where I was going on the subway train." Steve added that "it was really a big deal to spend my day in Manhattan and then come home to my neighborhood in Queens," and that going to Stuyvesant "was the first time, for me by myself, to have my own place in that world," in that Emerald City.

That liberatory sense was shared by Maria from above, who commuted from pre-gentrification Williamsburg in the 1970s. In Manhattan, though she initially went with "a little bit of a chip on my shoulder, feeling like I didn't want to be there, I was forced to go," she realized she could redefine herself. "I loved being at Stuy. For one thing, it was really great being in Manhattan instead of Brooklyn and nobody knew who I was—more importantly, nobody knew my parents." She had gone to a "small Catholic school, [where] everybody knew everybody, so you couldn't get away with anything. . . . Somebody's parents were always around somewhere and saw you doing something." She loved the school's diversity and the city's anonymity. "So for the first time, I felt this freedom. . . . Nobody knew me, nobody knew my family, nobody knew my parents. It was just this—sense of freedom."

Even Margaret, who lived in Manhattan, found "the city" inspiring. There were opportunities to explore and her Stuyvesant peers to explore with. She and her friends made regular trips to Broadway, buying half-price tickets at TKTS, which was located in seedy 1970s Times Square (tutoring gave her extra cash).[10] Margaret, her Chinatown friends, and her outer borough buddies found cultural capital together soaking in Neil Simon plays. She, like other poor kids, never had the chance to go to the theater when younger, but it was easily accomplished with Stuyvesant peers who knew what to watch. While it was rare and dangerous for her Queens crew to venture to Times Square alone, together they were unafraid.

Lisa Randall (White, '80 graduate) and Shirley Moy (Asian American, '80 graduate), Margaret's high school classmates, reminisced about going together to CBGBs to see the Go-Gos. They learned quickly that no one bothered to check IDs at the clubs since the legal drinking age was eighteen and they must have looked close to eighteen years old. Stuyvesant encouraged them to be bold and see more of the world, to try different activities on their own. Margaret would have never showed up at a club without her Stuyvesant friends. This is stuff their parents would have never approved of and probably would have scolded them for, but it is what their peers did anyway. These bits of boldness reshaped Margaret's relationship with her parents—allowing her to push to leave the New York City area for college.

Emily Mollenkopf ('01), whom we met earlier, also felt that being in Manhattan was a huge deal, even though she was from Park Slope and had professor parents. She said,

> It felt like, you know it was like I was growing up, I felt like I was almost adult. It was an incredibly kind of mature thing to be doing. I had been walking four or five blocks to go to school my whole life so getting on the train and going into Manhattan was—I think it made me feel more independent. It was also terrifying. . . . But by and large, I really enjoyed—you know it's so New York, I enjoyed being kind of part of the blood pulsing through New York's veins and seeing all the different people who live and work in that city and kind of being amongst them and it's something I really miss, having moved to Los Angeles.

Syed asked Emily about hanging out in the city, to which she replied, "That was another big adventure for me, getting to know Manhattan and hanging out there with my friends. You know we would skip out on school sometimes if there was a fire drill or I guess as we got older I think we were more flagrant about it." She and Syed shared a laugh. "We would just—I think the usual destination would be like Canal Street or kind of that Broadway-Lafayette area shopping. It's funny because I think in many ways, you grow up so much faster in New York than almost anywhere else, and that certainly happened at Stuyvesant. And I found everything very quaint when I went to college. So that's another kind of bittersweet thing about Stuyvesant, probably New York City in general."

The slackers were changed by Manhattan, too. Eric Presti, a White 1984 graduate who commuted from Maspeth, Queens, said that being at Stuyvesant and being in Manhattan was a cultural awakening. He would roam around Manhattan going to clubs like the Peppermint Lounge. He would cut class and go to the Frick Museum. "Who does that?" he asked rhetorically. Certainly not kids from Maspeth.

And for Syed, being in the city was also life-changing. He would cut school and walk all over Manhattan. He would go to the many art house movie theaters near the school, which was at the edge of the East Village, and watch all the indie and foreign language films that he read about in the alt-weekly *Village Voice*, which he would devour cover to cover on Wednesday mornings, soon after they were delivered to red plastic boxes all over the city where you could get your copy. (Never the top one—who knows who's doing what in there!) Syed's grades were poor by Stuyvesant standards, but he was culturally enriched. Going back to Staten Island at the end of the day was a punishment. There was no way he would be a doctor (stereotype alert!) after this education, much to the chagrin of his mother, who has told him repeatedly for nearly three decades, "I regret sending you to Stuyvesant." But he loved it and it expanded his horizons in a way they never would have been expanded if he had stayed at Saint Peter's High School for Boys in Staten Island.

Long-Term Transformations

Study after study on educational outcomes credit—or blame—teachers and administrators for the way kids turn out. Certainly, the legendary Frank McCourt (who quit teaching after publishing the Pulitzer Prize–winning book *Angela's Ashes*) profoundly affected Stuyvesant students; Jordan Sonnenblick (White, '87 graduate), now a writer of young adult and children's books, fully credits McCourt for his success. Other students credit administrators like Murray Kahn, a long-serving assistant principal, with literally saving their lives. Still, few graduates in our interviews stressed the importance of these adults in their long-term trajectories. The vast majority instead credited their Stuyvesant peers with helping them go far in life.

In a way, that *is* a credit to the teachers and administrators at their high school: those are the adults who, declining to follow other public and charter schools in "teaching to the test" and focusing on discipline, helped construct a generative "social architecture" for students. In it, students are given a great degree of academic and social freedom to "find themselves." Perhaps the best adult interventions were the least direct.

One consequence of the school's structure was its lenience toward cutting class. Officially, it was frowned upon, but administrators did little to curb the practice. Kids decided what was worthwhile in school and what was not (these were the days before electronically encoded ID cards). They were not labeled "at risk," because administrators knew implicitly that the work, as we said before, got done; the cutters were essentially given the freedom to make executive decisions and work through the consequences. Syed actually went so far with cutting at one point that it got the attention of the dean of students, who required him to get every teacher's signature for two weeks to attest to his attendance and turn it in at the end of the day. He did this for a week, then tired of it. The dean of students, who was his photography teacher, never followed up.

Every school has a hidden curriculum. Basically, it is the whole package of things you learn in school without them being taught in a classroom—the skills and knowledge that schools (wittingly or not) organize or allow, and that kids often pick up from each other. Through the independence allowed and encouraged at the school, Stuyvesant students learn to take risks. They develop self-confidence, too. From our interviews and personal experiences, it is clear to us that Stuyvesant has long-lasting effects on its graduates. That theme threads throughout all our interviews.

Marlon Williams ('99), a Black graduate who grew up working-class, returned repeatedly to the idea of the unique degree of freedom afforded students at Stuyvesant, educationally and socially, and how it gave him a certain "audacity." At age fifteen, Marlon was the drama program's stage manager, with a squad of twenty students under him and a ten-thousand-dollar budget to handle. The privilege of being at Stuyvesant, he explained, "gives you a sense of audacity. And that's really powerful, because there is a difference between the *capacity* to do a thing and then the *audacity* to do the thing. And I think we underestimate how important that is. The audacity comes from experiences. I have this belief that people can only dream as big as their experiences allow them to imagine." A more recent Stuyvesant alum confirmed that Marlon's experience was not unusual—serving as business manager of the school newspaper, the *Spectator*, he had been solely responsible for raising enough funds to print it for the entire year. These kinds of opportunities to sink or swim, to rise to the occasion, were transformative.

Being surrounded by achievers can sometimes make kids feel like "little fish in a big pond." It can be an ambition killer. Yet, we found the opposite: the peer effect at Stuyvesant is student driven, and though it makes it obvious that you are never the smartest kid in the room, it drives you to admire and aspire to be like the ones who bested you. Alexander Friedman, who went to Stuyvesant in the late 1990s, was one such student.[11] A Russian Jewish kid in heavily Italian Bensonhurst, Brooklyn, he got bullied, a lot. He was also usually one of the smartest kids in his class. But not at Stuyvesant: "Going to Stuy was incredibly good for me. I think if I didn't, I would have grown up to be an insufferable, arrogant prick." That is where he learned he had to do the work to keep himself at the top of his game—and that being smart did not always come with a chip on your shoulder.

This disinclination to be intimidated stood out particularly among the women in our interviews. While Alexander was helpfully humbled by all the smart kids at Stuyvesant, others realized that they absolutely deserved to be there, among the high flyers at the school—and they never felt the pain of "imposter syndrome" later in their careers. Kate Dominus (White, '89 graduate) recalled becoming a middle manager at an insurance company, often interacting with, but never cowed by, senior management: "That's the thing that Stuyvesant gave me—this sort of overarching confidence that I belonged there. Wherever 'there' is. And I think that that's helped me extraordinarily on a professional basis. But it's not the traditional academic stuff that you would have thought of."

Asian American alum Brian Ma* ('94) echoed Kate's account, finding the "audacity" to speak up though he was a minority in his corporate job. By his own admission quieter than most of his colleagues, he said he nonetheless spoke out more often, "realizing that it was in my interest to fight and push back." He gained that confidence in high school, where he played sports, tried lots of activities, and became used to going out on a limb. As he put it, "Stuy made me comfortable in my own skin." Maria ('79), the Puerto Rican graduate from pre-gentrification Williamsburg, similarly found her stride when she left her small Catholic school for Stuyvesant, where she was exposed to other "intellectual equals, more or less. [It was] intimidating at first because there were so many White people, except they were pretty cool and didn't make me feel funny."

Economic transformations of the sort that made parents clamor to send their kids to this school were equally common among the graduates who shared their stories. It really *was* a mobility machine, said Elizabeth Reid Yee ('85), a White graduate who grew up poor in Greenpoint, Brooklyn, which back then was a violent neighborhood in economic decline with lots of drugs. Today, she fully credits Stuyvesant with keeping her from a life of poverty. If Margaret had not gotten in, she would have been shunted off to her local, zoned school, Brandeis High, where she would have been marginalized and more likely to have gone into service work. Instead, Stuyvesant, she recalls, opened a variety of pathways toward social and economic mobility. There, her interest in computer science was nurtured, allowing her to join an NYU summer program she would eventually be tapped to teach—and *that* became one of the many entries, including race on her application that she credits with nabbing her a spot at Harvard.[12]

For all the rhetoric around STEM and STEAM curricula and the intense focus on standardized testing, it seems the ability of US students to keep up with their global competition need not hinge on coursework.[13] The peer culture and intentionally permissive structure at this one New York City high school are remembered, in our study, as far more important to the transformations that really made a difference in their lives.

Another direct, long-term transformative effect of the school upon its graduates is achieved through the school's name recognition. Like Harvard graduates, Stuyvesant alumni benefit from the school's reputation. We asked on a Facebook post if graduates put Stuyvesant on their resumes. A great many do, even a few decades after they graduated. One hiring manager told us, "[When] I see Stuy [on their resume] I definitely give the candidate extra props." He added, "I've gotten deals done in California because the other side found out I was a Stuy grad. Honestly, it's given me more cred than college or grad school combined." A recruiter answered the question saying, "100 percent I would leave it on, even if you're interviewing outside of NY." Another woman told us about the professional power of the Stuyvesant name: "Got almost every single job I have ever worked professionally because I had it on my resume." Rudi-Ann Miller ('10), a Black graduate we met earlier, told us that she thought having Yale on her resume would be a big deal when she went to start interviewing for jobs. It wasn't. She said the interviewer at the New York Fire Department, for a research associate position (which she was offered and accepted), did not just comment on her having gone to Stuyvesant. "In fact it was just like all the questions—not all of them; he did ask me the usual resume questions or interview questions like why do you want to work here and like what do you think you have to offer to this position and this organization—but he was just very, very interested in my experience at Stuyvesant."

Black graduates, in particular, noted that, at elite colleges and in the workplace, they might be assumed to be "affirmative action beneficiaries" in the negative way, rather than the positive way wherein beneficiaries are selected because they already have talent and affirmative action allows a greater equality of opportunity than otherwise for them to rise.[14] When people learned that they had gone to Stuyvesant, those suspicions of being undeserving melted away, just as they did for other Stuyvesant graduates. The association with Stuyvesant gave them instant gravitas and legitimacy. On the same Facebook post, one Black female graduate, Sheila* from the 1980s, told us of her friend, "[She] had been at her job for a few years and happened to mention she was a Stuyvesant grad. Her supervisor was upset he had not known. She was given a promotion without asking. I guess her never hiding that she was a sharp-as-a-tack Black woman wasn't enough to have gotten the promotion offer before then." Another Black female graduate, Janice,* said, "As a Black Ivy Leaguer, folks act like they lowered the bar for you. Once they learn you went to Stuyvesant, they realize you raised that shit."

Friendship and Diversity

So many of the graduates—ourselves included—emphasized the lifelong bonds they formed at Stuyvesant. These friendships and connections were ultimately far more consequential than the ones they found in college or in workplaces later in life. Jenny Che (Asian American '10 graduate), for instance, said that while she "didn't really know anybody going into Stuyvesant," she found a "solid group of friends" through her classes and Sing, a school-wide musical theater competition. "We are still," she commented, "I mean, they are still some of my closest friends and I really care a lot about them."

They also bonded over their being different. Kim Kindya, a Cuban American ('86), who, like Alexander Friedman above, had been teased as a high-scoring test taker in middle school, felt relieved arriving at Stuy. She was one of the crowd. They "understood her references" and made her feel normal. All of a sudden she found it easy to make friends. This is something we heard repeatedly. Eric Presti, whom we met earlier, echoed this sentiment: "You meet kids that were from everywhere. And the other thing that was really good was—I said I was picked on and bullied [in elementary and middle school]—everyone was a geek so there was no one picking on anybody. Everyone accepted your strangeness. Because every kid was kind of like that smart, weird kid. So it was nice. Like you felt safe. Safe amongst your own people."

Kate Dominus, the '89 grad who never suffered imposter syndrome, told us, "Stuyvesant was the first place that I had ever been where there were enough weirdoes like me that I had a crew." Soon, she had a "huge number of friends" and cut classes just to hang out with them. Two in particular—her "closest friends in the world"—have been by her side since sophomore year. "I'm close enough to them so that one of them ended up moving in with my family and is effectively a sister. The other one . . . is coming over for Christmas dinner. I mean, it's that kind of a close relationship. We are the guardians of each other's children. . . . I would have never gotten that anywhere else, and I didn't even get that in college, which is where most people make their best friends for life."

Racially, the school was one of the most diverse spaces these people ever recalled being included in. "I miss the diversity of people," noted David J. Cumberbatch, a Black graduate from 1980 with a Dartmouth BA and a Howard Law degree. "Only then, at Stuyvesant, did I have a diverse group of friends." And why was that important? "I learned to be open to listen to other people's ideas." Without that, he figured, "I would have not been admitted into a good college. Stuy was the *best* educational experience. . . . The students came from so many different walks of life. I was watered with knowledge . . . from many taps: teachers, but mainly by my peers. The students all knew they would go to college, because the students educate[d] each other."

With gratitude, David said the other kids' "ambition rubbed off onto me. You have this group of people who come together, and they're all doing different, interesting things. You hear about them, and you learn from them. I always tell people . . . I learned a lot from classmates. Just people doing science research or this or that or winning debating tournaments or athletics. . . . It's just a diversity of interest and diversity of backgrounds. I think it just bolsters your experience."

The same was true for Steve Marchese ('82), whom we met earlier, the White son of a trucker who would go on to be a first-generation college graduate—with a Yale diploma, no less.

I think it was a learning experience and a really great experience to be with kids who are also smart kids from a variety of different backgrounds. And I feel like, at the time that I was there, it was diverse in a way that it seemed like Stuyvesant is not diverse anymore, in a sense that there was a large community of Asian American students and there was a large contingent of White students from a variety of backgrounds from around the city. But there also were a significant African American and Caribbean contingent and Latino students. So, . . . I think it was very informative for me. . . . We shared this common experience at Stuyvesant that, as intense as it was, it really was a bonding experience. . . . We could do intense academic work and talk about things and do things socially and kind of bridge those differences to a large extent, because we were in this special kind of place. And I think it made it feel, for me, very unique.

Steve highlighted the camaraderie across social, ethnoracial, and class boundaries as crucial to his later success. He said this was not the case with other kids from his neighborhood, "kids that I know who went to the Catholic [school] with predominantly other White kids or kids who went to some elite private schools like Fieldston or Horace Mann."

Among our interviewees, this was another recurring theme. People told us that, when they walked into Stuyvesant, they found "I belonged." Adolescence is tough, and so is starting a new school. Before we, your authors, got to our first days at Stuyvesant, our heads were spinning with the idea of our eight hundred classmates and the cliques they would surely form (and exclude us from). Instead, we found a flattened, broadened peer group with many, many ways to prove yourself, compete, make friends, and direct your own education. Recently, the school boasted as many as two hundred clubs and activities! With all those outlets and all those energetic students, it was more likely than not that different students' paths would cross and produce lasting connections. The diversity of the student body, remarkable in retrospect, was just the norm for us then. Margaret found her crew by going back and forth between her wealthier, Whiter homeroom friends and her Asian American, Chinese, working-class peeps, while Syed found his on the Staten Island ferry, playing Frisbee, and hanging out in Stuyvesant Park.

Neal Ungerleider (dropped out in 1998 and got a GED), a former business journalist and now writer, summed up quite nicely how many of the people we interviewed felt about Stuyvesant. Neal was from a lower-middle-class White family in Staten Island, and he "paid more attention to friends and partying than to grades." He wrote,

> Attending Stuy opened my eyes to a world I didn't know existed. To my freshman brain, going to Stuy meant going to a school where I wouldn't be bullied for reading books or could meet other people into heavy metal music. But Stuy pulled a dirty trick; while I was excited about being in Manhattan, attending Stuy meant making friends I never would have met in my closed Italian/Irish/Jewish world in Staten Island. Even if I wasn't paying attention in class, I was subtly learning how to interact with future CEOs, surgeons, artists, and (God forbid) writers. I met people from every culture, nationality, financial status, and background. It took me years before I realized what an amazing gift that was.[15]

Neal wrote of his successful academic and professional career after attending (though dropping out from) Stuyvesant, "I don't think any of that would have been possible if I hadn't attended Stuyvesant." Again, this is something we heard repeatedly, and time and again, people like Neal credited the peers they were surrounded by and the peer culture they found themselves in.

Demographic Changes

By the 1990s, the demography of Stuyvesant began to change rapidly. The number of Black and Latino students dropped significantly in that decade, and the number of Asian American students (not a homogenous group by any means!) increased. The White student population remained steady at about 40 percent from the late 1980s to the early 2000s, but then dropped dramatically as Mayor Bloomberg expanded the number of "screen" schools, which gave White students more schooling options. There are three main reasons for the decline in the number of Black and Latino students, and the rise in the number of Asian American students. One is increasing Asian immigration to New

York City, especially notable from the 1980s on. Another is that honors classes (in New York City these used to be called Special Progress [SP] classes), which used to be in almost every middle school, began to disappear in the 1990s. They were replaced with smaller numbers of honors classes or schools in fewer districts, thus making them less accessible. Some districts did not have any. These SP classes were important for Black and Latino students, who most often attended segregated schools in their own neighborhoods, as they gave them good preparation for the entrance exam. The third major factor is the attention the test-prep industry gave to the entrance exam starting in the late 1980s/early 1990s.[16] Among people we interviewed, those who graduated before the late 1980s hardly did any test prep. But from the 1990s on, nearly everyone we interviewed had done commercial test prep.

Today, there are few Black or Latino students at Stuyvesant (4 percent Latino, 1 percent Black in the 2020–2021 school year; the Asian American population is 72 percent). The tiny number of Black and Latino students has led to many different proposals to increase their numbers, including tutoring, offering the test during the school day (instead of on a Saturday), more advanced curriculum in segregated schools, and so on. None of these have panned out. In a simulated model of different possible changes to the admissions process, Sean Corcoran found that the only way to effectively start to change the school's demography would be to adopt a version of the "Texas Ten Percent" plan, where top students from every middle school would be guaranteed admission to Stuyvesant or one of the other specialized schools.[17] Any change to the admissions process would mean doing away with the 1971 state law mandating the exam. But de Blasio's proposal to do away with the entrance exam was killed in committee in the New York State Senate, and it does not look as though there will be a change to the law, or the admissions process, anytime soon.

We do not want to say that there is a lack of diversity at the school—again, "Asian American" covers a lot of very different ethnic/nationality groups. (Asia is a continent, after all.) But the absence of Black and

Latino students at the school is a big deal. It is a big deal for Black and Latino students who will miss out on the benefits of going to this kind of school with these kinds of kids. And it is a big deal for the White and Asian American students who miss out on the benefits of being peers with Black and Latino students. The White and Asian American students we interviewed who graduated in the 1970s and 1980s commonly commented about how one of the most important parts of their Stuyvesant experience was being able to befriend Black and Latino peers, and the ways that made them better, and these friendships were transformative and long-lasting. That is now largely a thing of the past.

* * *

Most of the upper-middle-class White kids who went to Stuyvesant were going to be fine, and would likely come out on top in life wherever they went to school. From Manhattan, from Brooklyn's Park Slope and Queens's Forest Hills and the Bronx's Riverdale, they had plenty of financial and cultural resources. Their parents were high achievers with educational cachet and retirement funds. The kids went to "feeder" middle schools, assuming they would get into Stuyvesant or whichever elite private school they selected—and they were not wrong. But where Stuyvesant really shone through, where it was at its absolute best, was in the lives of students from the outer boroughs, children of immigrants, Black and Latino students, and poor kids. They went from being the "weirdos," the odd ones out in their middle schools, from being raised among "provincial" views and tastes, to gathering all kinds of new social and cultural capital, all kinds of belonging. They suddenly had kids around them who shared their interests and who could tell them where and how to further those interests. Take a peer-driven culture of achievement, add structured independence, and start transferring cultural capital, and, well, you have made a mobility machine.

Better yet, you have made a *durable* mobility machine. It has been working for over one hundred years. Kids from humble and racially diverse backgrounds and elite families alike have cycled through Stuyvesant, and the former find that they are eventually welcomed into the professions and social circles of the latter. So, can the hard-to-quantify benefits of going to Stuyvesant be replicated in other schools? We say yes. The majority of kids who go to Stuyvesant are "good testers," but they are quite regular in most every other sense. The school's social chemistry takes these kids—strivers and slackers and everyone in between—and encourages them to perform to their highest abilities; its *informal* lessons are what set them up for success for decades to come.

4

Problems in the Office

At six feet four inches and 240 pounds, Jose Canseco was an imposing presence at home plate. He had a seventeen-year career in major
league baseball, tallying 462 home runs (currently thirty-seventh-most
all-time) and 1,407 runs batted in (RBIs). He was major league baseball's
Rookie of the Year in 1986 and its MVP in 1988, when he became the
first player to steal forty bases and hit forty home runs in a single season.
He played in the All-Star Game six times and won two World Series. He
even made it onto *The Simpsons*.

How did he do it all? If his 2005 memoir's title, *Juiced*, doesn't make it
plain, Canseco's self-adopted nickname did: he called himself "the godfather of steroids." In his account, he was responsible for kicking off the
league-wide use of anabolic steroids, personally injecting six big-time
hitters and spreading the gospel to countless other players and trainers.[1]

We will probably never know the extent of the league's steroid problem that can be personally attributed to Jose Canseco (though the six
players he claimed he had injected were, in fact, shown to have used steroids). It just cannot be measured. But economists Eric Gould and Todd
Kaplan ask a question more pertinent to owners, managers, and fans:
Did players' performances get better after they played with Canseco?[2]
That's something we *can* measure.

To examine whether Canseco affected other players' performance,
Gould and Kaplan gathered data on the performance of baseball players from 1970 to 2003. In particular, they looked at players who played
on teams with Canseco, and compared the performance effect to that
of thirty other power hitters of the same era on their own teammates.
Controlling for a number of variables, including experience, ballparks,
league divisions, managerial quality, and so on, the authors confirmed

that playing with Canseco had a significant, positive effect on others' batting performance. Among the data, it was clear that the six players he said he helped "juice" accounted for a lot of the Canseco effect. But when the authors removed those six from the analysis, the godfather still had a significant, though smaller, effect on performance at the plate of other teammates.

Though Gould and Kaplan importantly point out that there is no direct evidence that Canseco's teammates learned about steroids directly or indirectly from him, their findings support this conclusion.[3] For example, the diminished effect on players further from Canseco's direct orbit, combined with Canseco's self-styling as a "chemist," would suggest that players further from him simply had less knowledge regarding the ins and out of steroid use. Further, none of the other thirty power hitters of the era whose data they considered had anywhere near Canseco's effect on teammates' performance. Nor did the six hitters that Canseco injected. To Gould and Kaplan, "Jose Canseco had an unusual influence on the productivity of his teammates."[4]

Canseco played for ten different teams over his career, but his effects on teammates interestingly shows up *after* they no longer played with him. Hypothetically, the players might not have taken steroids while they had this outsized player on their team, but did so afterwards to help make up the difference, or it is just that most players, with the league's various trades and moves up and down, to and from other divisions, spent more time as ex-teammates than as current teammates of Canseco's. Either way, Gould and Kaplan estimate that after playing with Canseco, power hitters gained almost three home runs a season and a 22 percent bump to their RBIs.[5] The rest of the batters who played with him did not gain in home runs, but their batting averages and slugging percentages (another measure of power) rose.

Gould and Kaplan use their case study of Canseco to demonstrate that workers affect the productivity of other workers. People can learn valuable skills and work habits from their coworkers. They can also learn and normalize unethical practices. Gould and Kaplan clearly label these as peer effects and lay out the mechanism: "Once one worker adopts questionable methods which seem to be effective, competitive pressures may lead others to follow suit in order to get ahead, or perhaps just to stay even with other workers who are adopting similar techniques."[6]

* * *

Like high schools, workplaces are face-to-face social environments where workers are in a somewhat closed social circuit and spend more time with each other than with almost anyone else. (And, yes, a baseball team is a workplace!) It makes sense that peers in the workplace will affect each other's behavior. And just as high school students have teachers and parents looking over them, workers have managers and executives. They, like parents and teachers, usually do not know much about the day-to-day informal social interactions that impact employees, even if the bosses spend a lot of time around them. In the workplace and in high school, workers and students are the ones who create the rules of interaction (i.e., social norms) that define the informal peer culture, and they create rewards and punishments for following or breaking the norms.

Here, we are going to delve into a couple of aspects of the social life of workplaces that have direct bearing on how firms operate: misconduct, and diversity. These, we argue, are related. Misconduct, including sexism and racism, is another way of talking of "bad apples." Diversity, meanwhile, is now a highly sought goal for managers (it is known to do a lot of things that businesses like—including raise productivity and profit); a lack of diversity, conversely, allows the "bad apples" to thrive and affect the tenor of the peer culture's norms. Effectively, we are talking about how peer culture can encourage malfeasance, but also serve to curtail it.

Economists have thought about these things from many angles, noting in various studies that coworkers, for instance, influence each other's parental leave decisions, retirement timing, dedication to putting in long hours, and choices about employee stock purchase plans.[7] As we have seen in the previous chapters, social behavior is contextual: the way we act is in large part a product of the peer cultures we find ourselves in. This is not just for children.

Misconduct

Many organizations proudly tout their company culture to anyone willing to listen (and quite a few who are not). Usually, what they mean by "company culture" is the top-down culture defined by the aspirations of executives and human resources staff. It is closer to a values statement from the C-suite than a comment on the way the organization runs, because the bosses actually do not determine the peer culture of their average workers. That is done by the workers themselves, through their daily tasks and office-based social lives. In large organizations with multiple offices, the office culture may actually vary from site to site. What constitutes misconduct can, too.

Soldiers Behaving Badly

In the early 2000s, as the second Iraq War progressed, US unemployment was low, and it was becoming really hard to recruit soldiers. Desperate times call for desperate measures, as they say, and the US Army started granting so-called morality waivers. Though they had previously prevented recruits from enlisting, acts including nontraffic criminal convictions, recent illegal drug use, and even adult felonies were waived to bring in more soldiers.[8]

This policy "shock" gave army researcher Francis Murphy a unique opportunity: he could very clearly examine how changes in recruitment strategy affected individual workplace performance. From 2005 to 2008, more "bad apples" were allowed into the army, where they became other soldiers' peers (by 2008, 25 percent of recruits required morality waivers). He studied US Army data that included the units that soldiers were assigned to, which let him explore whether exposure to waiver-dependent soldiers affected known occurrences of "major misconduct."

"Major misconduct," in the case of the army (the "organization," as it were), covers a range of behaviors treated as serious disciplinary offenses, from public intoxication, minor property damage, and disorderly conduct to aggravated assault and major theft (the last two can lead to a soldier's permanent discharge).[9]

The upshot? When the army changed personnel standards, its new recruits had a direct negative influence upon other army members. That is, soldiers who were exposed to a larger number of people with morality waivers and who committed major misconduct were more likely to commit minor misconduct, and somewhat less likely to commit major misconduct. This effect was concentrated among young soldiers (seventeen to twenty years old), and was more likely to occur in the same month that the waivered soldier committed major misconduct. Where this happens is also important; it doesn't happen during boot camp, which is a somewhat transient phase in a soldier's tenure. It happens when soldiers are assigned to a "company," which consists of about sixty junior enlisted soldiers who live and work in close proximity, plus officers and sergeants—the leaders and managers.[10] That is, it occurs once they have settled into a bounded sphere of peers.

Why doesn't the peer effect work the other way around? Why wouldn't the waivered soldiers, if placed in units full of presumably "good apple" soldiers, stop doing bad things? While Murphy does not explore this in his research, it seems clear to us that there is something going on with the culture here. Specifically, it could be that "good" behavior is not normatively promoted in the rank and file, and that "bad" behavior is not looked down upon. If it were, the good apples would not be dragged down by the bad apples; rather, the bad apples would emulate the good.

Garment Workers' "Misconduct"

According to many entrepreneurs and owners of corporations, unionized workers behave badly and constantly try to agitate and gain some kind of control over their work day, including duties on the job. This mindset leaked onto shop floors, where in the factory, on-the-job friend-ships among Chinese immigrant garment workers created peer effects. Their face-to-face shop culture cemented behaviors that furthered their own particular interests rather than that of the owners.[11]

Margaret observed Chinese women on their shop floors in the 1990s and early 2000s.[12] Each factory, which had on average forty workers, frequently defined its own rules while the women worked within the confines of piece-rate wages that were acceptable to the International Ladies Garment Workers' Union (ILGWU). Strong ties bound individuals to each other because on the shop floor, they are usually a team. Among those webs of connections, you can see the peer effect.

In her many months of observation, there was one factory, out of four, that had children on numerous occasions. How was that possible? A forelady/worker of the factory explained that "during school holidays there would be numerous kids in the shops. If the kids didn't want to play with the other kids, they would sometimes help their mothers. If the factory owners' kids were there, they might play together. You would also see kids congregating in the owners' offices, where they ate, played, and did homework."[13]

This garment shop had been around for at least fifteen years. The owners were themselves former garment workers, and most of the work-ers were experienced and excellent sewers. On this shop floor, a few of the workers had children within a few years of each other.[14] They cel-ebrated their children's births, birthdays, and milestones together. And when the children got older, many of the kids went to the same elemen-tary school. Quite innocently, a couple of them brought their kids to the shop floor one day after school, and before long, other women were doing it too. Why wouldn't they? This solved the endless childcare prob-lem. Children in the factory became a regular affair, especially on school holidays. Some did homework, others played with each other, and still others helped their mothers.

While this solved childcare problems for the women, it was illegal to have kids on the shop floor, according to New York State labor laws and ILGWU rules. The shop owners could be fined for having children near dangerous machinery. However, it was too late. The unspoken rules changed and changed quickly. Children on the shop floor during school holidays let the workers put in a full day's work while also keeping an eye on their children. This arrangement was quite appealing and was available to all the employees, including those just joining the shop. The ILGWU had no comment.[15]

After 9/11, Margaret went back to interview workers who had lost their jobs.[16] The Chinese garment workers lamented the loss of their friendships and of the peer effect. It was quite clear that the camaraderie built on the shop floors was significant, and they missed those relationships dearly. Most of them ended up in elderly people's homes as home health aides, working alone.

Like baseball teams and army units, each group of garment workers on a shop floor had its own peer culture. Once the garment industry evaporated, each locale with its own norms disappeared too.

Mergers and Misconduct

Stephen Dimmock, William Gerken, and Nathaniel Graham set out to see whether financial fraud among financial advisors was contagious.[17] (They defined "fraud" as "customer complaints for which the financial advisor either paid a settlement of at least $10,000 or lost an arbitration decision.")[18] To study this, they focused on mergers between financial advisory firms with multiple branches. In these mergers, financial advisors met new coworkers from one of the branches of the other firm, which led them to new ideas and behaviors. The researchers thus compared merged branches where advisors were introduced into workplaces where advisors had already engaged in misconduct (where new people came into an environment with "bad apples") with merged branches without known cheaters. The incentives to cheat were the same in the branch offices, of course, but the personnel were different.

What they found should be horrifying to investors, managers, executives, and regulators: "Financial advisors are 37% more likely to commit misconduct if they encounter a new coworker with a history of misconduct."[19] Further, "Peer effects in misconduct are stronger between advisors who share the same ethnicity; the contagion effect is nearly twice as large if an advisor meets a new coworker with a history of misconduct and who shares the advisor's ethnicity. Thus, similar individuals, who likely interact more, have stronger effects on each other's behaviors."[20]

The many of findings here are powerful: "bad" peers are going to have a strong effect on turning their coworkers bad, and if they share the same ethnicity—and, let's be honest, they are likely to be White, as the vast majority of financial advisors are White—that effect is more pronounced.

Like many of the studies we have mentioned so far in this chapter, this study on peer effects in organizations was conducted by economists. The big thing they are missing is the importance of peer *culture* within organizations. Or perhaps they are not missing it so much as dismissing it—culture is not quantifiable, or precisely countable, the way economists' preferred phenomena tend to be.

One person who has studied peer culture in business settings is Gillian Tett, editor-at-large at the *Financial Times*. She is a trained anthropologist who explored the insular culture of investment bankers working with a poorly understood (at least to outsiders) financial "product" called "collateralized debt obligations" (CDOs). (Eventually, CDOs would become a key contributor to the 2008 financial crisis.) What she called the "CDO tribe" had, Tett found, created their own mythology and peer culture that set them off as different, and in their eyes, better than others in their field.[21] At a conference for investment bankers in Nice in 2005, she found that these investment bankers were creating network ties, but also detailed how they were creating a cultural system of meaning, inventing a language that made them distinctive. (Recall our discussion of group boundaries and culture in the introduction: boundaries tell us who we are; culture tells us what we are and helps to reinforce the boundaries, drawing distinctions between "us" and "them.")

Tett wrote, "In the first couple of days I sat there, they almost never mentioned the human borrower who was at the end of that securitization chain. They were also very exclusive. There was a sense that 'we alone have mastery over this knowledge.'"[22]

These bankers of the CDO tribe, whose statistics-heavy work executives tended not to understand and so were largely left alone, also had what Tett calls a "founding mythology": back in ancient times, bankers made loans and kept them on their books. This was inefficient. Then bankers figured out that they should spread the risk. This would make the economic system safer.

These investment bankers thought of their specific idea of spreading risk across the system as superior, cutting-edge, and, in general, a societal good. "In retrospect," Tett wrote, "it turns out that these ideas led to disaster." These bankers wanted to be like each other, they were following the norms of the culture they created, they thought like each other, and because of this insularity, they could not foresee the horrors their new forms of securities (the sliced and diced subprime mortgage debt) would eventually unleash. These bankers operated within a cultural system they created, saw nothing wrong with it, and did not listen to, or value, any critiques that came from outside their peer group. This worldview was reinforced by a lack of outside regulation by governmental bodies, or even by superiors within their own firms.

How to Do Diversity Programs in the Workforce Better

Why should companies engage in diversity? Initially they did so because they had a legal obligation to. In 1961, President Kennedy issued Executive Order 10925, which required federal contractors to engage in "affirmative action" to end racial discrimination. Closely following this was the passage of the federal Civil Rights Act of 1964, which forbade discrimination on the basis of race, color, sex, religion, and national origin in the private sector.[23] The Nixon administration, oddly for Republicans, expanded affirmative action, requiring government contractors to hire minority workers under the "Philadelphia Plan." In 1972, Congress passed the Equal Employment Opportunity Act, which empowered the Equal Opportunity Employment Commission (EEOC) to sue for discrimination on behalf of plaintiffs. The number of discrimination lawsuits went from a few hundred a year to five thousand by 1980. Frank Dobbin and Alexandra Kalev point out that at this time, managers were looking for ways to cover themselves legally, and they came up with ceremonial civil rights compliance, which makes it look as though they are doing something without "rocking the boat."[24]

Dobbin and Kalev argue, though, that the civil rights revolution at work ultimately has largely failed. The gutting of antidiscrimination laws and agencies from the 1980s onward left companies with little legal incentive to promote change. They found that diversity in upper echelons of corporations has increased only incrementally, and that, even though there was a broad adoption of diversity training and grievance procedures, the deeper structures that reproduce inequality have been left intact. So firms largely cover themselves legally with diversity trainings to make it look as though they are engaging in practices that will lead to diversity, but really, they don't.[25]

Diversity for its own sake arguably should be enough, but a big reason why corporate firms *should* want more diverse workplaces is that—as studies conducted by consulting firm McKinsey & Company over the past few years have shown—this makes them more profitable than firms with less diversity.[26]

But since the police killings of George Floyd and Breonna Taylor in 2020, and so, so many other Black individuals, there has been a renewed interest from the corporate side in diversity. This is seen in the growing demand by companies for diversity, equity, and inclusion (DEI) training for antiracism and implicit-bias workshops—consultants cannot fill the demand fast enough.[27]

The problem, as Frank Dobbin and Alexandra Kalev show, is that such approaches, especially bias training in the workplace, do not always increase diversity or reduce biases.[28]

So, then, what can help? The basic problem if an organization needs a DEI training or program is twofold: the firm's employee base is not diverse *and* the culture of the employees is inhospitable to non-White and female employees. We argue that for diversity and inclusion to take root, managers and executives need to pay attention to horizontal peer culture and peer effects among workers. Top-down organizational culture is simply not the same. Companies have a better chance of achieving and maintaining diversity in their ranks if they can find a way to change the peer culture so it becomes more hospitable to workers who are not White men.

First, What Doesn't Work?

Let's focus on implicit bias training, as that is the most popular program foisted on workers by human resources departments. The idea of implicit bias is basically that we have many biases and blind spots that we are unaware of or that we do not express consciously (hence, implicit). If we can be made conscious of these through training or testing, perhaps we can eliminate them.

Implicit bias training often starts with a sort of revelatory exercise, meant to make participants recognize that they *do* harbor stereotypical racist or sexist views. The most well-known test of implicit bias is the Implicit Association Test (IAT), developed by Anthony Greenwald and Mahzarin Banaji in 1998. There are multiple versions of the test; we are just talking about the first and most well-known one, which deals with race. It has been taken by well over seventeen million people worldwide.[29] One problem with the test is that it has a very low test-retest reliability (r=.42), meaning that if you take the test today and then take it tomorrow, it is likely you will have very different results. (A good test has high reliability, with r=.7 or higher, meaning that if you take it today and tomorrow, your scores should be pretty close.)[30] This is a problem, because the originators of this test, which is widely used in work and schools, regularly assert that it predicts discriminatory behavior that is hidden even from the individual. Well, if it is not statistically reliable, then the results are suspect.

Another problem is even bigger. Greenwald, Banaji, and Brian Nosek wrote, basically agreeing with their critics, that psychometric issues with the race IATs "render them problematic to use to classify persons as likely to engage in discrimination." They also noted that "attempts to diagnostically use such measures for individuals risk undesirably high rates of erroneous classifications."[31] The journalist Jesse Singal, who has done a fascinating deep dive on the IAT, paraphrased by saying, "In other words: You can't use the IAT to tell individuals how likely they are to commit acts of implicit bias."[32] Further, he writes, it is not clear *what* the IAT is measuring. Basically, your IAT score is a measure of how quickly you associate "good" or "bad" words with African Americans versus European Americans (in the categories used by the test itself). Higher scores are meant to show that the test taker has implicit bias. For example, if you are slow to associate good words with African Americans (or, you make more mistakes hitting the buttons), then you have more anti-Black bias.[33] But, Singal explains, some people who feel that the plight of Black people in this country is due to structural factors *also* score high on the test. He speculates that "high IAT scores may sometimes be artifacts of empathy for an out-group, and/or familiarity with negative stereotypes against that group, rather than indicating any sort of deep-seated unconscious endorsement of those associations."[34] And these are hardly the only problems with the IAT detailed by Singal and fellow journalist Olivia Goldhill.

Still, in spite of journalistic and academic criticism of the IAT and of the idea that implicit bias is measurable at all, implicit bias tests remain in widespread use.

A research team including Angela Duckworth and Adam Grant, in their publication "Does Diversity Training Work the Way It's Supposed To?," wanted to see if they could measure the impact of diversity training.[35] They gave three thousand employees at a large global firm, spread across sixty-three countries, one of three one-hour training sessions:

one on gender bias; one that addressed multiple kinds of bias (gender, age, race, sexual orientation); and a control group that talked not about bias but about "cultivating psychological safety in teams." The participants next took the IAT, then learned strategies to overcome bias. The researchers measured employee attitudes after the training and studied their behavior over twenty weeks.

"We found very little evidence that diversity training affected the behavior of men or White employees overall—the two groups who typically hold the most power in organizations and are often the primary targets of these interventions. . . . The absence of any observable change in the behavior of male or White employees overall suggests that we need to stop treating diversity training as a silver bullet," concluded the study's research team. Similarly, when reporter Olivia Goldhill spoke to people conducting implicit bias trainings—who would surely trumpet their quantifiable results if they could—she wrote, "None of the implicit-bias training-program instructors . . . were able to point to definitive positive results from their workshops."[36]

Like other pop psychology concepts widely applied in real-world settings—think *grit* or *leaning in*—implicit bias is a popular concept without any real scientific evidence to support it.[37] Why do we lap these things up? Many smart and successful people love ideas that focus on the individual. If the problems are individual, the individual can fix them. Implicit bias? Show them and they will change. No grit? We can teach it. Women who are underpaid and want to go up the organizational ladder? Lean in! These are ideas and solutions that can be elegantly framed in a TED Talk.

But the world is messy and complex, and while these solutions sound smart, they are not right. And they ignore the history of how we got here. As the sociologist Victor Ray has pointed out, organizations in this country are not race neutral: they are White (and male).[38] They did not just become White (and male); naturalizing the segregation took decades and was reinforced every step of the way through discrimination in laws, educational institutions, banks, policing, societal norms, and more. All these factors shaped who ran the show, who organizations did and did not hire and promote, and who established the structures within which workplace cultures operate. Given that, can we really expect that a training session or two is going to make any difference?

"[In] quantitative terms, the literature on prejudice reduction is vast, but a survey of this literature reveals a paucity of research that supports internally valid inferences and externally valid generalization."[39] This is the conclusion of a major review of the *thousands* of studies on diversity/prejudice reduction in the journal *Annual Review of Psychology*. Translated out of academic-speak, that means that we are not cherry picking. Basically, nearly all the studies in this vein are poorly done, and we should not rely on them to try to understand how the world works or how to change it for the better.

What Does Work?

Sociologists Alexandra Kalev, Frank Dobbin, and Erin Kelly, in an article in the *American Sociological Review*, studied more than thirty years of data from over seven hundred firms and interviewed hundreds of line managers and executives to see which diversity programs work and which fail.[40] They found that "structures establishing responsibility (affirmative action plans, diversity committees, and diversity staff positions) are followed by significant increases in managerial diversity. Programs that target managerial stereotyping through education and feedback (diversity training and diversity evaluations) are not followed by increases in diversity. Programs that address social isolation among women and minorities (networking and mentoring programs) are followed by modest changes."[41]

"Programs that target managerial stereotyping" do not increase diversity—that is, feedback (diversity evaluations) and education (diversity training) for managers do not work. Interestingly, "networking and mentoring" lead to only modest changes. Though these practices give mentees access to internal knowledge about how the organization works and who is actually important for what purposes, they do not do as much as we might hope to raise diversity or lower discrimination. It is possible that what is important here is the *type* of mentoring. Informal mentoring may be more effective than formal mentoring, because people will see the informal relationship as expressing social, as well as professional, approval, and this could enhance the mentees' status in other people's eyes.[42] Status by association works better when it seems organic. Thus, the reaction to an informal mentoring relationship could be something like, "Oh, Jim the VP has taken Helen, the Black woman from accounting, under his wing. She must be something special," while a more formal mentorship would elicit, "Oh, I see Jim the VP has taken on Helen, the Black woman from accounting, as his mentee in that program. Good for them." The informal relationship would be understood as an implicit endorsement of Helen, while the formal one could be established for any number of reasons.

It is critically important that these authors found so definitively that "structures establishing responsibility" (affirmative action plans, diversity committees, and diversity staff positions) significantly increase managerial diversity. The organizations that are serious about increasing diversity are establishing permanent staff positions, new policies, and mechanisms for feedback about how it is all going.

Unfortunately, very few companies have put up the resources to do this correctly, and affirmative action has faced so many attacks in the courts and in the courts of public opinion, in spite of the fact that affirmative action works.[43] The number of Black women and men in management positions today is minuscule; in the C-suites it is tiny. The number of Asian Americans past midlevel positions is minimal given their numbers in entry-level jobs.[44] The number of White women in senior management across all sectors is still relatively small, too.

Why Do "Structures Establishing Responsibility" Work to Effect Diversity?

Peers. Let's think again about Stuyvesant High School. There, peers directly affect each other's behavior, and they also have a part in creating and sustaining a student culture of excellence that is independent of teachers, administrators, and parents. The peer effect at Stuyvesant makes good students better than they otherwise might be by promoting certain norms of behavior, like doing your work conscientiously and fastidiously. While Stuyvesant has slackers and potheads like any other high school, the peer dynamic there is such that they learn early on that no matter what "extracurriculars" you engage in, your work must get done, or you will face social disapproval from your peers (is there a worse punishment in high school?). So, no one at Stuyvesant is surprised when their druggie classmate becomes a surgeon. They *expect* them to.

This is why organizations that take diversity hiring seriously can find that changing the composition of peers leads to pleasant surprises in the culture. Take the University of Houston for example.[45] In 2017, helped by a relatively small $3.3 million grant from the National Science Foundation, the university set out to hire more minority faculty. Just two years later, in 2019, it had about 42 percent more tenured and tenure-track faculty of color. But hiring was not the end of the story. The university also created an Underrepresented Women of Color Coalition, whose members shared tips on writing, teaching, and research, and who acted as an informal social support network and role modeling group. This is hugely important to academic careers, since many of us scholars are hidden away in our departmental silos rather than interacting with our peers across campus. A third change was that the university altered the way hiring committees reached out and evaluated potential hires—a move that increased minority recruiting.[46]

This resulting dramatic change in personnel has, in turn, led to a shift in the peer culture. One Black female professor who was at the university before the new programs said, "I don't have to hold my breath anymore and worry about being under the White gaze or, 'How can I just tone myself, my dress, my speech down so that I can not disrupt, so that I won't be seen as an outlier?'" Rather, she reports that she can now walk into a space like the faculty café and have the sense that "I belong here, because she probably uses the same hair product that I use, she has the same curl pattern that I have." People smile at her and want to talk with her. This is no small thing. A welcoming culture goes a long way toward making people comfortable and committed to the job.

What Can Organizations Do?

As we have made clear, we believe that the programs that will be most effective in increasing and retaining a racially diverse workforce do so through direct peer effects, and indirectly through changes to the peer culture in the face-to-face environment. Executives and managers can try to govern the peer culture directly from the top, but a more effective way is for workers to do it themselves. This idea may be scary for executives as it points to their lack of control. To help effect change, they would have to have trust in, and give more freedom to their employees than perhaps they are comfortable doing. The informal peer culture at work, which is horizontally organized, can change internally under certain conditions—for example, through staff with strong personalities and a little know-how, who put in time and effort to change norms in this informal culture. Management can help *indirectly* by identifying and developing employee catalysts of change, and creating an architecture of support for them to work to change norms.

Diversifying the workplace, as we saw with the University of Houston above, can help to change culture and norms, and can embolden change agents to change culture and norms further. Once the norms (and with them, rewards and punishments for behavior) change, the behavior of toxic people could change. They will have to adapt to the changed norms (no more White men interrupting Black people and women and others in meetings and taking up all the time speaking and other subtle, harmful workplace practices), or possibly they will leave.

Organizations need to also pay attention at the upper, middle, and lower levels to peer composition and hiring practices, because having more diversity in a workforce can change the norms of the informal peer culture. A small number of hires would have to assimilate to the workplace culture; a larger number can be bolder in trying to change the culture. Is this the only way that peer cultures can change? No. But if you have the same personnel, or little change to the personnel, it is unlikely that the culture will change. A newly diversified workplace that is diverse at all levels can change the culture and norms. And if you have a diverse team at leadership levels, who intentionally consider these very peer effects, they are going to hire, and more importantly, promote, talented individuals who represent diversity and who have shown skill at catalyzing these changes to peer-influenced norms. Historically at elite firms, the people whom managers hire are overwhelmingly White, and graduated from elite universities.[47] Having managers of different backgrounds in charge of hiring is crucial to the diversity project. So if organizations have diverse peer groups, because they have enough women and Black men and other minorities in key roles, even when there is turnover the changes to the organization's informal culture among its workers could take hold. Once that happens, it will be difficult to undo those changes to the norms in the informal peer culture, and the goal of diversity will become a workplace fact.

Hedge Funds: Why Office Culture Is So Hard to Change

While the state of diversity in corporate America is still rather appalling, corporations are at least talking about it and doing *something* (no matter how ineffective that something may be). But there is one sector where diversity is not even really thought of as a concern: hedge funds. In her 2022 book, *Hedged Out: Inequality and Insecurity on Wall Street*, Megan Tobias Neely takes us on a tour of this industry. Her rich data include deep interviews with dozens of hedge fund insiders and ethnographic descriptions of various hedge fund–related events. And her analysis of the hedge fund industry can help us understand why changing peer cultures within organizations is such a difficult task, even when the organizations are actively trying to change their ways.

Hedge funds, in stark terms, are private financial firms that get money from rich people and large institutions to invest in the stock market. To qualify as a hedge fund investor, individuals are required by the US Securities and Exchange Commission to have a net worth of at least one million dollars and an annual income of at least two hundred thousand dollars. Meanwhile, nearly 60 percent of hedge fund investment money—the funds the investors get to play with—comes from pensions, governments, universities, and other nonprofit endowments.[48]

This is a very White and male industry, more so than almost any other. Firms run by White men manage 97 percent of all hedge fund investments. The industry employs about fifty-five thousand people in the United States; women account for only about 20 percent of hedge fund workers (10 percent in senior positions). The workers in this industry make a lot of money: hedge fund portfolio managers get roughly $1.4 million a year, and even entry-level analysts make around $680,000 a year.[49] While hedge fund investors are relatively few in number, their impact is felt globally.

Hedge funds have an exclusive clientele and high fees, and they generate high profits for their firms. The fees charged are taxed as capital gains, not income, so the tax rates on hedge funds are substantially lower and personal earnings substantially higher than in other industries. US-based hedge funds manage assets worth about 12 percent of the country's entire GDP. In 2010, Bridgewater Associates, the world's largest hedge fund, had investment returns of fifteen billion dollars, more than the profits of Google, eBay, Yahoo, and Amazon put together. But it only had twelve hundred employees, against Amazon's, for instance, one hundred thousand workers at the time.[50] Because they do not have a product, in the traditional sense, hedge funds do not need a lot of people.

Many large companies engage in diversity programs because of societal pressures, client pressures, and sometimes legal pressures. Hedge funds do not feel these pressures in the same way. The organizations tend to be very small and "flat"—hardly any have human resources departments, and they do not have layers of bureaucracy. They even outsource many key functions, like IT and payroll. There is not much room for advancement in these firms.

A big part of Neely's story of hedge funds is fleshing out the reasons why the industry is so exceedingly White and male. It starts with hiring. As Lauren Rivera has shown for high-end, white-collar jobs, hiring managers hire people "like them"—elite-educated, usually White people. Because hedge funds are so small, the people doing the hiring are even more conscious of "fit" and "similarity." The key decision makers are nearly all White men, wealthy, from upper-middle-class or upper-class economic backgrounds with elite private school educations, and they are very much looking to reproduce themselves. To give an example, one woman told Neely about the freedom hedge fund managers (again, White and male) have in hiring: "I've actually sat next to a hedge fund guy who told me that he doesn't hire any woman, because he really doesn't like women in the workplace."[51] Even in the worst corporate environments, there are HR departments to curb these excesses. But as Neely notes, in this rarified space, there is "no scrutiny or repercussions for discriminatory employment practices."[52]

These hedge fund managers shape who is in the group, and the "who" are mostly White men, some women, and precious few non-Whites. The culture of the group will be a reflection of this world building, curated by the hedge fund managers (with very, very few exceptions), to be a very White, elite, male world.

Given the financial stakes in the hedge fund world, the culture Neely describes is one of elite, White masculinity, defined by "being bold, taking risks, amassing fortunes, and mastering uncertainty." At the same time, it "hedges against some of the ugliest, most overt forms of masculinity, such as open sexism and physical violence."[53] Their work never ends as the markets are global, and their drug of choice is not alcohol or cocaine, but rather Adderall, to enhance the singular focus on money making. Theirs is not the toxic, finance bro masculinity we see in movies like *Wall Street* or *The Wolf of Wall Street* (though there is no shortage of overt sexism and harassment). And yet, the effect is similar—a certain class of White men can gain access, while women, and minorities especially, are largely held at bay.

This is not to say that the bro culture is over, but that it has mutated. Women can gain entry to this world, but they have to conform to its cultural norms. One of Neely's female respondents said that the women who can fit into the culture "are not easily offended," and they are "women who engage like men." Talking about their personal lives and feelings is discouraged. And women should be willing to "work really, really, really long hours, and place their careers the clear and obvious number one priority."[54] Because networks are so crucial to getting hired, women working in this world know that to report harassment could spell the end to their hedge fund careers. So they mostly keep quiet about it.

To reiterate a theoretical point from the introduction, boundaries tell us "who" we are as a group; cultures tell us "what" we are. The "who" in the hedge fund world are carefully crafted through discriminatory hiring practices to be mainly White and male. The peer culture within the "flat" hedge fund world is bound to reflect that. Indeed, for women and minorities in this world to thrive, they have to conform to the norms of what Neely calls "hedgemonic masculinity," a type of masculinity that works to "hedge" out women and minority men, and makes it difficult for them to conform to the norms created with White men in mind. Yes, there are Asians and Blacks and Latinos in this industry, but their paths to success or just staying in this world are far more difficult than the paths open to elite White men, and because they do not have the same depth of networks, if they find themselves out of a job (common, as turnover rates are high), it is much harder for them to get another one.

Cultures Are Conservative

To end this chapter, let us return to the question at its beginning: Why is it so difficult to change the peer cultures of work organizations? Cultures, once they come into being, are extremely resistant to change. They have norms and traditions and taken-for-granted ways of doing things. These are, by definition, conservative. In the hedge fund world, the people who make these norms—elite, White men—are in no hurry to change their ways, and there are no external pressures on them to do so. They reproduce themselves by hiring other elite, White men, and long after they are gone, the people in this world will still look the same.

In many other corporate and nonprofit firms, there are internal and external pressures to change culture. But, even with near-universal discussions of "diversity," not much has changed in terms of demographics. The Coca-Cola Company is a notable exception, largely because it has made bold moves to change the "peers"—to actually diversify its workforce at every organizational level. (The impetus was a high-profile discrimination lawsuit in 2000 that was settled for $192.5 million, the largest settlement for racial discrimination in legal history, with payouts to nearly twenty-two hundred Black employees.)[55] No matter how many diversity training sessions HR orders people to attend, anodyne commitments to corporate cultures will not be realized in actual worker diversity.

5

Cops, Peers, and a Culture of Violence

"Some days," said a Vallejo, California, police officer in the months after George Floyd was murdered in the streets of Minneapolis, Minnesota, "I feel like I work with a bunch of thugs who take pleasure out of hurting people."[1] Indeed, in the United States, officers sworn to "protect and serve" regularly dole out beatings, kill civilians, and withhold life-saving efforts from critically injured people.[2] They are not supposed to—and surely know that—but they do. And when they do, there are usually very few repercussions for the police officers or departments. Cities pay out the lawsuits (to the tune of millions of dollars each year) from their general funds, not police budgets, officers pull some desk duty or take administrative leave (at full pay), and the public is unconvincingly assured that the violence was an aberration, evidence only of a few "bad apples" among those holding the "thin blue line" between order and lawlessness.[3]

New York City has a police force that is bigger than the armed forces of many countries—at least thirty-six thousand officers strong. Its budget is roughly eleven billion dollars per year (including roughly five billion dollars for fringe benefits and pensions).[4] Between 2014 and 2019, the city's general fund paid out more than one billion dollars in settlements related to police misconduct (with the costs rising almost every year for a decade and counting now).[5] Just over two thousand of the city's cops (6 percent) are plainclothes (i.e., they do not wear uniforms), but they are involved in 31 percent of all fatal police shootings.[6] One of them, Daniel Pantaleo, choked Eric Garner to death in Staten Island in 2014. Garner was suspected of but denied selling loosies, individual cigarettes, and pulled his arms away as Pantaleo made contact. Within moments, the man was on the ground in a chokehold. A widely circulated video of the incident made his last words indelible: "I can't breathe," which he repeated eleven times. He lay unconscious on the sidewalk for seven minutes before an ambulance arrived. An hour later, Garner was declared dead. Though Pantaleo had already been subject to seven misconduct complaints in his eight years on the job, including two that resulted in civil rights lawsuits, the NYPD, the mayor, and Staten Island's district attorney collectively dragged their feet, and a grand jury declined to indict.[7] The federal Department of Justice refused to file charges. It took five years of desk duty at full pay (with a base salary over one hundred thousand dollars, supplemented by a heap of overtime pay) before Pantaleo was even fired.[8]

And guess what? Getting rid of that bad apple did not stop police misconduct.

Arthur Rizer, a former cop who heads the criminal justice program at a center-right think tank in Washington, DC, told *Vox*, "That whole thing about the bad apple? I hate when people say that. The bad apple rots the barrel. And until we do something about the rotten barrel, it doesn't matter how many good fucking apples you put in."[9] In other words, the problem is not cops, but cop culture.

Peers

Knowing what we do about the peer effect, we argue that Pantaleos are *made* by their fellow cops. Sure, some already have violent (and racist and sexist) tendencies, but those are undoubtedly amplified by their surroundings: a culture that values violence, within an organization that rarely punishes it. And it is very much a White, male culture, as about 70 percent of the over 486,000 police nationwide are White, and more than 85 percent are male.[10]

In a groundbreaking study of peer effects, researchers examined police misconduct in London from 2011 to 2014. They followed police over time as they changed roles and were able to identify their peers. Seeing changes in behavior over time allowed them to see what happened when cops changed peer groups, in turn allowing the researchers to make causal claims. They found that "a ten-percentage-point increase in the fraction of peers with misconduct would raise the incidence of misconduct by an absolute 8 percent. These results are consistent when an officer switches to an entirely new group or when he receives new members to his current peer group."[11] That is, as the number of cops who engage in misconduct increases, misconduct among other officers they work with increases. In other words, cops who hang out with bad apples *become* bad apples. Thus, the authors suggest, "Moving a bad cop to alternative locations will increase the risk of spreading misconduct."[12]

Another study looked at gun violence among Chicago cops from 2010 to 2016. In a total of 435 shootings, cops wounded 170 civilians (35 Latino, 14 White, and the rest nearly all Black), and killed 92 (80 of whom were Black). The researchers wanted to know whether "an officer's exposure to a shooting by a neighbor on his network increases the probability that he will engage in a shooting in a subsequent encounter with a civilian."[13] In line with the London study's authors, these researchers found that police violence was "contagious," and that being exposed to a single shooting more than doubled the likelihood that a "network neighbor" (i.e., another cop who is connected to the first one) would be involved in a future shooting. In their data, contagion affected about 30 percent of the shootings. "Officers who are exposed to multiple shootings appear to be particularly at risk, as the effect of exposure is cumulative."[14]

Taking the two studies together, we have reason to pause: Why would anyone think it was a good idea to reassign New York City's problematic plainclothes cops? If, as it appears statistically, they were a particularly violent subculture of the NYPD, spreading them to different parts of the force, the Chicago and London studies imply, will spread violence. They can be expected to bring their attitudes and tendencies with them, pick up new "tricks" in their new working environments, and help to develop violent behavior among the cops in their new precincts and units.

Culture

The London study's big finding, that cops are affected negatively by their peers, makes complete sense when we take into account our earlier point, that norms and sanctions are most well developed within intense and interactive peer groups. Cops work in intense, closed, face-to-face social worlds. They have a peer-driven culture, like the one we saw at Stuyvesant High School, in which higher-ups have little practical say (the "adults," as it were, administrators and superior officers, are not exactly riding in every patrol car), and extremely well-defined boundaries between "us" and "them." Further, new police officers "assimilate" to an existing and durable peer group. Like high school kids, they will want to be like the other officers and avoid being outcasts, so they will usually follow the behavioral expectations enforced by these new peers. They will hew to the "hidden curriculum" of informal norms no cop needs to be taught and every cop knows exists, or they will face the consequences. Follow the rules and you will be fine; break the rules, and there will be hell to pay. (Arguably, ostracism has more dire and direct consequences for cops, who work in a sometimes-dangerous profession, than for high schoolers.)

One of the London study's coauthors said in an interview, "I don't think this is a police problem as much as a human being problem."[15] They were right, in that peers affect all people's behavior within the group, but otherwise, the study actually showed that this is *very much a police problem*. That is the case because their report was not about the overall behavior of cops—it was about *on-the-job misconduct*. These behaviors of these cops occur as a result of influencing, and being influenced by, their police peers within a culture that tolerates a wide variety of misconduct (except for snitching on a fellow cop or otherwise violating the "blue wall of silence" norm, which is absolutely not tolerated). One resident of rapidly gentrifying Crown Heights in Brooklyn said in an interview that the plainclothes cops "act tough, like they're from the hood, like they're from a gang."[16] But those cops' friends, family, neighbors, and their kids' teachers may well see the same people as sweet and sensitive. (Pantaleo started dating and married a woman while on desk duty *after* killing Eric Garner.)[17] A bad cop may be a horrible person in every aspect of their lives, but most bad cops probably aren't. It is just like the way high school kids may act one way at school, and another at home. Police misconduct, however, is an institutional problem born out of policing's organizational structure, the power that unions and police departments wield in local, state, and federal politics, and the "us versus everyone else" culture that would put them above the law.

To talk seriously about police culture, we should remind ourselves about our working definition of culture. Many people define culture as a set of ideas and practices, including values, norms, food, dress, music, etc. And this culture belongs to a "people"—Americans, Texans, Christians, high school kids, people living in a retirement community, etc. Culture and identity are bound together, so that culture defines "our" way of life, reinforcing boundaries between insiders and outsiders.[18] But that definition assumes a sort of intentional, democratic, participatory, and consensual creation of culture. In the real world, "we" (the people in the group) do not have to agree on all the specifics of our culture (values, traditions, norms, music, etc.), and it doesn't even take a majority to define the culture. A powerful minority, able to compel others because they are rich, have political authority, or control cultural symbolism (like those in the clergy or a high school's popular clique), can establish "how things are done." Over time, the idea that these aspects of the culture are "our tradition" is all the justification anyone needs to continue doing things (and to not *change* how things are done). Think female genital mutilation, flying the Confederate flag, or having different curfew times for teenaged boys and girls in the same house—all seen, by many, as traditional, therefore appropriate, cultural practices.

Can cultures change? Sure, but there has to be an impetus, whether it comes from the inside or from the outside. There is always a struggle between preserving and changing, though the default is inertia. People do the things that "their" people have always done, and it is difficult to get them to even think it is possible to do otherwise.

Culture is also, you will have noticed, about power. Those powerful few get to determine the various elements of the culture, define its norms, and establish sanctions for violating those norms.[19] Because culture is decided by power and not consensus, change requires defying or defeating or displacing those in power. It is worth repeating that not every member of the group has to agree with every aspect of its culture nor follow all the norms. They can be deviants; they can develop countercultures; they can develop subcultures. But, they—everyone in the group, and often people outside the group—understand the ground rules and know that there *may* be consequences for breaking the rules.

So, for instance, Black cops may not agree with or do everything White cops do. But there are some norms that everyone knows are paramount, like not snitching. We can tell that "not snitching" is a central norm in cop culture because the penalties for violating it are so severe—as the story of Adrian Schoolcraft, related later in this chapter, so viscerally demonstrates. Other cops, even "friends," will abandon a cop who steps out of line to snitch when another cop commits a crime. Higher-ups and unions might even decline to support them. Whistle-blowing ruins careers, while, say, beating or killing a civilian will see the "blue wall" rally behind their fellow officer.

Another police norm we can infer from behavior we observe is that a cop must never take the side of/defend civilians over cops. When violent behavior by cops at protests gets out of control, the "good cops" hardly ever step in. And when they do step in, it is newsworthy. For instance, in New York City days after the City Council made it illegal for cops to use chokeholds, a cop made the news for tapping another cop on the shoulder and stopping his chokehold on a person who had become unconscious. (And why did he intervene? He noticed a bystander filming and another yelling, "Yo, stop choking him bro!")[20]

More usual is the behavior that occurred when Derrick Chauvin had his knee on George Floyd's neck for at least eight minutes and forty-six seconds, slowly choking him to death; two other cops restraining the man were rookies, and though bystanders being held at bay by a third officer begged them to intervene, only one suggested their supervising (and former training) officer turn Floyd over to let him breathe. The fact that these three officers were convicted, two years later, of federal civil rights violations for their failure to intervene was far more surprising than their hands-off approach on the scene.[21] As the *New York Times* reported, "At the heart of this case was a more widespread problem, experts say, than a single officer's act of violence: the tendency of officers to stand by when they witness a fellow officer committing a crime."[22] Later in the same article, a professor at Georgetown University's Law Center said the verdict "forces you to move beyond the bad apple narrative. . . . Now you're like, 'Oh, everyone on the scene played a role in this.' It shifts the entire narrative."

Teaching Fear

The culture of policing has actually shifted significantly toward even greater, and more lethal, violence in recent decades. Specifically, it has shifted to a shared "knowledge" that policing is inherently—and always—lethally risky. Though training that makes this explicit is present in only some departments, the cultural understanding has saturated police ranks extremely thoroughly and throughout the country. Cops are taught, informally by their peers and officially through department trainings and messaging, that it is "kill or be killed" out there on the mean streets of Anytown, USA.

A reporter for the *New Republic* recently took his dad, a retired cop, to a seminar for police called "The Bulletproof Mind: Prevailing in Violent Encounters . . . and After." It was led by Dave Grossman, a retired army Ranger and former West Point instructor who runs what he calls the Killology Research Group (yes, that's correct). He is among the nation's most popular police trainers. As the journalist wrote, Grossman looked out to a crowd of 250 cops, crammed into a high school auditorium in

Elizabethtown, Pennsylvania, and declared, "We. Are. At. War. And you are the front-line troops in this war. There is no elite unit showing up to save your bacon when the terrorists attack. You are the Delta Force. You are the Green Beret. You are British SAS. Can you accept that? Every single one of you is in the frontline of a live ammo combat patrol every day of your life."

The reporter's dad was from a different generation of cops. He had served thirty-five years on the police force of Syracuse, New York, before retiring in 1998. He told his son that the mindset, the culture of police, had undergone an enormous change. In 2017, he told his reporter son, "The younger cops are a little different, you know." He marveled, "Christ, they pump fucking iron, got shaved heads, got fucking tattoos," and said they acted like Special Forces soldiers. "I think they're being trained that way."

"You guys didn't get trained like that?" his son asked.

"No. You were just an ordinary person that happened to be a cop."[23]

A former Chicago Police Department officer who is now a private investigator who aids cops accused of excessive force says that now that cops have gotten the idea that *any* situation could be fatal, they cannot accept any degree of being out of control. That makes them exceptionally violent: "If you are gonna use force, you have to use a lot of force, or you are going to die. You can't be a namby pamby."[24] This is corroborated by an article in the *Marshall Project*, in which cops, their defense lawyers, prosecutors, and law enforcement researchers agree that police culture has reoriented toward asserting dominance.[25] It is also evidenced by a 2016 incident in which a West Virginia cop ended up being fired for *not* using his gun on a man he thought was trying to commit "suicide by cop" (that is, trying to get a cop to kill him). He thought that because it is what the man's girlfriend told the 911 dispatcher. She also explained that the man was drunk and, though he had a pistol, it was empty. So, the cop was trying to talk him down when two other police arrived. They, too, knew the gun was empty, but they almost immediately shot the man in the head (they also managed to shoot the ground, a car in a neighboring driveway, and another neighbor's front door).[26] The first officer on the scene was fired for putting the lives of his fellow officers on the line—for, as *ProPublica* reports, not using *enough* force. Looking at what gets rewarded and what gets punished tells us a lot about which norms are crucial in the violent culture of policing.

Tom Nolan, a criminologist and a former lieutenant and twenty-seven-year veteran of the Boston Police Department, says about police culture, "I have seen, throughout my decades in law enforcement, that police culture tends to privilege the use of violent tactics and non-negotiable force over compromise, mediation, and peaceful conflict resolution. It reinforces a general acceptance among officers of the use of any and all means of force available when confronted with real or perceived threats to officers."[27] The militarized police response to protests, he says, "is in part due to a policing culture in which protesters are often perceived as the 'enemy.' Indeed teaching cops to think like soldiers and learn how to kill has been part of a training program popular among some police officers."

A critical, but often overlooked part of the story of this shift is visceral. In 1998, a Georgia sheriff's deputy, Kyle Dinkheller, pulled over a speeding driver. The whole encounter was caught on the deputy's dash cam. In the video, now shown in police academies around the country, the car's driver, a White Vietnam veteran with PTSD, gets out of his car and says, "Here I am, shoot me." Things escalate, and the man returns to his car, pulling out a rifle. There is an exchange of gunfire; both men are shot, but the deputy is hit worse. The man then approaches Dinkheller, yells "Die, fucker!," and shoots and kills him. Peter Moskos, a former Baltimore police officer and now professor at the John Jay College of Criminal Justice, says, "Every cop knows the name 'Dinkheller'—and no one else does."

Even though the number of killings of police officers has dropped dramatically since 1970, police academies and field training officers greatly emphasize the risk of violent death to officers. Indeed, this preoccupation with death can be seen clearly through the ways that police departments commemorate deaths of officers killed in the line of duty. These commemorations centralize this kind of death in police culture, as the sociologist Michael Sierra-Arévalo has shown.[28]

But police are almost as likely to die in a car crash as they are to be shot. (And in 2020–2021, COVID-19 was by far the leading cause of death among police officers nationwide, accounting for nearly five hundred deaths.)[29] According to twenty years of recent FBI data on officer fatalities, 1,001 officers have been killed by firearms while 760 have died in car crashes. But cops don't worry about dying in a car crash, and a great many don't wear a seat belt.[30] Why? The warrior mentality is so engrained that they think they have to be ready to jump out of a car to chase a suspect—a seat belt would only slow them down.[31]

The Department of Justice has ordered at least five major cities to overhaul their field training programs, as these programs, and the low standards for accepting people as field trainers, "fuel the toxic street-cop culture."[32] Police trainees may not know the hours they spend on various topics of study, but we do: of an average of 833 hours of training (roughly twenty-one weeks—the amount of training varies greatly from state to state), cadets will receive eighteen hours of training on "de-escalation/verbal judo." They will also get 154 hours of training on firearms, nonlethal weapons, and self-defense.[33] It is hard to miss that skewed ratio—and that the number of hours spent in all training is paltry. For comparison, in North Carolina, cops require 620 total hours of training, while barbers require 1,528 hours to be licensed.[34]

In other countries, recruits will also have more education coming into the police academy; US cops rarely need more than a high school education. And they will spend way longer than 833 hours training in many other countries; German recruits, for instance, spend three years studying with professors who are experts in their fields, as well as with law enforcement and former military members.[35] More importantly, police in many countries, like Germany, Canada, and the United Kingdom, are not trained in this warrior mentality, to always think in an "us versus them" mentality.[36]

When we say that this stuff is visceral, we mean it rather literally. Cops increasingly work to embody warrior policing. Remember the reporter's father, shocked at the ways cops had changed since his day? He emphasized the physical. "Matthew," a six-year veteran Pennsylvania cop who was jailed, then forced to resign for illegal anabolic steroid use, told a reporter that he took the drugs because he "was looking for an edge" in a police department where he estimated that more than one in seven cops was juicing. In three months, his weight went from 172 to 190 pounds, and his bench press went from 225 pounds (strong guy) to 300 pounds (beast!).[37] Anecdotally, these drugs are on the rise among police; undeniably, steroids increase users' rage (an especially bad side effect for people whose jobs already involve violence). The problem got bad enough by 2004 that the US Department of Justice updated its website with a report: "Steroid Abuse by Law Enforcement Personnel: A Guide for Understanding the Dangers of Anabolic Steroids."[38]

But it is hard to do anything about police violence when not only is the "warrior mentality" baked into cop culture, but it is also supported from without, by legislators who rhetorically support cops and pass legislation shielding cops from criminal and civil penalties for misconduct; police unions, which are highly successful at negotiating contracts that shield cops from these same penalties; district attorneys, who routinely shy away from taking on cases of police brutality; and courts, where police are routinely allowed to get away with violence during encounters and judges and prosecutors allow them to lie repeatedly in court.[39] Cops lying in court under oath is so widespread it even has a name—"testilying." Judges know that cops lie, and prosecutors know that cops lie. And they are all loath to do anything about it.[40]

White Police, White Protestors

The protests of the past few years have made it pretty obvious—with video clips posted online and broadcast across our TV and computer screens—that there is at least one segment of "civilians" exempted from cops' "us vs. them" outlook. The police have a long history of treating White pro-police or anti-Black protestors with kid gloves, even if the protestors get violent. We saw this during protests in August 2020 in Kenosha, Wisconsin, when a seventeen-year-old White man name Kyle Rittenhouse, armed with an AR-15, walked right up to and chatted with police. One officer tossed bottles of water to the boy's militia partners and said, "We appreciate you guys, we really do." Rittenhouse then proceeded to kill two people. He tried to surrender after he killed the two people, but the cops walked right by him, even though bystanders were telling the cops he had just killed two people.[41] Rittenhouse was charged and tried, but it almost goes without saying that he was found not guilty of all charges.

This is not an isolated incident, but rather this appreciation for armed White men is baked into policing in this country. The sociologist Jennifer Carlson interviewed seventy-nine police chiefs in three states and found, basically, that they are very happy to have White people owning guns as they say they help police by protecting themselves. But armed Black people in cities? Not so much. The police chiefs don't come out and say "Black people," but their racial coding is not subtle.[42]

Police have long "appreciated" these White mobs and "good guys with guns." Rittenhouse is not the only one they have protected. When White mobs protested against integration during Jim Crow and again in the 1950s and 1960s, when they protested against busing in the 1970s and 1980s, and against groups and causes considered anti-cop, like #BlackLivesMatter, no hoses or dogs or rubber bullets were turned on them. In Charlottesville, Virginia, a 2017 White supremacist rally was allowed to move forward, even as the neo-Nazis violently attacked counterprotestors. Violence spread through parking garages and city streets, a White counterprotestor was killed with a car, and then president Trump famously claimed, "There are very fine people on both sides." The US Department of Homeland Security had alerted local police three days prior to the "event" (really a sort of orchestrated terroristic threat) that White supremacists there were expected to be exceptionally violent—

you would think, given what we know about warrior policing, that they would have shown up fully prepared to shut it all down. They did not.

The affinity of White police toward aggrieved Whites is not incidental; cops are often drawn from the same pool of people, live among them, share the same politics and ideologies and racism.[43] A 2015 FBI counterterrorism guide warned agents that "domestic terrorism investigations focused on militia extremists, white supremacist extremists, and sovereign citizen extremists often have identified active links to law enforcement officers." In the not-so-distant past, law enforcement and the Ku Klux Klan overlapped, and more recently, police in departments big and small have made their affiliations with far-right racist/militant groups like the Oath Keepers and Three Percenters and Proud Boys known, and have faced hardly any repercussions.[44] So when the Kenosha police applaud the White militia members, they are applauding *their* people.

This parsing out of "us" and "them" is affected by the tendency of White cops to be more politically and socially "conservative" than other people. A nationwide email poll by *Police Magazine* found that 84 percent of police supported Donald Trump in 2016, and only 8 percent supported Hillary Clinton.[45] This is something that should be obvious but rarely is reported or researched. And, given the politics of cops, it should not be surprising that White kids protesting in the street or on college campuses against the police temporarily lose their White privilege as, for the moment, their class/educational/political identities are different from those of the police, and that makes them subject to beatings and shootings by the police—though Whites who protest tend not to be killed. So to be clear, the warrior mentality is only applied to people who are unlike (White) cops. Even Black and Latino cops have to think this way.

Hardened Boundaries, Hardened Cops

The cultural shift to "warrior policing" has unfolded over the last few decades. Violence has always been central to policing, writes journalist Radley Balko in his 2013 book, *Rise of the Warrior Cop: The Militarization of America's Police Forces*, but a handful of changes since the 1970s have disproportionately changed the tide.[46] Now, violence (the threat of and the need to exert) is the default and organizing principle of American policing. To find the roots of today's warrior cops, Balko traces back to the creation of SWAT teams in the 1960s, the War on Drugs begun in the 1980s, and the influx of surplus military equipment into police departments in the early 1990s.

Special Weapons Attack Teams were originally specialized units charged with addressing particularly dangerous situations, like hostage taking. In 1970, there were *maybe* two SWAT teams in the country, but by mid-decade, five hundred police departments had them. By 1980, nearly 45 percent of cities bigger than fifty thousand people had a SWAT team, a proportion that doubled by 1995. Astoundingly, researchers found, 65 percent of smaller cities (populations from twenty-five to fifty thousand) had them, too. In those cities, nearly 20 percent of all the sworn police officers worked on the SWAT teams. It was evidence, criminologist Peter Kraska commented, of "the militarization of Mayberry."[47]

The Reagan-championed War on Drugs was in full swing by the mid-1980s, and earmarked federal money was flowing to police departments to aid in the crackdown. It had to be used for drug policing, which meant for SWAT teams, narcotics units, or overtime pay for police working drug cases. Federal policy also allowed for asset forfeiture—the practice of police seizing any property even remotely *thought* to be linked to a crime—which greatly benefited local police (who can keep these assets), who assisted federal agencies in drug cases in any way they could.[48] Together, the policies of the early "tough on crime" period in the United States heavily incentivized local police to spend more time and dedicate more personnel to drug-related crimes and ignore "less profitable" cases like rape and murder and robberies.[49] Nationwide, SWAT-team deployments ballooned from about three hundred incidents in 1980 to about thirty thousand in 1995, at which point SWAT teams were not really responding to cases like hostage situations.[50] They were mostly breaking down doors for drug raids.[51]

And, as Balko explains, to truly militarize, the police needed military equipment. In 1987 a federal law established an office in the Pentagon to facilitate the transfer of military equipment to local police. Congress even established a toll-free phone number (phone calls were expensive back then) so police chiefs and sheriffs could call to see what the military had on hand, ready to be transferred.[52] Then, in 1997, the federal 1033 program expanded the effort. With all the free tanks and artillery, with the War on Drugs grants and proceeds from asset forfeitures, any town, no matter how small (like Middleburg, Pennsylvania, population 1,363) could have a SWAT team.

Why would small-town police departments *want* SWAT teams and all this unnecessary equipment? The notion that large cities need the heavy toys because their criminals have big guns is not even true; handguns are the weapons of choice for most murderers and drug dealers.[53] Peter Kraska, the scholar who wrote about the "militarization of Mayberry," found that smaller police departments appeared to have a kind of inferiority complex: they saw that larger departments had all these toys, and they wanted them, too.[54]

The intensification on homeland security after 9/11 became another boon for police departments. The Department of Homeland Security has handed out antiterrorism grants, not to mention armored vehicles, aircraft, guns, and an assortment of other military-grade equipment, like candy.[55] These DHS grants, which far outpaced the 1033 program ones, went to urban centers as well as out-of-the-way hamlets, like Fon du Lac, Wisconsin. While waiting for terrorists to show up (the non-White ones), the departments mostly use the gear for drug raids.[56]

Police Killings and Misconduct

We have a lot of very reliable data about cops killed in the line of duty. But we do not actually know how many civilians are killed *by* on-duty cops each—or any—year. We can only assume the counts we have— that about a thousand people were killed by the police each year in the mid-1990s and about seventeen hundred every year nowadays—are undercounts.[57] Prior to 2015, the numbers are composites gathered from various government agencies. Since then, a project created by the *Washington Post* called the Fatal Encounters Database has cross-referenced these sources with media accounts, Freedom of Information Act requests of local agencies, and verified crowd-sourced information to create more reliable estimates. Interestingly, in the same period, the number of police killed on the job *and* nearly all categories of violent crime have dropped significantly. Yet killings by police have risen from no more than 6 percent in the late 1960s through the early 2000s to 8 percent of all violent deaths in the United States.[58]

When we consider all kinds of police misconduct (including un-justified shootings), the "bad apples" idea starts to make a little sense. A sizeable minority of cops receive a *lot* of complaints, but most cops have hardly any. The "sizeable" in that sentence is key. Take the 2018 stats for New York City's active police. In that year, the Civilian Complaint Review Board received no complaints for 41 percent of officers, one complaint for 21 percent, and six or more complaints for about 9 percent.[59] Many incidents will go unreported, some complaints will be substantiated, and many complaints will be dismissed. In the extreme, these complaints can end up as lawsuits that result in large sums being paid out by cities' general funds (see above for a reminder on just how large).

In 2020, section 50-a of New York's Civil Rights Law was repealed. It had protected police misconduct records from public scrutiny for decades. Now, thanks to *ProPublica*, we know that data show that one in nine NYPD officers has a confirmed record of misconduct at some point in their career. Again, we are talking undercounts. The Civilian Complaint Review Board, which investigates complaints, has limited investigative powers and resources, and is often stonewalled by individual police and the department, regardless of the legal requirement for the NYPD to cooperate.[60] Most likely, plenty of the dismissed complaints actually had merit.

As with the White agitators we mentioned earlier and with the cops convicted after Derek Chauvin murdered George Floyd, we can "see" cop culture not only in what they do but in what they don't do. What they *say* is less reliable. For instance, in a 2016 Pew survey, 84 percent of all cops surveyed said that they should be required to intervene when another cop is about to use what they think is unnecessary force.[61] But their stated beliefs and best-case-scenarios do not match their actions on the ground. Those are a product of immediate circumstances and a police culture that tolerates excessive force and heavily sanctions anyone who disagrees. In police norms, Black men can be murdered on camera by officers of the law, and cops and unions will stand behind those actions. Norms against racism, drug dealing, drug taking, even murder are simply no match for the Golden Rule: no snitching. Stop another cop from beating on a suspect or, worse yet, tell a superior it happened, and you are in for a lot of trouble back at the station.

Police Unions

Labor unions tend to be great for workers, and police unions have negotiated enviable job protections for their members. They do as well as or better than other public-sector unions at negotiating wages and benefits (especially overtime and pensions), and they have been spectacularly successful in protecting their members from disciplinary measures. Criminologist Joshua Page points to the 1980s, when a major recession intersected with the Reagan-era antitax fervor, as a turning point in the relationship between police unions and their cities. Cities *could not* offer raises, so they made concessions on police demands for watered-down disciplinary proceedings.[62]

The result is that it is nearly impossible for a police officer to be convicted and sent to jail for a crime committed on the job. Police get what is called "qualified immunity"—essentially, the legal benefit of the doubt when it comes to their intent and assessment of the situation at the time of the actions in question. Even if police get sued for civil violations, they are not personally liable. The departments are not even liable. The cities are on the hook for mandated payouts. In 2017, a Reuters report on eighty-two police union contracts found that most required departments to erase officers' disciplinary records, sometimes after only six months, and eighteen cities removed suspensions from disciplinary records in three years or less. Almost half of the contracts allowed officers to see their disciplinary files—including witness statements, photos, and videos—*before* being questioned about any complaints; that's a clear leg up in disciplinary interrogations, and it risks exposing information that could lead to retaliation against complainants.[63]

Worse, multiple studies have shown a positive relationship between the presence of police unions and increases in occurrences of police violence, including killings of civilians, which, again, today amounts to over seventeen hundred civilians killed by police a year.[64] A recent report looked at the varying times at which different states introduced collective bargaining rights to police unions, starting in the late 1950s, and their data cover the time frame from 1959 to 1988.[65] The lead author said in an interview, "We found that after officers gained access to collective bargaining rights that there was a substantial increase in killings of civilians—0.026 to 0.029 additional civilians are killed in each county in each year, of whom the overwhelming majority are non-White. That's about 60 to 70 [more] per year civilians killed by the police in an era historically where there were a lot fewer police shootings. So that's a humongous increase."[66] Another way to say this is that they found that police having collective bargaining rights accounted for 10 percent of the total number of killings of non-White civilians. Importantly, there was no increased killings of Whites.[67]

Police unions are among the country's most effective and untouchable labor organizations. They draw on some standard tactics to successfully thwart reform efforts and strengthen their overall positions vis-à-vis mayors and other politicians (the idea is to intimidate to get their way). It is no wonder that politicians are generally unlikely to stand up to these unions.

Joseph McCartin, a labor historian, asserts that police labor unions "have more clout than other public-sector unions, like the teachers or sanitation workers, because they have often been able to command the political support of Republicans."[68] This is critical—Republicans are typically no friends to unions, but they are staunch supporters of police unions. They cannot risk the ire of the cop union when it comes to election time. (Neither can Democrats, for that matter.) Again, Joshua Page points to the tried-and-true tools police have on hand when it comes to taming politicians.[69] For instance, they can invoke the moral authority of the badge to decry critics as anticop and anti–public safety. Trying to increase police accountability? You are obviously attacking the good men and women in blue who put their lives on the line for us! In fact, police have a long-standing reputation as, by and large, good and selfless people unless proven otherwise. In a 2020 survey of trustworthiness of occupations conducted before the police murders of Breonna Taylor and George Floyd, cops came in sixth, behind nurses, engineers, doctors, pharmacists, and dentists. At the bottom of the list were senators and members of Congress.[70] So, politicians are eager (like high schoolers) to associate themselves with those who have better reputations—like cops. It is a sure route to gaining status. Conversely, people who are critical of the police, even if they are right, risk losing status.

Another tactic police unions use to maintain the upper hand, Page points out, is to play into public fears about crime and political instability. If police are seen as "the thin blue line" between "us" (coded to mean the White middle-class) and anarchy (understood to be Black people and/or criminals), imposing changes to the way police work is framed as basically an invitation to chaos.

Even under a supposedly liberal mayor, New York City's Bill de Blasio, police budgets marched steadily upward, though serious crime has been on the decline for decades. When de Blasio took office in 2014, the NYPD's operating budget was five billion dollars per year; it would increase by another billion before 2020. (This does not include "centrally allocated" costs such as benefits and pensions, which account for another five billion dollars a year.)[71] The mayor heard the pleas of many city councilors, calling for drastic budget cuts, and felt the flex as the police made his own daughter's arrest at a protest following the murder of George Floyd public information, but stayed true to the blue. That is how powerful police unions are in one of the most liberal cities in the country. Police departments are now so big and politically entrenched, there is little possibility of any kind of meaningful reform—though, in the aftermath of the national and international summer 2020 antipolice protests over the killing of George Floyd (and so many others), there *seemed* to be the possibility of change. We will come back to this.

Should Cops Live Where They Serve?

A big policy question is, Should cops live in the "communities" they serve? Can they effectively police these places if they do not live there?

In about two-thirds of US cities with the largest police forces, the majority of police officers commute to work from elsewhere. The proportion of cops living in the cities where they work varies greatly. In Chicago, 88 percent of police officers live within the city boundaries; in Philadelphia, it is 84 percent. On the other end of the scale, only 23 percent of cops both live and work in Los Angeles, that number is 12 percent in Washington, DC, and just 7 percent of officers in Miami live in the city.

Of seventy-five cities that one study examined to see where cops live, 49 percent of Black police officers and 47 percent of Latino officers live within the city limits, but only 35 percent of White police officers do. The variation is greatest in cities with largely Black populations. In Detroit, only 8 percent of White officers live in the city, whereas 57 percent of Black police officers do.[72]

In New York City, 62 percent of police live within the five boroughs, but this papers over big differences—77 and 76 percent, respectively, of Black and Latino police officers live in the city, but only 45 percent of White officers do. (When people argue that police need to be paid more to live in the cities where they work, they gloss over this racial divide. Black and Latino cops *already* live in one of the most expensive cities in the country. White cops *could*, but they choose to live in the suburbs.) New York City cops often retire after twenty years of service, with pensions averaging $74,500, and with plenty of time to start another career, often in security.[73] To put that in context, the average pension for individual cops is higher than the median household income ($61,000) in New York City.[74] And the pay and benefits for cops nationally are exceedingly good for a high school graduate. A former cop turned criminology graduate student said this: "I became a police officer for the health insurance and economic security, and because the people I'd looked up to as a working-class kid had told me being a cop was a respectable career. I was married with two small children and saw policing as one of the few remaining paths to the middle class available to an army veteran without a college degree."[75]

But would it make a difference if cops—and let's be honest, we are talking about White cops—lived in the cities where they worked? We would say no. For instance, in New York City, again, only 45 percent of White cops live in the city, but they generally live in suburban areas within the city. They live in Staten Island—mostly in the lily-white South Shore, like Daniel Pantaleo, not in the North Shore, where more Black individuals live—or in a handful of other White enclaves in the city that are mostly middle-class, and are peppered with single-family and two-family houses and townhouses, with few apartment buildings. The only thing distinguishing these areas from the actual suburbs is that their residents have to pay New York City income taxes.

While some people argue that residency requirements root officers in the community, a city is not a community, but a collection of communities or neighborhoods. White officers are going to largely live in segregated, White communities. Communities are places (well, they don't have to be physical places) where people are known to each other—by this definition, cities do not qualify as communities. And, again, Pantaleo lives in New York City; that did not make any difference in his attitude and actions toward Eric Garner. In fact, Pantaleo lived only a few miles from Garner in Staten Island. (And a quick aside—Pantaleo's childhood friend Joseph Imperatrice founded "Blue Lives Matter," whose name is a response to #BlackLivesMatter, which is a movement created after his friend killed Eric Garner in Staten Island and another cop killed Michael Brown in Ferguson, Missouri.)[76]

A more important factor to consider is how representative the police force is of the locality. In nearly every city, Whites are overrepresented on local police forces.[77] Cop culture is described as blue, but it is really White. Until and unless the numbers of Black, Latino, and Asian American cops hit a critical mass *at all levels*, a Black chief of police will not make a difference. And the police culture and its norms of behavior will continue to be defined by White cops. Black and Latino and Asian American cops will follow, or be punished by, their peers.

Even in New York City, where the police force is 57 percent non-White, the further up the chain of command you go, the Whiter it becomes. And if you are not White, police departments are not welcoming places. A recent *Wall Street Journal* article found that "black officers across the country say they commonly face harassment, discrimination and even abuse from their own departments."[78]

That Black officers should find themselves the subjects of racism within police departments should not surprise anyone; the institution of the police in this country draws a direct line to the pre-abolition slave patrols in the South.[79]

Policing from the late 1880s into the early twentieth century concentrated on enforcing Jim Crow laws in the South, and generally criminalizing Blackness in the North. In Philadelphia, arrests of Blacks, a little more than 7 percent of the population, went from 11 percent in 1911 to about a quarter of the Black population by the 1920s. We know that Black veterans returning from World War II were often beaten by police, even while in uniform. And the reaction from police to the civil rights movement in the 1950s and 1960s throughout the country was vicious.

Even after the civil rights movement and the changes in laws, Blacks disproportionately faced policing and beatings. Then, as today, police disproportionately patrol Black neighborhoods and arrest Black people, prosecutors charge and juries convict Black people disproportionately, and judges hand them longer sentences.[80] If anything, it might even be worse today as the number of people, again, disproportionately Black, whom we jail has astronomically increased since the beginning of President Reagan's War on Drugs, and especially under Presidents Bush, Clinton, and Bush Jr. (There are nearly 1.4 million people in prisons and jails in the United States, and Black men are nearly six times more likely to be incarcerated than White men. About one in twelve Black men in their thirties is in prison or jail on any given day.)[81] Part of the story is about disproportionate sentencing. One common example of disproportionate policing/sentencing arose with the Anti–Drug Abuse Act of 1986, which gave the same penalty for possession of crack cocaine as for possession of one hundred times the same amount of powder cocaine. Reader, you will not be surprised that crack cocaine at the time was largely consumed by Black people, and powder cocaine by Whites.

The racism of police today, as then, is not hidden; it is easily seen, and it has not changed dramatically since the 1800s. Police beat and kill Blacks at far higher rates than they do Whites. For instance, Black residents in New York City were 21 percent more likely than Whites to be held at gunpoint, shoved, pepper sprayed, or beaten with batons. Blacks are more likely to encounter violence from the police *even when police say they are fully compliant.*[82]

Black cops are still Black, and they face the same reactions from White police, whether they are in uniform or not. Eric Adams, the current mayor of New York City, who retired from the New York Police Department as a captain in 2006, said in a 2020 interview of his time as a Black man in the NYPD, "The same hell that Black people were experiencing on the streets, we were experiencing inside the department." He said that the dynamic has not changed today.[83]

In Arkansas, Sergeant Willie Davis, who was suing the Little Rock Police Department, said Black officers did not always trust White commanders to take action if they reported misconduct. "Officers who look like me learn early that if you keep your mouth shut, you'll be fine. So you develop this attitude of 'going along, to get along,'" he said.[84]

Little Rock police chief Keith Humphrey, who is Black, said that a small group of racist White officers had caused problems for Black officers. Given what we have been discussing about police culture and peer effects, this should not be a surprise. They are the bad cops, but there are no "good" White cops who are going to step in, or step up, to do anything about this, or to support their Black cops, like Sergeant Willie Davis. The idea of police brotherhood has many caveats, and one of these is to exclude Blacks, women, and other minorities.[85] In fact, since Humphrey was appointed in 2019 as police chief, he has faced insubordination from White cops and the White-dominated union on a scale unfathomable if the police chief were White. (The article cited in this footnote goes into great detail about how this Black police chief is being hounded by lawsuits and HR complaints by White cops. So many lawsuits came in that Tuesday was renamed "lawsuit Tuesday." The article shows really clearly how reform, even if the mayor and police chief are on board, gets stymied in myriad ways by the White rank and file and their union.)[86]

Black cops are expected to be "blue" and to swallow any racism that comes their way. For instance, Captain Yulanda Williams of the San Francisco Police Department sued the city and police department in May 2019, saying she had been targeted by coworkers and management for speaking out about sexism and racism. A supervisor told her that she needed to choose the police over her identity as a Black person. "Pick a side. You seem confused about this," the supervisor supposedly said. Captain Williams said that trying to change the culture in the department was "like trying to turn the Titanic."[87]

Some departments have developed such toxic cultures that the federal government has had to step in. The Department of Justice wrote a scathing report in 2017 on the state of the Chicago Police Department:

We found that some Chicago police officers expressed discriminatory views and intolerance with regard to race, religion, gender, and national origin in public social media forums, and that CPD takes insufficient steps to prevent or appropriately respond to this animus. As CPD works to restore trust and ensure that policing is lawful and effective, it must recognize the extent to which this type of misconduct contributes to a culture that facilitates unreasonable force and corrodes community trust. We have serious concerns about the prevalence of racially discriminatory conduct by some CPD officers and the degree to which that conduct is tolerated and in some respects caused by deficiencies in CPD's systems of training, supervision and accountability.[88]

The report went on to say, "Our review of files for complaints that were investigated revealed consistent patterns of egregious investigative deficiencies that impede the search for the truth. . . . We also found that investigations foundered because of the pervasive cover-up culture among CPD officers."[89] While the language is harsh, the thing is, this is very common, and given that municipalities either cannot or will not police the police, we should expect this.

No Longer One of "Us"

Adrian Schoolcraft was a whistleblower cop. When he was eight years into the job, in 2008–2009, he began surreptitiously recording hundreds of hours of the goings-on in New York City's 81st Precinct, in Bed-Stuy, Brooklyn.[90] His tapes captured precinct roll calls, precinct commanders and other supervisors chatting, street encounters, and stationhouse banter. On them, we hear precinct bosses threatening street cops over their arrest and stop-and-frisk quotas and ordering them to bury robbery reports in order to manipulate crime statistics. We hear command officers call crime victims directly in order to intimidate them into dropping criminal complaints. This is not quotidian managerial productivity banter, but the transfer of an imperative: maintain high "activity"—including stop-and-frisks—and record fewer actual crimes.

Schoolcraft's tapes shine a light on one aspect of what policing actually is—in practice, it means productivity. That gets defined from above, and that means making arrests (valid or wrongful) and writing tickets. Lots and lots of tickets. Another thing the tapes demonstrate clearly is that not only do the higher-ups in the NYPD have "productivity goals," but they have clearly defined quotas, and if the officers do not meet those quotas, they face possible punishment. For example, the tapes feature a "Lieutenant B" discussing the summons target, saying, "The XO [second-in-command] was in the other day. He actually laid down a number. He wants at least three seat belts, one cell phone, and 11 others. All right, so if I was on patrol, I would be sure to get three seat belts, one cell phone, and 11 others. Pick it up a lot, if you have to. The CO [commanding officer] gave me some names. I spoke to you." The journalist who wrote about these tapes for the *Village Voice* explained, "If you've ever had the feeling that you see more cops out, and are more likely to get a ticket at the end of the month, well, you're right. The pressure [to give tickets] is the worst at the end of the month and at the end of every quarter, because that's when the precinct has to file activity reports on each officer with the borough command and police headquarters. (Put another way: If you want to avoid getting a ticket, stay away from police officers during the last few days of the month, when the pressure for numbers is the highest.)"

David Simon's classic HBO show *The Wire* made viewers cringe with frequent scenes in which politicians and top police obsess over numbers. The kicker is that these scenes happen all the time. Police are pressured by higher-ups to refuse to process criminal complaints for the flimsiest of reasons (say, if the victim of a robbery will not come to the precinct—which, sometimes you have to work or watch your kid); to downgrade charging recommendations (so that, for instance, felonies become misdemeanors); and, administratively, to simply not enter data into the city's computer tracking system. Together, such actions artificially deflate crime statistics.

When Schoolcraft (who is White), seeing that the NYPD was not addressing what he saw as grave complaints, gave his tapes to the local, independent alt-weekly publication, the NYPD retaliation was swift. One day, three weeks after meeting with investigators, Schoolcraft went home sick from work. "Hours later, a dozen police supervisors came to his house and demanded that he return to work. He declined, on health grounds. Eventually, Deputy Chief Michael Marino, the commander of Patrol Borough Brooklyn North, which covers 10 precincts, ordered that Schoolcraft be dragged from his apartment in handcuffs and forcibly placed in a Queens mental ward [in Jamaica Hospital] for six days." More damningly, Schoolcraft's father noted that "his son's requests to the Patrolmen's Benevolent Association [PBA, the union for New York City's rank-and-file police] for assistance [with his confinement] were rebuffed, with attorney Stuart London offering no more than a referral to civil-rights lawyer Norman Siegel. A spokesman for PBA President Pat Lynch declined comment on that claim."[91]

Pat Lynch, we should note, has always been dogged in his defense of cops who beat and kill people, including Daniel Pantaleo. But Schoolcraft had snitched. Even being White cannot mitigate that. Schoolcraft was suspended without pay for nearly six years, he faced departmental charges, he was placed under surveillance, and his application for unemployment benefits was blocked by the city. All this even though the city's independent investigation corroborated *all* of Schoolcraft's claims (and despite the fact that a cop like Pantaleo could, instead, receive full pay plus overtime for five years after choking Eric Garner to death).[92] Schoolcraft sued the city and Jamaica Hospital; in September 2015, the city settled for six hundred thousand dollars and back pay and benefits, and in November 2015, the hospital settled for an undisclosed amount.[93]

Other whistleblowers' experiences are often similar. It turns out, police departments and police unions generally are not too bothered by bad apples; it's the *good* apples they crush.[94] Unprotected by his union, Schoolcraft has moved on—the union was helping Pantaleo sue to get his job back but ultimately lost its bid.[95]

Who Is Us?

The weight of the PBA gets thrown behind police officers like Pantaleo, officers who get into trouble because of violence and killing on the job. But not all cops in this situation get the benefit of the PBA. In November of 2014, Peter Liang was a Chinese American twenty-eight-year-old rookie cop who was patrolling with his White partner in a dark stairwell in the Louis H. Pink housing complex in East New York in Brooklyn. He heard a sound, and fired off his gun, he said accidentally. His bullet ricocheted off a wall and killed Akai Gurley in the stairwell. Akai Gurley was with a friend, and they were both walking down the stairs as the elevators were broken. Neither Officer Liang nor his partner did CPR or even called an ambulance. Liang was indicted and convicted for manslaughter, while his partner was not.

We know that White NYPD officers have been involved in even worse actions that also resulted in deaths and have never been indicted, or lost their jobs. But the PBA clearly does not protect everyone.[96] The thin blue line, a symbol of police solidarity, can also be color-coded. It is understood that Black cops are expected to be "blue" and to swallow any racism that comes their way, but what about Asian American cops? Does the union provide protection to them like that of other police, especially White police officers who had been in confrontations with Black victims?

The Akai Gurley killing unfolded in an intense moment for the #BlackLivesMatter protests across the states. The shooting occurred only four months after Eric Garner was killed in July 2014. Daniel Pantaleo, as noted above, was not indicted. Just three months before, in August 2014, Michael Brown had been shot dead in Ferguson, Missouri, and Darren Wilson was not indicted. Just two days later in November 2014, Tamir Rice, a twelve-year-old, was shot dead in Cleveland and neither Timothy Loehman nor Frank Garmback was indicted. In fact, the charges were dropped for all these officers.[97]

With protests flaring across the United States, Peter Liang was indicted in February of 2015, and he was convicted during his January 2016 trial.[98] He was the first NYPD officer convicted in over a decade. In this extraordinary moment, the PBA was not willing to extend its protection to an Asian American cop.[99]

Shortly after the shooting, according to Peter Liang's mother, the union did not respond as she tried to reach them to find a lawyer to represent her son. When assigned, the PBA lawyer, Stephen Worth, also did not put Liang in front of a grand jury.[100] Worth said that Liang "didn't testify in the grand jury because my instinct was it wasn't going to be a fair grand jury."[101] Peter Liang's partner did testify and was granted immunity. Daniel Pantaleo testified, on advice from his PBA lawyer, and was not indicted. Many believe that if Liang had testified, he would have been found not guilty.

Because of lack of support, Liang's mother decided to hire private attorneys.[102] At his trial in January 2016, there was a notable absence of the PBA. Only two officers attended. The lack of presence hinted that Peter Liang would not be treated as a White officer would.[103] In the end, Liang was found guilty of second-degree manslaughter.[104]

#defundthepolice

In the wake of protests in the spring and summer of 2020 after the murder of George Floyd by the police, people across the country shouted for the police to be defunded or abolished. These demands had been on the political outskirts for decades, and momentarily, they became central, and feasible.[105] The question is, What does that mean and what would it do?

"What about rape and murder?" is the common retort to calls to defund the police. But acts of violence account for less than 10 percent of the average officer's time on duty. Even with homicide, police have a mediocre record, only clearing around 50 percent of cases in the typical American city. And as for rape, most rapes and sexual assaults go unreported, in large part due to horrible interactions rape victims have with police.[106]

The average officer spends 90 percent or more of their time addressing "infractions of administrative codes—rules dictating how and where Americans sit, walk, eat, drink, drive, and participate in commerce."[107] Most of our contact with the police is car related, dealing with collisions or police-initiated stops.[108] A 2015 report from the Bureau of Justice Statistics found that every year, fifty million people come into contact with the police at least once. Nineteen million people are pulled over in a car they are driving and another six million, in which they are a passenger. Eight million are involved in a car accident, and another nine million said that they called the police about a noncrime—mostly traffic accidents.[109]

So then, "Most police interaction with civilians involves driving around in cars talking to other people driving around in cars."[110] Much of the rest of their time is occupied with minor, administrative infractions. And police statistically are not great at solving crimes. So can we do with fewer police, and spend less money on them?

The other question the idea of defunding and/or reforming the police raises is whether those things could effect a real change in cop culture and cop violence. It is possible that a reimagined police department that has had its funding cut, has its functions slashed, and has real civilian oversight and real consequences for actions of police—it is possible that if the police's political power and ideological control over mayors and city councils were reduced, that could effect a change in cop culture. If violence had consequences, it might reduce cop violence. If whistleblowers had actual protections and the people whom they blew the whistle on faced real consequences, it could change the norms and punishments regarding snitching.

But—there is always a but—despite the nationwide protests, and despite the financial hardships localities all over the country faced because of the COVID-19 pandemic in spring and summer of 2020, police budgets across the country actually saw *increases*. And even where budgets were cut, as in New York City, they were not really cut; numbers were just moved around spreadsheets.[111] Black lives may matter in the protests, but elected officials still care a lot more about blue lives—the public pressure they exert and their ability to sway elections.

Can't We Just Train the "Bad" Away?

Sociologist Rashawn Ray, as part of his police research, has overseen "implicit bias" training programs with about twenty-five hundred officers, trying to teach them to see their own racial prejudices. But he found that the programs did not really work. "We're sitting in a classroom and I'm telling them a bunch of stuff, [and] rarely do any of them think, 'This is me.'" While he was conducting an anti-bias training recently, dozens of Prince George's County officers walked out in protest. Not long after this happened, a report on racial discrimination within the Prince George's County department was issued. Police Chief Hank Stawinski resigned later the same day.[112]

While anti-bias training may sound like a good idea, it probably would not work with the police—specifically with White police—because they have no incentive to take it seriously, as, again, there is little a municipality can do to them. For instance, a human resources manager in San Francisco's city government recently quit after spending two years conducting anti-bias training for the city's police. In an exit email he sent to his boss and the city's police chief, he wrote that "the degree of anti-black sentiment throughout SFPD is extreme," adding that "while there are some at SFPD who possess somewhat of a balanced view of racism and anti-blackness, there are an equal number (if not more)—who possess and exude deeply rooted anti-black sentiments."[113]

* * *

So we just took a deep dive into one example of peer effects and peer culture in one type of workplace, that of the police. The boundaries around the group are well defined, and even symbolized with the notion of the "thin blue line," the cops that protect us, the law-abiding (ahem, White) citizenry, from anarchy and bad guys. There is even a thin blue line American flag that flies in White neighborhoods all over the country. Including Daniel Pantaleo's neighborhood in Staten Island.

Cop culture is very deep, and greatly developed. Every new cop who goes through training learns the policing process in a formal way, departmental dos and don'ts. But they also learn the informal norms of the culture from their training officers, like Derrick Chauvin, and from other officers they get to know in their units. Here they learn the actual dos and don'ts of on-the-ground policing. They learn about the things that get rewarded, and the actual things that will get you in trouble—the central norms. As we saw above, there are precious few things that get cops in real trouble, the most important of which is snitching on other cops. Nobody hates a whistleblower more than the police.

Another important aspect to understanding this insular peer group and peer culture is the degree to which it is supported from the outside. Politicians of all stripes acquiesce to police and police unions, looking for their money and approval for elections. Any criticism they have of individual police or departments, they keep to themselves. Police are largely left free to deal with misconduct internally, with little to no oversight. A point that we have intermittently made over the course of the book is that cultures are inherently "conservative" and slow to change, and that there has to be either internal or external pressure for that change to happen. This change will be resisted by people who have power in these groups and their cultures, the power over who is a member, and the power to define the norms.

Conclusion

What Can We Do?

Aging can bring lots of woes. Besides declining physical health, there is also loneliness, depression, and barriers to socializing. What can be done? Some people bring the elderly animals to play with. Some high school kids looking to beef up their college applications volunteer to do stuff with old people.

These efforts are nice, but have not really been shown to have any effect. You know what does, though? That's right. A recent study, for example, examined lonely, isolated, lower-income adults in San Francisco. The researchers matched them with peers of similar backgrounds (age, race, LGBT status) and similar interests. Initially the peers, paid healthcare workers, took the study participants to health visits, then later on to social functions. The participants were happy to have the company, and the researchers found that there was an "intrinsic value of having someone they felt emotionally and socially connected to consistently checking in on them over an extended period of time." The time frame of the study straddled the pandemic, and "participants and peers noted these relationships helped to buffer the impact of COVID-19, which limited in-person interactions."[1] Loneliness decreased, depression decreased, and barriers to socialization fell away. Participants found that they had the motivation to reach out to people in other areas of their lives, and their moods improved.

* * *

To this point, the book has looked at how our peers affect who we are and who we become. We have examined how parents are cognizant of peer effects, and how they let that understanding shape what they consider to be good schools and bad schools. We have looked at how peers affect the behavior of high school and college students, and whether our peers and peer culture from these settings continue to affect us into adulthood. Turning to adults, we showed how peers affect each other in the workplace, especially how misbehavior spreads through peer effects. And then we considered a very particular example of workers and workplace culture: the police. What is the story behind the cop culture of violence, and why can't we seem to curb it? It should not surprise you that our answer is the durability of peer-driven norms, including the "warrior" mentality and the no-snitching imperative, which encourage violence and discourage accountability.

Now the question is, *So what?* How can knowing about the importance of peers help to make the world a better place?

In these closing pages, we will go back and look at some of the situations we examined earlier and pose possible solutions for the problems that arise. We will offer "pie-in-the-sky" solutions that would really address the problem but would be quite difficult to implement for various reasons (sometimes money, often politics, quite often racism), and we will present some more immediately realizable, if smaller-scale, solutions. In general, academics are good at analyzing, but really, really suck at giving advice. Still, we are going to try, and hopefully we will be less sucky than most.

Let's start!

Better Schools, Better Outcomes

The problem with segregated schools, as we laid out in chapter 1, is that they may benefit White, racist parents, but they harm kids. (Okay, we can be kinder: the White parents may or may not be racist themselves, but they certainly benefit from the structural racism of educational institutions.) The simple "solution" is to integrate the schools, which, nationally, are still highly segregated. Interestingly, they are segregated in ways that look like the 1930s. A recent study of the country's one hundred largest school districts found that the boundaries between pairs of neighboring schools correlate really closely with race and with 1930s-era redlining maps, which were used as the basis for housing loan decisions—or, more specifically, making loans to the "right" White people, and denying loans to Blacks and the "wrong" White people (working-class Jews and Italians, largely, where they lived near Blacks).[2]

School districts in places like the urban-suburban school districts in Wake County in North Carolina and in Louisville, Kentucky, had integrated and demonstrated the academic benefit for poor and minority students without "harm" to White and Asian American students.[3] The idea is that, when students of various academic abilities are mixed, peer effects work to lift the lower-ability students' achievement—and that is exactly what happened in Wake County.[4]

Not many suburban-urban areas integrate their schools in this manner. More commonly, as a result of White flight from cities to suburbs from the 1950s onward, urban areas (and urban schools) in the United States have a higher Black and poor population, and suburban areas (and suburban schools) tend to be richer and Whiter. In 1973, the Supreme Court's *Milliken* decision undid a lower court ruling that forced suburban Detroit schools to participate in busing to better integrate schools in the city and its surroundings. That aligned White suburbanites' preferences with precedent, and it is unlikely that towns will voluntarily choose to implement such a busing program today.

We saw something different when Brooklyn's District 15, itself one of the largest school districts in the country, undertook its own integrative measures. In 2019, it ended academic screening (test scores, interviews, auditions, etc.) for admission to middle schools. Instead, the district implemented lotteries weighted to favor admissions for poor kids and English language learners. The "Whitest" four of District 15's eleven middle schools saw an immediate increase in the number of Black and Latino students. Though the seven other schools have seen smaller growth in the number of White students, it is early days. While naysayers predicted that White parents would run away from the district if their kids *had* to go to school with higher numbers of Black and Latino kids, that did not happen. Nor, though, did an expansion of District 15's approach. Then New York City mayor Bill de Blasio declined to undertake a city-level operation of this kind, making it clear that this kind of desegregation had to happen at the district level, and was subject to local approval. And no other district has been willing to go so far in integrating its schools—some districts even explicitly stated that they would do nothing of the kind. Though there was not any city plan in place to desegregate one racially divided district in Queens (District 28), the entire 2022 season of the podcast *School Colors* was devoted to the neighborhood's White and Asian American parents who so vigorously fought district integration![5]

As of late 2022, as we are finishing the book, integration measures that started under de Blasio appear to be dead in the water. Mayor Adams is reviving the testing requirement for the gifted and talented program (again, the test is of four-year-olds) and expanding it.[6] The screens that were in place in many schools (tests, portfolios, grades, etc.) that were suspended during the pandemic (from 2020 to 2022) and that led to slightly more integrated student populations at some of these schools are being revived in many schools.[7] And there is no change for Stuyvesant and the other specialized high schools—admission is still strictly by the two-and-a-half-hour standardized exam. The one glimmer of hope for desegregation in the school system is that Brooklyn's District 15 plan remains in place, and the mayor has not tinkered with it or struck it down. As of yet, anyway. Another glimmer of hope is that the schools' chancellor left to school superintendents the decision to bring back screens to middle schools. As of the end of 2022, superintendents in twenty-six out of thirty-two districts either reduced or eliminated screens for admissions. Now, only fifty-nine middle schools screen for admission, down from 196 in 2020.[8]

Fighting Integration

Desegregation, while an obvious and effective fix, is a matter of political will. As we noted way back at the start of this book, it works when it is mandated and system-wide (otherwise, it is ridiculously easy to circumvent). But politicians rarely have the backbone (or willingness to "spend" their political capital) to tell White parents that their kids will have to go to school with Black and Latino kids. These White parents can be expected to protest, saying in so much coded language that they do not want their child's educational experience diluted by diversity. Nor are they ready to tell Black and White (and Latino and Asian American and Native American) parents that their kids will have to commute an hour to school. The courts have routinely struck down race-based integration and busing programs, and that is enough cover for most elected officials to demur on the question of desegregation.

A big sticking point comes from our collective idea, in the United States, that neighborhood schools are good and just and inevitable—and, by rights, *ours*. They are none of these things! Our schools are segregated because our neighborhoods are segregated because, well, racism. These are public schools, there to serve the public interest. Because we know it is in the public interest to have integrated schools (better academic outcomes for all kids, to start), kids will need to be moved around, even if it means little Janie cannot go to the primary school across the street. Janie can go to one a fifteen-minute walk away. So be it.

Another barrier to integrated schools is the federal government's willingness to consider them a "states' rights" issue (a phrase that has long been coded to mean "states' rights to control women and minorities"). Most states are not going to desegregate their schools unless they are forced to, and the courts are backing away from such orders. If liberal cities in "red states" even try to make it so White kids have to go to school with Black kids, their more conservative state legislatures might take a cue from Minnesota, where state law makes it easy to leave urban schools for suburban schools—but only if you have your own private transportation! (An incredible 10 percent of Minnesota students make use of this policy to attend White-dominant, "good" suburban schools.)[9] But we can't have a public school bus transporting Black kids. (Does that even need to be said?) To neutralize such a possibility, states committed to integration would have to redraw district maps to traverse urban-suburban lines. They would also have to deal with the elephant in the room—funding. Schools in this country are largely funded with local property taxes, so school districting lines are often based on cities, towns, and/or counties; funding corresponds, then, to the local property tax base. Richer areas have better-resourced schools. Could states rewrite the way they fund education and draw lines to say who goes to which schools? In theory. But it is extremely unlikely. State-level progressive lawmakers do not have the votes or the chutzpah to make it happen.

A big problem with segregated schools is not just unfairness, inequality of resources, and differential academic performance and reputation. It is also the unspoken stuff that comes with privileges of race and class. Richer, White kids already have a leg up because they have *social capital*, the intangible privileges of broad networks of loose social ties, and *cultural capital*, an understanding of implicit cultural rules of getting ahead. This is the legacy of well-off and racially privileged parents—and it is something that can be transferred, as we saw at Stuyvesant High School in chapter 3, through peer effects if kids (like Syed and Margaret) have diverse peers. At private and public schools, kids without these kinds of nonfinancial capital can acquire them from the kids who have them.[10] Students who gain social and cultural capital in this way develop a sense of how the world really works, and they become able to navigate it skillfully. Meanwhile, the White, wealthy, and high-achieving kids do not lose out—in fact, they, too, learn more from integrated environments (and they might turn out a bit less racist).[11] Everyone wins!

Oops. Except parents. That is how we ended up with school-choice policies. Parents—White parents, especially—are pretty sure they can nudge their kids toward better school and social outcomes and away from being screw-ups by carefully choosing neighborhoods and schools, effectively choosing their kids' total population of peers. Remember, kids choose their own peers, so the best that parents can do is try to find neighborhood and school populations with more "good" kids who are academically inclined or at least engaged. And who are mostly White, and not poor. But combine parents' varying ability to choose "good" schools with all the problems already noted, and you will almost inevitably get disparate outcomes. If some schools are good, then by definition, other schools will be bad. And these middle- and upper-middle-class parents, wittingly or not, are contributing to the worsening of those "bad" public schools.

What if you are poor and cannot choose "better" (Whiter, richer) neighborhoods or schools for your children? Then the game becomes a lot harder, and your kids will be at a decided disadvantage. In the end, school choice is great for a select few, but the choice really should not be on parents. That is very unfair and shortsighted—and it predictably increases inequality. Again, decreasing educational inequality has to be done at the systemic level. When we look to the "amazing" results of, say, Finnish schools, where the kids are the world's best educated, one thing really sets them apart: Finns do not think in terms of "good" schools and "bad" schools. They make sure that *all* schools are good schools. We have never done that in the history of this country.

Using Peer Effects

Dealing with segregation has to happen in a systemic way to affect the learning and social outcomes of kids. But it is super-hard to accomplish that at the city level, even with sympathetic politicians and school board chancellors. There are ways, though, that we can affect learning at the school or classroom level, without spending all our time fighting City Hall.

Children can be made to be responsive to adult influences broadly, if these can be applied in such a way as to affect the values and norms of peer culture. For instance, students in many Asian countries have very different school cultures from what we have here, and study way more on average than our students do, because getting into college is simply a matter of doing well on an entrance exam.[12] So while parents and teachers push students hard on their yearly exams (which are way more high-stakes than ours) and on their college entrance exams, that pressure is almost superfluous. The kids are already driven to study because doing well on standardized exams or end-of-year exams is how you get status from your peers in school, how you get promoted from grade to grade, how you gain entrance to college, and how you eventually get a good job.

In the United States, where we do not have such high-stakes exams, school-based peer cultures are responding to different external stimuli. Our high schools here are very different than in other countries—we have clubs, sports, and other activities that do not exist in schools in other countries. This affects how the school-based peer cultures look, as well as how important they are to American students.

What we want to emphasize is that peer cultures are responsive to external forces. But in this country, we are not going to do something so radical as to try to change the way students approach learning by instituting that degree of high-stakes exams. So then, practically, what can adults do to affect a peer-defined culture of achievement? First, you have to be sneaky. Indirect influence is often key. Kids do not respond well to adults trying to shape their behavior—other than maybe changing their behavior *in front of* those adults—but they respond to their peers. You also have to be courageous: changing individual children's behavior is difficult; changing their culture is ridiculously difficult. But you should keep in mind, it *can* be done.

Take, for example, bullying. Most approaches are top-down. And most approaches are ineffective. What kind of anti-bullying strategy works? One that, as we detailed in chapter 2, centers on making use of peer effects. One study used "influential" students in fifty-six New Jersey middle schools to get the word out online and in person about the dangers of bullying and school conflict. This masked the role of the researchers, ensuring that these student influencers were not seen as "stooges" or "confederates" of the researchers, but as independently motivated anti-bullying activists. After a year, these schools saw a 25 percent reduction in student conflict. High-status kids were able to change school peer norms around conflict, which led to dramatic results in conflict reduction.[13] No administrator or nonprofit organization could achieve such results. If administrators want to see change among students, they have to empower students to make that change, then step back.

What about teachers? The basic dynamic in a classroom is the classic "us" (students) versus "them" (teachers). Great teachers can get their classes to achieve at higher levels by motivating/manipulating their students to come together with the teacher as a group, rather than being split into competing factions, the bane of classroom management. Judith Harris, for instance, tells the story of "Miss A," a primary school teacher in the 1940s who was so good that her students performed well years after her class. Harris argues that what Miss A did so well was that instead of allowing the usual factionalism in a class, she created a sense of "groupness," of us (the entire class plus Miss A) versus the world. This made her so mythically amazing that Harris notes many of the school's alums recalled having been in Miss A's class, even though they weren't![14]

But most teachers are not great. Like, well, one of your authors, Syed. He was an English as a Second Language teacher in Coney Island, Brooklyn, in 1990, right when the Soviet Union was collapsing and thousands of Soviet Jews arrived as refugees. Many came straight to Syed's classes. And he was, at best, a mediocre high school teacher. (This is a very generous assessment he is giving himself.) One day his class was so out of control, he just dropped his head down on his desk in defeat. Irina, who sat right in front of him, turned from her conversation to face him and said sweetly and with compassion, "Mr. Ali, what is wrong?"

"Irina, you guys are killing me."

Irina, who had been in the country just a few months, reminded him how the world of schooling worked: "Mr. Ali, we love you. But you are the teacher, and we are the students. This is what we do." This was a moment of clarity for Syed, a mediocre teacher, that the educational system was inherently oppositional. Miss A, a great teacher, was able to convince the kids otherwise, to get all the kids to work with her. Syed could not even get the kids to settle down, and he lasted just a year and a half as a high school teacher.

(Side note on the sociology of classroom management. College classes generally do not have problems with classroom behavior. Why? College students do not have to be in the class—attendance, even if mandatory, usually isn't, and students do not have physical restrictions as they do in high school, like having to get a pass to go to the bathroom. Since high schoolers cannot leave the classroom and usually the building without permission, they often develop an oppositional stance to teachers, their jailors. College? You can leave the class anytime, so such an oppositional stance, even if you were an especially ornery and contrary student, would be pointless and find no support among fellow classmates. Also, individual classes in high school develop a kind of bounded identity [for the time they exist], and develop their own culture. Individual college classes tend not to develop bounded identities like high school classes, nor do they develop peer cultures, particularly for large classes.)

It is really hard to create a group dynamic that promotes learning for the whole class. So what should not-great teachers do? Anything that helps foster informal peer dynamics that promote academic achievement. For instance, they might start by imposing formal peer dynamics, like assigning study/work groups so that some, but not all, group members are high achievers. (We are not talking about assigning group projects, though! They are notoriously awful, because there is always the "free rider" who doesn't do anything. Any teacher who actually solves the free-rider problem deserves the Nobel Prize.) It is possible that through their interaction in these groups, the formal dynamic *could* turn into an informal one, even something resembling friendship. And that can improve academic performance. (Tina Rosenberg has a great description of this process and how it raised the calculus grades of Black and Latino students in Texas.)[15] We are emphasizing the word "could" because there is no guarantee here. And if the group is composed of all low achievers, it will not work, as the drive for academic achievement has to come from peers. Again, you can lead a horse to water, but you can't make it drink. If they are not studying or learning, that is not the teacher's fault. Or the parents'. On the flip side, if the kids are studying and learning, that is probably not a credit to teachers or parents—just a reflection of the norms of peer culture.

Syed's friend Gary, who used to teach physics at the Bronx High School of Science, the second-best public high school in New York City (after Stuyvesant), offers another example of peer effects. Year after year, he explains, his "regular" students did perfectly fine, B level work. Then one year, four honors students were placed into one of his four regular physics classes. So now he had a natural experiment: three classes full of regular students, one class with an additional four honors students. Since the regular students were randomly placed into their required physics classes, the presence of the honors kids was the only variation. And it absolutely changed the dynamic of the class. Classroom and laboratory discussions were better, performance on class exams was better, and scores on the New York State Regents Exams were better in the "experiment" classroom. Like the Stuyvesant grad quoted in chapter 3 who said that you did your work to avoid looking like a schmuck in front of your peers, the thirty or so "regular" kids in this one section of Gary's physics class seemed to not want to look like schmucks in front of the four honors kids.

Peer Effects and College Graduation Rates

College graduation rates in this country are pretty abysmal. In 2019 (looking at first-time, full-time students who started in 2013), the six-year graduation rate at public institutions was 62 percent, at private nonprofit institutions it was 68 percent, and at private for-profit institutions it was an appalling 26 percent. The overall six-year graduation rate for males was 60 percent and 66 percent for females.[16] That is a lot of students starting but not finishing undergraduate studies.

When President Obama took office in 2009, he made increasing college graduation rates a priority. Reports from major educational think tanks like the Gates Foundation and the Pell Institute followed, as did a major book from the president of the Spencer Foundation.[17] By and large, these reports found that major factors affecting graduation rates included financial aid (and the ways it is disbursed), student preparedness, university selectivity, and institutional effects.

One major factor present throughout most of these reports, yet often overlooked, is the importance of the social aspect of the university experience to graduation rates. While most view "social" as meaning the interactions students have with faculty, staff, and administration, others specifically point to peers. In his bold book, *What Matters in College? Four Critical Years Revisited*, Alexander Astin emphasized, "The student's peer group is the single most important source of growth and development during the undergraduate years."[18] In a similar vein, William Bowen, Matthew Chingos, and Michael McPherson wrote an authoritative 2009 book (authoritative because of their access to a broader and more detailed dataset than anyone else has had access to), *Crossing the Finish Line: Completing College at America's Public Universities*. They made the point that controlling for students' high school GPAs, SAT/ACT scores, and demographic characteristics still could not account for all the variation in graduation rates. They hypothesized that the remaining differences were principally driven by five broad sets of factors, the first of which was peer effects—academically capable peers improve the learning environment and promote graduation rates.[19]

Nearly all the major agencies and scholars who are active participants in this discussion about graduation rates are using state- or national-level data, and/or survey data. But for the individual university seeking to reflect and improve upon its own graduation policies and rates, Bowen, Chingos, and McPherson advise that "there is no substitute, at the end of the day, for addressing completion rate and time-to-degree issues at the level of the individual institution."[20] That is, they encourage individual schools to conduct a "micro-analysis," unlike the macro studies (including their own) that look at the problem as a nationwide problem.

We have not found any studies of individual schools that tried to ascertain why their graduation rates are what they are, or why they vary between students, but we are pretty sure that *informal* peer interactions will have a profound effect on graduation rates and time to degree. This is not to say that other factors such as financial aid, the classroom experience, interactions with administration, family obligations, outside work, and other factors do not affect graduation rates—they do. But informal peer effects will likely prove to be significant.

At the school where Syed works, Long Island University at Brooklyn, the vast majority of students are commuters, mostly from minority groups, often immigrants and/or the first in their family to go to college, and most take out loans for their education. In 2010, the six-year graduation rate for the campus was about 20 percent—to say it was not great would be an understatement. It was much higher, though, for students in the honors program and in certain majors like visual arts and media arts. (The six-year graduation rate had risen to 28 percent by 2017, but that could have been due to changes in counting. This is a 40 percent rise in graduation rates, which should have been cause for celebration, if real. But there was no celebration.)[21] It was also higher for students at the school who were in New York State's HEOP (Higher Education Opportunity Program), a program for "educationally and economically" disadvantaged students, at about 35 percent in 2010 (HEOP has since been discontinued at LIU).[22] The common factor that set apart the HEOP, honors, and visual and media arts programs was that all of them had their own physical space where their students could hang out, study, sleep—or do whatever. Unlike its peer universities, LIU-Brooklyn has no student center, and students who transfer out of the school often say they did so because there was little social life on campus. Students come, go to classes, maybe go to the library, then leave. The social glue of the hangout spaces created smaller peer groups and appears to have fostered the sort of peer culture that helps kids achieve.

Think back to chapter 2, in which the researcher Janice McCabe considered college students' friendship networks and how their structures corresponded to dropout and graduation rates. McCabe's "tight-knitters," who had only one group of close friends, graduated about half the time. But the students with more, and more varied, social connections with peers were more likely to graduate. In their huge study of public universities, Bowen, Chingos, and McPherson similarly found that students who lived on campus were seven to eight percentage points more likely to graduate than students who lived off campus. Basically, students benefit from proximity to their peers. They *also* benefit from going to a college where more students live on campus, even if they personally don't![23] Those same students, if they went to a school that had no student center and less social engagement, would be less likely to graduate, and if they did graduate, would take more time to do so.

For peers to affect each other, they have to be in contact with each other. "Good" colleges and universities all have dormitories, and the vast majority of students live in them. Schools without dorms could build them and require (or seriously encourage) students to live in them. Schools that do not have student centers could build them, and schools that have underused student centers could redesign, adding bells and whistles to encourage students to congregate and socialize.

There is even a much, much cheaper fix. Dorms and student centers are essentially physical spaces that allow students to congregate and interact informally, and importantly are not commercial spaces where you have to buy stuff (like a food court). Administrators could repurpose central spaces on campus as plain old hangout spots for students. We are *not* talking about space for clubs or other formal organizations. And you don't really need anything fancy, just open space, maybe with a handful of couches and pillars to lean your bags against. A somewhat open physical architecture that invites socialization would cost next to nothing and could have a huge impact on retention and graduation rates. Big change need not break the budget—provide places for hanging out, and you are halfway there.

Lessons from Stuyvesant High School

Stuyvesant High School is clearly a unique institution. The question is, Can we take the lessons we have learned from it about peer effects and peer culture and apply them to "regular" schools?

Every school has a peer culture, but not every peer culture places a premium on achievement as at Stuyvesant. Teachers and administrators, who widely want their students to graduate, go to college, and do well later in life, cannot force children to be achievement oriented, no matter how many college-focused assemblies they hold or college banners they tape to the walls. Few schools or school districts or cities will be able to devise a student body like Stuyvesant's, full of working-class and middle-class high academic achievers and strivers, but they can help shape a "social architecture" that will allow students the academic and social freedom to find themselves, in turn encouraging a peer culture that values achievement.

How can schools do that? They can start by bucking the trend of heavy discipline to trust students and increase their freedoms—say, to leave campus for lunch, etc. That is a risky move that requires responsibility on the part of the student. It is also politically difficult, because so many parents and politicians love having cops—sorry, armed "school resource officers"—roaming the halls and being surrounded by teenagers (what could go wrong?). That is, the barriers come from the fact that responsibility is not simply an individual's characteristic, but a learned and contextual behavior. If responsibility is part of the student culture (as at Stuyvesant) then giving students freedom is not that big a risk, even if some students do abuse it (as Syed did).

Nonetheless, freedom is the major element in re-creating Stuyvesant's peer culture. We cannot stress this enough. Kids will not be able to develop a peer culture that rewards—or at the least does not denigrate—academic curiosity and achievement unless they are given a long leash to explore. This is intellectual freedom, as well as a basic kind of physical freedom to roam, to get up out of your chair in a classroom as you listen to a lecture or to leave campus as needed. We can think back to the American study abroad student whom the writer Amanda Ripley observed in Finland. The American student commented that back in Oklahoma, she would never have had long stretches of time during the school day to herself or be allowed to go to the village coffee shop in the middle of the day, if she so chose. This was most certainly not how they did things in Oklahoma, she reported.[24]

Freedom also breaks down the likelihood that student culture will be oppositional, us versus them. That is helpful, because good luck teaching kids who are resistant to learning before you even start. The most extreme forms of nonfreedom, found in schools where kids walk down the middle of the hallways in silence and have to be quiet, with hands folded, in their classrooms (these are policies at an awful lot of "no excuses"–type charter schools), are almost comically ineffective when we imagine trying to promote a positive peer culture.

The second major element to promoting a positive peer culture within a school is trust. The peer effect works through informal mechanisms. Sometimes formal mechanisms work if they are *seen* as peer driven, like the anti-bullying campaign we have described. Another big success in recent years has been the implementation of restorative justice programs in middle schools and high schools throughout the country; rather than have administrators or the criminal justice system punish students, they have the students' peers work through issues and come up with solutions together.[25] Students in schools with restorative justice programs often feel that their schools are safer, and teachers feel closer with students. Out-of-school suspensions decline, and graduation numbers go up. This practice also interrupts the school-to-prison pipeline, which greatly benefits Black students especially, who are assessed out-of-school suspensions in public schools at roughly triple the rate of White students.[26]

The broader point is that schools can use a lighter touch in dealing with their students. By working on creating an indirect "social architecture" rather than attempting to directly shape students, administrators could create the conditions under which students themselves can successfully evolve a peer culture of achievement. That, in time, could lower rates of negative behavioral issues; spur better school performance, higher retention and graduation rates, and higher college attendance and graduation rates; and increase graduates' rates of occupational success. There are no guarantees that this will work, and it relies on school administrators to radically shift their basic thinking about kids to trust them and give them freedom. But it holds a great deal of promise and will not break the budget.

Defend Diversity, Affirm Diversity in Colleges

On many residential campuses, there already exist dorms (where roommates are often assigned randomly), open places to hang out, and students of different racial backgrounds.[27] Race-conscious affirmative action played a huge part in increasing the non-White student body, especially among the more selective colleges. The population of eighteen- to twenty-two-year-olds at these institutions is now close to or more than half non-White.[28] Affirmative action has made real cultural change on college campuses but not in society overall.[29] However, these changes are threatened. According to data in the 2018 *Students for Fair Admissions (SFFA) v. Harvard College* case, if race (as one of over two hundred factors) were removed, White student admits would increase over two times the percentage of Asian Americans, and the percentage of Blacks and Latinos would be reduced by nearly a half.[30]

The Coalition for a Diverse Harvard (CDH), of which Margaret is a board member, helped organize the rallies in Washington, DC, on October 31, 2022, as the Supreme Court had its historic five-hour hearing on affirmative action. Leading up to that day, she saw firsthand the real results of what a multiracial college student and alumni body looks like and how they can work together. CDH, along with the other amici represented by the Legal Defense Fund, planned teach-ins, cultural programs, op-eds, and social media campaigns.[31] Look at any news coverage of the affirmative action advocates outside of SCOTUS and you will see supporters representing a multiracial, pluralistic United States. Among the hundreds of students in DC that weekend from Harvard, University of North Carolina, Yale, Morgan State, University of Maryland, Howard, and more, Margaret met Kylan Tatum, a Harvard sophomore, whose ancestry includes his mother's connection to American enslavement and his father's connection to Vietnamese wartime.[32] Kylan said it succinctly to a reporter: "If you have a decreased number of Black, Latinx, Indigenous students on campus, there's going to be less opportunity to create diverse friend groups that expose you to worlds that you may not be aware of. . . . It'll have systemic effects, but it'll also have very personal effects on all students at these institutions."[33]

Workplaces and Precincts

Affirmative action works, full stop.

If you, a hypothetical manager, have a toxic workplace culture (a peer culture you have no say over), and you are serious about changing it, you need to hire better. You have to make sure that your many racist and sexist White male employees (let's be honest here) are surrounded by people who are not racist and not sexist. If you hire enough of these new people, they may be able to establish new norms that are less racist and less sexist. If that happens, and if it upsets racist and sexist White men (*It's too woke! It's too PC!*), well, they will have to either conform, quit, or get fired.

When it comes to changing workplace culture, nothing else comes close—not mentoring (mild effect), not diversity training (no effect and big expense)—to the effectiveness of affirmative action. Affirmative action works because it changes the composition of peer groups; if you make enough of a change to the peer-group composition, that can effect change to the peer workplace culture. If the end goal of management is retention and promotion of people whose paths in these organizations have been historically blocked (i.e., women and minorities), this is the most effective way to do it, as we discussed in chapter 4.

Firms are, however, reticent (or flat-out refuse) to hire and promote enough minorities to make the difference, let alone weed out the hold-outs who are reticent (or flat-out refuse) to change their ways and embrace diversity and its many benefits. These types of firms are probably happy to keep having diversity, equity, and inclusion (DEI) implicit-bias seminars that we know do not work but give the appearance of an attempt (which, crucially, provides legal cover from discrimination lawsuits).[34]

In a direct sense, leaders of companies cannot change aspects of the worker peer culture. Yet that anti-bullying program we have discussed offered a good idea for changing things indirectly. Basically, the researchers in that experiment trained a few key group members to influence the other group members. The cool kids already hold sway and define norms; their role here is in defining new norms. So, this is about finding the influential "cool kids" in the organization's lower echelons and tapping them as change makers. One possibility is for managers to hold events like "leadership training" seminars for their lower and midlevel workers. There, they could take the "cool kids," the ones other workers listen to, and try to instill in them the need to change certain norms (say, wouldn't it be cooler to have a chill office where women and minorities don't feel uncomfortable?). Even if it is just standard DEI messaging, its coming from peers could amp up its effectiveness. Managers train their influential employees in the norms they want spread, and the employees spread them, but without a direct connection to management (so that there is no devaluing of the peer message). The middle school kids did it, after all.

If organizations are willing to go further in their honest attempts at diversity, hiring non-White people to actually diversify the ranks, they need to pay attention to peer composition at the middle and lower levels, where informal peer culture is created. Hiring a new Black executive or two and appointing a Black female to the board are great efforts, and they can make for nice headlines, but they do not directly affect the peer culture in which most workers operate. The number of hires must be substantial, too. A small number of hires would have to assimilate to the already existing, possibly toxic workplace culture; a larger number can be bolder in trying to change the culture. Is this the only way that peer cultures can change? No. But with little change to personnel, the culture is not likely to change.

While doing talks for her book *Stuck*, Margaret learned that hiring more diverse workers at all levels is important, and it is even more important to retain them.[35] When companies consolidated or merged, less tenured Black, Latino, or Asian Americans employees were often lost or fired. There are lots of experienced non-White workers out there. Hire, retain, and of course promote them.

Again, at elite firms, the people managers hire are overwhelmingly White graduates of elite universities.[36] Midlevel hiring managers with diverse backgrounds, however, could make more diverse hiring decisions. Then, with enough women and minorities at every level, organizations' diversity can become self-sustaining, even with employee turnover. That is how you know you have changed the culture. Once that happens, it will be difficult to undo the norms in the informal peer culture, so the goal of diversity will become a workplace fact.

Police departments are totally different kinds of workplaces. As we argued in chapter 5, changing cop culture is an even bigger challenge. External supports for the status quo—legal, political, social—are incredibly deeply entrenched. You could completely change the demographics of the force, but unless it is done radically and quickly, cultural change probably would not take hold. Why? Because when they enter the force, cops learn to be "blue." Non-White cops learn that being "blue"—being police—is now their primary identity, while White cops, because Whiteness is a bedrock of cop culture, learn to be blue, but they are never asked to downplay their Whiteness. This is true even in New York City, where the majority of the police force is non-White. But the hierarchy there gets Whiter as you get to the top, including in the unions.

Could you change cop culture and peer relations as they did in the anti-bullying program? No. There is no incentive for White cops to change their behavior. Reform measures have been tried for decades, and they have all failed to ensure public safety, tamp down misconduct, or help departments clear (that is, solve) the worst criminal cases. Nothing short of a radical reorganization of policing as a concept will change anything. The police are one spot where we simply have to recognize that incremental change is not always possible. It will just be subsumed by the self-replication of cop-ness.

The easiest thing if you want to make police more respectful and less abusive and violent to the people they are supposed to protect and serve (especially the non-White ones), according to the peer socialization theory we have described, is two-pronged. First, fire the bad cops. That changes the peer group. Second, try to indirectly change cop culture by eroding all the incentives to bad behavior. For instance, local governments can change the terms upon which they negotiate with unions—only negotiating financials, and making disciplinary issues administrative rather than contractual. Municipalities can make cops personally liable for bad behavior by forcing them to have malpractice insurance, the way doctors do.[37] Along with those sticks, you might try some carrots: bonuses for not shooting your weapon, or successfully de-escalating situations, or having no citizen complaints in a given period. It is possible that changing formal regulations and personnel could do the trick. After all, cops have not always been trigger happy. The warrior mentality was developed, and it has been consciously spread and reinforced. Doing the opposite will mean facing considerable headwinds.

The London study we discussed in chapter 5 showed that bad behavior is transmitted, cop to cop, through peer effects. Can good behavior also be transmitted? Well, that depends on the culture. If good behavior is a norm that is rewarded, then yes. That is what happens at Stuyvesant, where the kids do their homework not because adults tell them to but because it is what their peers do—and if they don't do it, too, they will earn the disdain of their peers.

Unfortunately, good behavior is not a norm that is often rewarded in police culture. Cops get fired for *not* immediately shooting citizens. They get ostracized for speaking up about misconduct. All but the absolute very worst cops are kept on the job. When Breonna Taylor and then, only weeks later, George Floyd were murdered by police, it seemed as though change was viable—some of the largest crowds ever recorded, around the world, took to the streets to demand it! And yet, the movement really only succeeded in changing the conversation about police brutality, not in forcing real consequences or stopping it altogether. It did not change department funding, disband departments, or bring about that elusive "transformative change in policing."[38]

Cities and police departments will continue futzing around the edges, tinkering with things like considering requiring police to live in the cities they serve in, and administering even more DEI sessions. We know, however, that nothing will change in a substantial way until would-be change makers address the roots of police peer culture and leverage peer effects. Among the most pie-in-the-sky-est suggestions we have on reforming this particular workplace culture is to go big: start over. This is radical, threatens entrenched power brokers, and is by far the least likely thing to happen of all the ideas we have put forward in this book. Yet disbanding and reforming police forces around the goals of public safety and human dignity may be the only real way to build a new, safer cop culture.

The Promise of Peers

The approaches we take to so many different types of social problems we face tend to be ineffective and often quite expensive. Schools, politicians, and parents have convinced themselves that to have better outcomes for kids, we need some combination of better teachers, better curriculum, and more curriculum (more Advanced Placement exams! Take algebra in eighth grade!). None of this has really made a dent in improving learning outcomes overall, or increasing learning outcomes for minority students.

When talking about diversity in the workforce, managers are convinced that you can train bias away, and they have had a hand in building up a multi-billion-dollar DEI industry. Yet, DEI bias trainings have been shown time and again to be, basically, worthless.

And cops. Politicians, when forced by public protest, sometimes wring their hands and say we have to do something about police violence. Let's have more DEI anti-bias trainings. Let's have laws banning chokeholds. Let's have body cameras on officers. Though more often they just increase the funding for police and the number of cops (Put more cops in the subway! Put more cops in the community! Put more cops in schools!). None of these things has led to a reduction in police violence, or better community relations.

Kids, corporate workers, cops. When talking about social problems among groups in various situations, pundits think that the problem, and the solution, lie with things like parents, teachers, funding, and training. Maybe. We have tried a ton of possible remedies that address these problems. But we know from repeated experience that they do not work, and sometimes they make things worse.

The big idea we have put forward here is that we could take entirely different approaches to addressing these social problems. We have spent the pages of this book arguing that wherever you have a somewhat closed social loop, where groups draw boundaries around themselves, you will find that the behavior of group members is shaped by peer effects and the norms of a peer culture. If this is causing "problems" (killing, racism, bad grades) as defined by others, then changing that thing that is causing the problems very well might be your solution. Our peers affect who we are and who we become. We all instinctively know this. If peers are rotten and at the root of whatever problem it is we are talking about, we could try ways of changing peers, and hope that will affect peer culture.

Is it easy to do this? Of course not. If it were easy, it would have been done already. Cultures that are longstanding have a built-in legitimacy to them; to change them means that people inside and outside of that culture have to see aspects of their identity, their culture, as illegitimate, as immoral, as wrong. And then on top of that, they have to be motivated to change the culture, or at the least, to not stand in the way of change. People who have power in these cultures have a lot invested in them, and are loath to see them change in any significant way. To change a culture, and the peers in that culture, is a very long, fraught process. But it can be done.

ACKNOWLEDGMENTS

We'd like to thank the people who've been critically helpful to us for getting this book done. It took way too long to write, but we were in a pandemic, and what are you going to do?

Conceptually, our book owes a tremendous debt to Syed's graduate advisor, Murray Milner Jr., who passed away recently. His book on status processes and the Indian caste system and culture, and his book on status among American high school students had an indelible effect on much of Syed's earlier work, and Milner's influence on this book is crystal clear.[1] While we don't cite his work often in the book, it informs our analysis throughout.

For Syed, his wife, Eli Pollard, is an intellectual heavyweight who read the manuscript and challenged a lot of points in it. She made this book better. Their kids, Sami Ali, Noura Ali, and Jordan Pollard were somewhat helpful, too: they fed the cats.

Steven Thrasher is an old friend and brilliant journalist and scholar who has provided much merriment and company, and has been a critical sounding board over the years.

The fabulous author and Stuyvesant graduate Ada Calhoun taught Syed a lot about writing and publishing. She is very smart and helped Syed think through the book from a bird's eye perspective: What's it about? Who is it for? What's the big picture? These are obvious questions, but really, really hard to answer!

Syed's college friend and life mentor Will Seto helped Syed conceptualize many of the questions in this book. Chapter 4 grew out of a manuscript he wrote with Syed, "How to Do Diversity Programs Better." Unfortunately, no one wanted to publish it. Fortunately, though, it perfectly structured the chapter. Thanks, Will!

Herbert Gans, Margaret's dissertation advisor, always has keen insights, and his early acknowledgment (from his work in *Urban Villagers*) that we all live among our peer groups, including young children, helped shine light on concepts in this book.[2]

Margaret thanks her husband, Perry, who went to a Stuyvesant-esque public school in San Francisco—Lowell High School. He had many feelings on what we wrote, and we incorporated a few of his ideas. Alex, Meredith, and Winnie were also very opinionated, but not always on the Peer Effect. All were thoughtful and supportive.

In addition, Margaret is grateful to her Coalition for a Diverse Harvard Board members—Jane, Jeannie, Kristin, and Michael—for years-long conversations that sharpened her ideas on educational opportunity, work opportunity, social justice, racial justice, and affirmative action.

We are grateful for the PSC-CUNY Research Grants from the Professional Staff Congress, the union representing the faculty and staff of the City University of New York, and also to the Hunter College Presidential Advancement Fund, which supported the research and writing of this book.

We both want to thank Ilene Kalish and everyone at NYU Press for taking on this book and waiting patiently for a very, very long time while we got it done.

Lastly, we want to thank our wordsmith, Letta Page. While we were pretty sure that the book was good, once it got into her hands it got soooo much better. It helps that Letta, a degree holder in classics, knows more sociology than most sociologists. In fact, she has *forgotten* more sociology than most sociologists know. She pointed out flaws, she stressed good points, she suggested additions and subtractions, she said go read these things right now, and she gave the writing a good, spit-shine polish. We can't thank her enough.

NOTES

PREFACE

1   Syed developed the notion of peer effects among adult children of immigrants in these articles: Ali, 2005, 2008; Ali and Fokkema, 2014.
2   This is a critical point that Judith Harris makes abundantly clear in her book *The Nurture Assumption* (2009).
3   Lee and Zhou, 2015.
4   Carbado and Crenshaw, 2019; Harris, 2003; Katznelson, 2006; Lawrence and Matsuda, 1997; Williams, 2021.
5   Kao et al.'s *Company We Keep* (2019) is one exception.
6   Ali and Chin, 2018, 2019.

INTRODUCTION

1   See for example Burroughs et al., 2019.
2   Lareau, 2003. Two of the better, more recent sociological studies arguing for the importance of parents in kids' school lives are Jessica Calarco's *Negotiating Opportunities: How the Middle Class Secures Advantages in School* (2018) and Laura Hamilton's *Parenting to a Degree: How Family Matters for College Women's Success* (2016).
3   Chua, 2011.
4   Harris, 2009, 357.
5   Milner, 1994, 2004.
6   There are a great many ways to define culture, but this is not the place to go into that. Our discussion of culture, identity, and boundaries draws very heavily on the works of Fredrik Barth (1969) and Joane Nagel's (1994) discussions of boundaries and culture, and Murray Milner Jr.'s (1994, 2004) theorizing of status as a function of norms and intimate associations. People may disagree with how we conceptualize culture, finding it a touch idiosyncratic for their taste, and that's okay. The question for you, dear reader, is, Do you find that our conceptualization helps in analyzing the phenomena we are examining?

CHAPTER 1. GOOD SCHOOLS, BAD SCHOOLS

1   Christ, 2009.
2   Mader et al., 2018.
3   Thrasher, 2010.

4 Lance Freeman, an urban studies professor at Columbia University, is a big proponent of this idea. See Freeman, 2020.

5 Brooklyn Deep, 2019, episode 7.

6 See the data for K309 in New York City Open Data, 2022a.

7 New York City Open Data, 2020, 2022b.

8 Millheiser, 2014.

9 Waxman, 2020.

10 Delmont, 2016.

11 Turner, 1971.

12 Turner, 1971.

13 Delmont, 2019.

14 Delmont, 2016.

15 In the mid-1850s, the Chinese entered as all immigrants did—not needing any documents. There were also no medical examinations, or interrogations or supporting testimonies from White witnesses. At the finish of the construction of the transcontinental railroad, the relationship turned. The Chinese were no longer welcomed and were depicted as labor competitors, and morally inferior. On the streets the Chinese were often harassed, and there was an anti-Chinese movement with vigilante violence. In one example in 1871, eighteen Chinese were killed, some lynched, in Los Angeles, and there were many more violent episodes representing the driving out of Chinese from the United States. See also Lee, 2015, 2019; Pfaelzer, 2008. In 1882, just five years after Federal troops were pulled out of the South leading to the end of Reconstruction, the Chinese Exclusion Law was passed outlawing Chinese immigration and naturalization. Soon all Asians were excluded. Moreover, Japanese Americans were forcibly interned during World War II and faced discrimination even after the war. Interned Japanese American K–12 students had to go to makeshift schools located on the internment sites situated throughout the American West. See Okihiro and Ito, 1999.

16 Quinn, 2020, 11.

17 Quinn, 2020, 11.

18 Quinn, 2020, 11.

19 Lee, 2019; Quinn, 2020, 12.

20 Ngai, 2012.

21 Quinn, 2020, 13.

22 Berard, 2016; Lee, 2015; Ngai, 2012.

23 Madrigal, 2014; Sawyer, 2014. Areas such as the Western Addition (Black community), the Haight, Chinatown (Chinese community), and parts of the Mission (Latino community), where largely non-White populations lived, were marked as Fourth grade ("characterized by undesirable population or infiltration of it") in this map.

24 Bay Area Census, 1970.

25 Quinn, 2020.

26 The ethnic and racial groups were Chinese, Black, Latino, White, Filipino, Korean, Japanese, American Indian, "other."

27 Quinn, 2020.
28 There is a huge literature on the great migration. An accessible entering point is Wilkerson, 2010.
29 Massey and Denton, 1993.
30 Roberts, 2010.
31 Pinkney and Woock, 1970, 27.
32 Katznelson, 2006.
33 Nasheed, 2021.
34 Baum-Snow, 2007.
35 In New York City, a small number of schools, mainly charter schools, populated mostly by Black and Latino students, score seven or above.
36 Barnum and LaMee, 2019.
37 The Civil Rights Project, 2014.
38 Hannah-Jones, 2017.
39 Johnson, 2019, 12.
40 Orfield et al., 2016, 3.
41 GAO, 2016.
42 Jiménez and Horowitz, 2015, 42.
43 Jiménez and Horowitz, 2013.
44 Rosales and Walker, 2021.
45 Ali and Chin, 2018.
46 For example, see Renzulli and Evans, 2005.
47 Johnson, 2019, 3.
48 Stumpf, 2019.
49 Barshay, 2019.
50 Johnson, 2019, 210.
51 Johnson, 2019, 210.
52 Lassiter, 2021.
53 MacLean, 2021.
54 "Charter Schools," 2016; Loveless, 2013.
55 Barnum, 2019.
56 Monarrez et al., 2022.
57 There are thirty-two school districts in New York City.
58 Mader et al., 2018.
59 Mader et al., 2018, 11.
60 Mader et al., 2018, 12.
61 Mader et al., 2018, 20.
62 Ghartey, 2018.
63 Acs, 2011.
64 Stumpf, 2019.
65 Ripley, 2013, 138.
66 Ripley, 2013, 136–37.

67 Ripley, 2013, 139.
68 Barshay, 2021.
69 Barshay, 2019.
70 Viega, 2021.
71 New York City Department of Education, 2021.
72 Ali and Chin, 2018.
73 Shapiro, 2019.
74 Calder, 2022.
75 New York City Department of Education, 2022.
76 Gonen, 2018.
77 Shapiro and Wang, 2019.
78 O'Neil, 1992, 20–21.
79 Dwyer, 2018.
80 Oakes, 2005, 233.
81 Kahlenberg, 2016. For a detailed look at how Wake County did it, see Domina et al., 2021.
82 Potter and Burris, 2020.
83 Semuels, 2015.
84 Semuels, 2015.
85 Semuels, 2015.
86 Krauth and McLaren, 2021.
87 Wall, 2016.
88 Though that story is a little too involved for us to get into here, it is fascinating. The podcast is an excellent decades-long history of White parent involvement and disinvolvement with BHS and D15, well worth a listen. Joffe-Walt, 2020.
89 WXYStudio, 2018.
90 Viega, 2018.
91 Viega and Zimmer, 2019.
92 This was the subject of the second season of the podcast *School Colors*. Brooklyn Deep and NPR, 2022.
93 Hancock, 2011.
94 Ripley, 2013, 140.
95 Hancock, 2011.
96 Ripley, 2013, 8.
97 Ripley, 2013, 83–84.

CHAPTER 2. HOW THE PEER EFFECT WORKS IN SCHOOLS AND UNIVERSITIES

1 Milner, 2004.
2 Milner, 2013.
3 Chiang, 2017.
4 Chiang, 2017, 11.

5 Some highlights from these subfields: Crosnoe, 2011; Harding, 2009; Haynie and Osgood, 2005; Kandel, 1985; Kreager, 2008; Ueno, 2005.

6 For example, see Ali, 2005, 2008; Ali and Fokkema, 2014. Another earlier example comes from Herbert Gans's 1962 study of an Italian working-class neighborhood in Boston's West End. While peer effects are not the focus, he does note how as children start school, they learn the lore of their childhood group. In fact, their influence is so strong that both parents and school officials have difficulty competing with their peer group.

7 Harris, 2009.

8 How we choose peers is an important question. Arguably the most popular argument is that people choose peers on the basis of "homophily"—ethnic or racial similarity (Moody, 2001; Quillian and Campbell, 2003). However, Wimmer and Lewis (2010) looked at data from Facebook friends and make a convincing case that the emphasis on racial homophily is greatly exaggerated.

9 Westhill, 2021 is a very recent one—there is no shortage of them.

10 Fordham and Ogbu, 1986.

11 Lockhart, 2018.

12 See the recent review essay by Tyson and Lewis, 2021. Also see Desmond-Harris, 2017, which lays out the critique quite well, and in detail. Other major critiques have come from Downey and Ainsworth-Darnell, 2002; and Tyson et al., 2005.

13 Bouie, 2010.

14 Carter, 2005, 2006.

15 The classic monograph is by Willis, 1977. Also see Kruse and Kroneberg, 2022.

16 MacLeod, 2009, 188. By 1991, Blacks and other minorities made up 60 percent of the project's population.

17 MacLeod, 2009, 5–6.

18 MacLeod, 2009, 28.

19 MacLeod, 2009, 39.

20 MacLeod, 2009, 47–49.

21 MacLeod, 2009, 146.

22 MacLeod, 2009, 47.

23 MacLeod, 2009, 102.

24 MacLeod, 2009, 28.

25 MacLeod, 2009, 118.

26 MacLeod, 2009, 188.

27 MacLeod, 2009, 473.

28 Lewin, 2005.

29 Best and Bogle, 2014.

30 See Centers for Disease Control and Prevention, n.d.

31 New York State Bureau of Tobacco Control, 2021. Also see Richtel, 2021. As in the rest of the country, vaping in New York increased from 2014 (when they first

started keeping track) until 2018, so perhaps the 2018–2021 decline is also occurring in the rest of the country.

32 Brady et al., 2021; Best and Bogle, 2014.
33 England, 2016.
34 Armstrong et al., 2010.
35 Wade, 2017a.
36 Wade, 2017b.
37 Wade, 2017a, 35.
38 Wade, 2017a, 34.
39 Wade, 2017a, 36.
40 Wade, 2017a, 94.
41 Armstrong et al., 2010.
42 Wade, 2017a, 110.
43 Veenstra et al., 2018, is a pretty good, comprehensive review on youth peer effects. See also Cherng et al., 2013 on friendship networks. Many qualitative sociological studies focus on parents' influence, but give us glimpses of peer effects. See for example Dhingra, 2020; Louie, 2004; and Warikoo, 2022. Read also Sacerdote, 2011 about peer effects by economists.
44 Sacerdote, 2001.
45 McCabe, 2016.
46 See Jack, 2019.
47 Jack, 2015, 2019.
48 Illing, 2019.
49 Khan (2011, 80) writes,

> St. Paul advantages its students by giving them cultural resources that future institutions will then select upon and reward. . . . Students learn to be comfortable around such elite tastes and sensibilities and, more often than not, even be indifferent to them. The students at seated meal [a formal dining experience where everyone dresses up to eat surprisingly awful food] are not uncomfortable in their formal attire, nor are they anxious about dinner with faculty members. In fact, this is a non-event to them. They could care less. And this ease—which, it turns out, is far more valuable than merely revering and producing expertise—is what students at St. Paul's learn at seated meal and everywhere else.

50 Jack, 2019.
51 Paluck et al., 2016, 570.
52 Paluck et al., 2016, 568.
53 For the curious among you who look this paper up, in the text it says 30 percent, but in a correction, they amend that to 25 percent. Which is still pretty impressive.
54 Paluck et al., 2016, 571.
55 Mueller and Abrutyn, 2015, 131; Abrutyn and Mueller, 2014, 144.
56 Mueller and Abrutyn, 2015, 144.

57 Abrutyn et. al., 2020, 116.

58 Mueller and Abrutyn, 2016, 893–94.

59 Email communication with Seth Abrutyn, June 20, 2022.

CHAPTER 3. STUYVESANT HIGH SCHOOL, WHERE IRON SHARPENS IRON

1 Abdulkadiroğlu et al., 2014; Dobbie and Fryer, 2013, 2014; Taylor, 2015.

2 We asked to use people's real names, contrary to the unnecessary habit that sociologists have of anonymizing people's names by default. A few people chose not to use their real names. We have given them pseudonyms and put an asterisk next to their names when we quote them here. On why we shouldn't default to anonymizing people and places in qualitative research, see Murphy and Jerolmack, 2016.

3 Pinsker, 2015.

4 Data for 1986 come from Shapiro and Lai, 2019. Data for 2022 comes from New York City Open Data, 2022b.

5 Meyer, 2005, 144.

6 This park was right across the street from Beth Israel Hospital. Every now and again, especially as the weather got nice in the spring, there would be a student who was not a regular class cutter who drank way too much, and had to be dragged to the hospital to have their stomach pumped. This did not happen to the park regulars.

7 Shapiro and Lai, 2019.

8 The Century Foundation, 2019.

9 See Bowen et al., 2009, chapter 5.

10 Margaret worked summers, and during the school year she tutored middle school kids who lived in Stuyvesant Town. She earned enough to pay for excursions to the theater and such.

11 He started working in the summer before senior year and earned a GED rather than graduating from Stuyvesant. He matriculated at Northeastern University and now owns a test-prep/tutoring company.

12 Margaret noted on her college applications that she is an Asian American and a first-generation college student. Another activity that was included was her participation in the Youth Speak Out on NY conference, where she led a discussion on sexual health—including teen birth control and abortion.

13 Wade-Leeuwen et al., 2018.

14 Harris, 2003; Lawrence and Matsuda, 1997; Warikoo, 2023.

15 This is from a Facebook post he published on the Stuyvesant Alumni page in June 2018. Quoted with permission.

16 See Ali and Chin, 2018.

17 Corcoran and Baker-Smith, 2018.

CHAPTER 4. PROBLEMS IN THE OFFICE

1 Canseco, 2005.
2 Gould and Kaplan, 2011.
3 Gould and Kaplan, 2008, 19.
4 Gould and Kaplan, 2008, 6.
5 Gould and Kaplan, 2008, 12.
6 Gould and Kaplan, 2008, 1.
7 Brown and Laschever, 2012; Ouimet and Tate, 2020; Rosaz et al., 2016; Welteke and Wrohlich, 2019.
8 Murphy, 2019.
9 Murphy, 2019, 442.
10 Murphy, 2019, 438.
11 Chin, 2020b. From the 1970s till 2001, almost all of the garment shops in the New York City Manhattan Chinatown area were unionized by the International Ladies Garment Workers' Union (ILGWU). When large numbers of Chinese arrived after 1965 with the liberalization of immigration laws, the women entered the garment industry to replace the aging Jewish and Italian workforce. Sewing skills were learned on the job—as workers accepted lower pay for however many pieces of clothing they could finish. The Chinese women became the fastest-growing group in Local 23–25 of the ILGWU throughout the 1970s and early 1980s. It is no wonder since the ILGWU was known as a social union providing services such as English classes and family trips, in addition to health and dental benefits. Until 2001, most working-class Chinese women in New York City had a stint in a garment shop at some point in their lives.
12 Chin, 2005a.
13 Chin, 2017, 2020b.
14 Chin, 2012. Margaret was visibly pregnant when she did fieldwork, and many of the garment workers often gave her advice about parenting and how to manage work and children—including at this shop where they advised her to have kids alongside her as she worked.
15 The ILGWU needed these Chinese women members, just as much as the shop needed workers to sew union-contracted work.
16 Chao, 2021; Chin, 2005b.
17 Dimmock and Gerken, 2018; Dimmock et. al., 2018.
18 Dimmock and Gerken, 2018.
19 Dimmock and Gerken, 2018.
20 Dimmock and Gerken, 2018.
21 Tett, 2012.
22 Tett, 2012.
23 Dobbin and Kalev, 2021.
24 Dobbin and Kalev, 2021, 284.
25 Dobbin and Kalev, 2022.

26 Dixon-Fyle et al., 2020.
27 Kim, 2020.
28 Dobbin and Kalev, 2016, 2022.
29 See their highly influential book, Banaji and Greenwald, 2013.
30 Singal, 2017.
31 Greenwald et al., 2015.
32 Singal, 2017.
33 Goldhill, 2017.
34 Singal, 2017.
35 Chang et al., 2019.
36 Goldhill, 2017.
37 Dahl, 2016; Goldstein, 2018.
38 Ray, 2019.
39 Paluck and Green, 2009, 357.
40 Kalev et al., 2006.
41 Kalev et al., 2006, 590.
42 Milner, 1994, 36.
43 Chin, 2020a, 64, 68.
44 Chin, 2020a, 125; Lee and Chin, 2016.
45 Zahneis, 2020.
46 See also Wingfield, 2019.
47 Rivera, 2012.
48 Neely, 2022, 4.
49 Neely, 2022, 2.
50 Neely, 2022, 5–6.
51 Neely, 2022, 95.
52 Neely, 2022, 98.
53 Neely, 2022, 22.
54 Neely, 2022, 93.
55 Newkirk, 2020, chapter 6.

CHAPTER 5. COPS, PEERS, AND A CULTURE OF VIOLENCE

1 King, 2020.
2 Actually, the police have no legal duty to protect you, or save you. Listen to the incredible Radiolab episode by Parker and Qari, 2020.
3 Police departments' budgets tend to increase year over year, while the axe is always looming over other municipal departments. So, with every successful lawsuit against a cop, the Parks Department or Education Department takes the budgetary hit. See the set of articles by The Marshall Project, n.d.
4 Citizen Budget Commission, 2021.
5 Hayes, 2021. Also, see chart 8 and chart 12 in Office of the New York City Comptroller Scott Stringer, 2020, 12, 19.

6 In a very belated acknowledgment that plainclothes cops are a problem, the NYPD announced after two weeks of protests in June 2020 that it was disbanding units of plainclothes cops throughout the city and reassigning them. Then Eric Adams, who soon after became mayor, brought them back. Dorn, 2022; Joseph and Quigley, 2018; Pereira, 2020.

7 Greene, 2020.

8 Goldenberg, 2016.

9 Beauchamp, 2020a.

10 Hyland and Davis, 2019.

11 Quispe-Torreblanca and Stewart, 2019, 805.

12 Quispe-Torreblanca and Stewart, 2019, 805.

13 Horel et al., 2018, 3.

14 Horel et al., 2018, 29.

15 Wu, 2019.

16 Joseph and Quigley, 2018.

17 Li, 2017.

18 Our definition of culture may not accord with other people's. Again, we draw on Barth, 1969 and Nagel, 1994. They very astutely make it clear that culture and identity, and the boundaries that separate our identities, are inextricable, and you can't talk about one without talking about the other. The more cultural "depth" there is, the stronger the identity and the more defined the boundary separating people of that group from others.

19 The importance of norms—and the sanctions, or rewards and punishments, that uphold them—for culture is something that Milner, 1994 stresses.

20 The cop doing the choking, David Afanador, had earlier pistol-whipped a sixteen-year-old boy, breaking his teeth. He was tried, and, not surprisingly, acquitted. Finnegan, 2020; Lapin, 2020.

21 In an interesting side note, some websites noted that one of the cops, Thomas Lane, was known for tutoring Somali immigrant kids in his off hours—adding evidence that individual police can behave quite differently on and off the clock.

22 Arango et al., 2022.

23 Featherstone, 2017.

24 Weichselbaum and Lartey, 2020.

25 Weichselbaum and Lartey, 2020.

26 Sexton, 2018.

27 Nolan, 2020.

28 Sierra-Arévalo, 2019.

29 Treisman, 2022.

30 Associated Press, 2013.

31 Beauchamp, 2020a.

32 Weichselbaum, 2020.

33 Buehler, 2021.

34 Yan, 2016.
35 Finnegan, 2020.
36 Dingari et al., 2021.
37 James, 2009.
38 Drug Enforcement Agency, 2004.
39 Van Cleve and Trivedi, 2020.
40 Goldstein, 2018.
41 Beauchamp, 2020b.
42 Carlson, 2019.
43 Hvistendahl and Brown, 2020.
44 German, 2020.
45 This was a nonrandom sample, so is most certainly skewed to those inclined to respond, which seem to be Trump supporters. But Trump voters are largely White, and the police are largely White, so the results probably aren't *too* far off from the actual numbers. See Griffith, 2016.
46 Balko, 2013.
47 Balko, 2013, 202.
48 "Civil Forfeiture," 2014.
49 Balko, 2013, 158.
50 Balko, 2013, 202.
51 Balko, 2013, 185.
52 Balko, 2013, 158.
53 Balko, 2013, 259.
54 Balko, 2013, 205.
55 Balko, 2013, 244.
56 Balko, 2013, 245.
57 Stone, 2020.
58 This rate is roughly the same as Brazil and Bangladesh, and far higher than South Africa. Stone, 2020.
59 New York City Civilian Complaint Review Board, 2018, 22.
60 Robbins et al., 2020. For the database, see Umansky, 2020.
61 Morin et al., 2017.
62 Page, 2015.
63 Levinson, 2017.
64 Greenhouse, 2020.
65 Cunningham et al., 2021.
66 Aronczyk, 2020.
67 Cunningham et al., 2021.
68 Greenhouse, 2020.
69 Page, 2015.
70 Gallup, 2021.
71 Citizens Budget Commission, 2021.

72 Silver, 2014.

73 Finnegan, 2020.

74 United States Census Bureau, n.d.

75 Baker, 2020.

76 Devine, 2019.

77 Ungar-Sargon and Flowers, 2014.

78 Frosch and Chapman, 2020.

79 Lepore, 2020.

80 Lepore, 2020.

81 The Sentencing Project, 2019.

82 Fryer Jr., 2016. For similar research results in other cities, see a summary of research by Wihbey and Kille, 2016.

83 Frosch and Chapman, 2020.

84 Frosch and Chapman, 2020.

85 Frosch and Chapman, 2020.

86 Balko, 2021.

87 Balko, 2021.

88 US Department of Justice, 2017, 15.

89 US Department of Justice, 2017, 47.

90 Rayman, 2010.

91 Steier, 2013.

92 Rayman, 2012.

93 Goodman, 2015.

94 al-Gharbi, 2020.

95 DeGregory and McCarthy, 2021.

96 Rivlin-Nadler, 2016. For more demographic information, see New York City Civilian Complaint Review Board, 2022. As of November 2022, Asian Americans are 10 percent of the NYPD, while they are 14 percent of the New York City population. White police officers make up 43 percent of the force while they are 41 percent of the New York City population.

97 Fantz et al., 2015.

98 Katersky, 2015.

99 Board, 2022; Lee and Park, 2018.

100 Rivlin-Nadler, 2016.

101 Lewis, 2015.

102 Tso, 2016.

103 Rivlin-Nadler, 2016.

104 See Lartey (2016) for reactions to police accountability and reaction to Liang's probation and community-service sentencing. See Rankin (2016) for reaction from some in the Asian American or Chinese communities nationwide. Also, Nir, 2016.

105 See, for example, Kaba, 2020.

106 Cheney-Rice, 2020.

107 Smith, 2015.

108 Cheney-Rice, 2020.

109 Davis et al., 2018.

110 Thompson, 2020.

111 Olivier, 2020.

112 McCartney, 2020.

113 Beauchamp, 2020a.

CONCLUSION

1 Kotwal et. al., 2021, 3368, 3370.

2 Monarrez and Chien, 2021.

3 Semuels, 2015.

4 Domina et al., 2021; Parcel et al., 2016.

5 Brooklyn Deep and NPR, 2022.

6 Viega, 2022.

7 Amin and Zimmer, 2022.

8 Elsen-Rooney and Zimmerman, 2022.

9 Mervosh, 2021.

10 Armstrong and Hamilton, 2013; Jack, 2019; Khan, 2011.

11 Johnson, 2019.

12 See Ripley, 2013.

13 Paluck et al., 2016.

14 Harris, 2009, 228–31.

15 Rosenberg, 2011.

16 National Center for Educational Statistics, n.d.

17 Bowen et al., 2009; Engle and O'Brien, 2008; Hess et al., 2009; Johnson and Rochkind, 2009.

18 Astin, 1993, 398.

19 Bowen et al., 2009, 233.

20 Bowen et al., 2009, 235.

21 After 2017, LIU merged the data it reported to the federal government for its campuses, so recent numbers are not comparable to prior years. These and other graduation-rate data are available at the IPEDS (Integrated Postsecondary Education Data System) website of the National Center for Education Statistics of the US Department of Education (National Center for Education Statistics n.d.).

22 The HEOP graduation rate was shared with Syed by email by the then-director of HEOP. The numbers for HEOP were from a state report by the former director in 2009 (emailed to Syed January 7, 2010).

23 Bowen et al., 2009, 200.

24 Ripley, 2013, 97.

25 Augustine et al., 2018; Fronius et al., 2016; Gregory et al., 2016.

26 See for example, Morgan, 2021.

27 Sacerdote, 2001.

28 For example, see Harvard College data on the class of 2022. Chaidez and Zwickel, 2018.

29 Qiu, 2022.

30 Card, 2017.

31 DeVenny, 2022.

32 Kylan's father was born in Vietnam during the Vietnam War.

33 Rios, 2022.

34 Dobbin and Kalev, 2016.

35 Chin, 2020a.

36 Rivera, 2012.

37 Fields, 2020.

38 Subramaniam and Arzy, 2021.

ACKNOWLEDGMENTS

1 Milner 1994, 2004.

2 Gans, 1962.

REFERENCES

Abdulkadiroğlu, Atila, Joshua Angrist, and Parag Pathak. 2014. "The Elite Illusion: Achievement Effects at Boston and New York Exam Schools." *Econometrica* 82: 137–96.

Abrutyn, Seth, and Anna S. Mueller. 2014. "Are Suicidal Behaviors Contagious in Adolescence? Using Longitudinal Data to Examine Suicide Suggestion." *American Sociological Review* 79 (2): 211–27.

Abrutyn, Seth, Anna S. Mueller, and Melissa Osborne. 2020. "Rekeying Cultural Scripts for Youth Suicide: How Social Networks Facilitate Suicide Diffusion and Suicide Clusters Following Exposure to Suicide." *Society and Mental Health* 10 (2): 112–35.

Acs, Gregory. 2011. "Downward Mobility from the Middle Class: Waking Up from the American Dream." Pew Charitable Trusts, September 6. pewtrusts.org.

Ali, Syed. 2005. "Why Here, Why Now? Young Muslim Women Wearing Hijab." *Muslim World* 95: 515–30.

———. 2008. "Understanding Acculturation among Second-Generation South Asian Muslims in the United States." *Contributions to Indian Sociology* 42: 383–411.

Ali, Syed, and Margaret M. Chin. 2018. "What the Fight over New York's Elite Public High Schools Is Really About." *Atlantic*, June 14.

———. 2019. "It's the Peer Effect, Stupid: What Makes Schools like Stuyvesant Great? It's Not Test-Based Admission, but a Broader Culture of Excellence." *New York Daily News*, February 20.

Ali, Syed, and Tineke Fokkema. 2014. "The Importance of Peers: Assimilation Patterns among Second-Generation Turkish Immigrants in Western Europe." *Journal of Ethnic and Migration Studies* 41 (2): 260–83.

Amin, Reema, and Amy Zimmer. 2022. "Tensions High as NYC Soon Starts Middle and High School Admissions Season." *Chalkbeat*, September 14. chalkbeat.org.

Arango, Tim, Nicholas Bogel-Burroughs, and Jay Senter. 2022. "3 Former Officers Are Convicted of Violating George Floyd's Civil Rights." *New York Times*, February 24.

Armstrong, Elizabeth, and Laura Hamilton. 2013. *Paying for the Party: How College Maintains Inequality.* Cambridge, MA: Harvard University Press.

Armstrong, Elizabeth, Laura Hamilton, and Paula England. 2010. "Is Hooking Up Bad for Young Women?" *Contexts* 9 (3): 22–27.

Aronczyk, Amanda. 2020. "Police Unions and Police Violence." *Planet Money.* National Public Radio, June 5.

Associated Press. 2013. "California Study: Half of All Police Officers Don't Wear Seat Belts." *Denver Post*, December 11.

Astin, Alexander. 1993. *What Matters in College? Four Critical Years Revisited*. San Francisco, CA: Jossey-Bass.

Augustine, Catherine, John Engberg, Geoffrey Grimm, Emma Lee, Elaine Wang, Karen Christianson, and Andrea Joseph. 2018. "Can Restorative Practices Improve School Climate and Curb Suspensions? An Evaluation of the Impact of Restorative Practices in a Mid-Sized Urban School District." *RAND Corporation*. www.rand.org.

Baker, Thomas Owen. 2020. "As a Cop, I Killed Someone: Then I Found Out It Happens More Often Than We Know." *Guardian*, July 31.

Balko, Radley. 2013. *Rise of the Warrior Cop: The Militarization of America's Police Forces*. New York: PublicAffairs.

———. 2021. "Big Trouble in Little Rock: A Reformist Black Police Chief Faces an Uprising of the Old Guard." *Intercept*, December 18. theintercept.com.

Banaji, Mahzarin, and Anthony Greenwald. 2013. *Blindspot: Hidden Biases of Good People*. New York: Bantam.

Barnum, Matt. 2019. "Critics of Charter Schools Say They're Hurting School Districts: Are They Right?" *Chalkbeat*, June 11. chalkbeat.org.

Barnum, Matt, and Gabrielle LaMarr Lamee. 2019. "Looking for a Home? You've Seen GreatSchools Ratings. Here's How They Nudge Families toward Schools with Fewer Black and Hispanic Students." *Chalkbeat*, December 5. chalkbeat.org.

Barshay, Jill. 2019. "Gifted Classes May Not Help Talented Students Move Ahead Faster." *Hechinger Report*, April 15. hechingerreport.org.

———. 2021. "Proof Points: Gifted Programs Provide Little to No Academic Boost, New Study Says." *Hechinger Report*, April 19. hechingerreport.org.

Barth, Fredrik. 1969. "Introduction." In *Ethnic Groups and Boundaries: The Social Organization of Cultural Difference*, ed. Fredrik Barth. London: Allen and Unwin.

Baum-Snow, Nathaniel. 2007. "Did Highways Cause Suburbanization?" *Quarterly Journal of Economics* 122 (2): 775–805.

Bay Area Census. 1970. "San Francisco City and County, 1970 Census." Bay Area Census. www.bayareacensus.ca.gov.

Beauchamp, Zack. 2020a. "What the Police Really Believe: Inside the Distinctive, Largely Unknown Ideology of American Policing—and How It Justifies Racist Violence." *Vox*, July 7. vox.com.

———. 2020b. "Why Police Encouraged a Teenager with a Gun to Patrol Kenosha's Streets." *Vox*, August 27. vox.com.

Berard, Adrienne. 2016. *Water Tossing Boulders: How a Family of Chinese Immigrants Led the First Fight to Desegregate Schools in the Jim Crow South*. New York: Penguin Random House.

Best, Joel, and Kathleen A. Bogle. 2014. *Kids Gone Wild: From Rainbow Parties to Sexting, Understanding the Hype over Teen Sex*. New York: NYU Press.

Board, Marcus. 2022. "When Communities of Color Favor More Policing." *Washington Post*, May 19.

Bouie, Jamelle. 2010. "'Acting White' Just Standard Bullying, Racialized." *Prospect*, July 7.

Bowen, William, Matthew Chingos, and Michael McPherson. 2009. *Crossing the Finish Line: Completing College at America's Public Universities*. Princeton, NJ: Princeton University Press.

Brady, Hamilton, Lauren Rossen, L. Lu, and Y. Chong. 2021. "U.S. and State Trends on Teen Births, 1990–2019." National Center for Health Statistics.

Brooklyn Deep. 2019. *School Colors: Season 1—Brooklyn*. www.schoolcolorspodcast. com.

Brooklyn Deep and National Public Radio (NPR). 2022. *School Colors: Season 2—Queens*. podcasts.apple.com.

Brown, Kristine M., and Ron A. Laschever. 2012. "When They're Sixty-Four: Peer Effects and the Timing of Retirement." *American Economic Journal: Applied Economics* 4 (3): 90–115.

Buehler, Emily. 2021. "State and Local Law Enforcement Training Academies, 2018—Statistical Tables." US Department of Justice, Office of Justice Programs, Bureau of Justice Statistics, July. www.ojp.gov.

Burroughs, Nathan, Jacqueline Gardner, Youngjun Lee, Siwen Guo, Israel Touitou, Kimberly Jansen, and William Schmidt. 2019. "A Review of the Literature on Teacher Effectiveness and Student Outcomes." In *Teaching for Excellence and Equity*. IEA Research for Education, vol 6. Springer. https://doi.org/10.1007/978-3-030-16151-4_2 (retrieved August 18, 2021).

Calarco, Jessica. 2018. *Negotiating Opportunities: How the Middle Class Secures Advantages in School*. New York: Oxford University Press.

Calder, Rich. 2022. "Asian Students Are Biggest Losers in New NYC School Admissions System." *New York Post*, July 30.

Canseco, Jose. 2005. *Juiced: Wild Times, Rampant 'Roids, Smash Hits, and How Baseball Got Big*. New York: William Morrow.

Carbado, Devon W., and Kimberlé W. Crenshaw. 2019. "An Intersectional Critique of Tiers of Scrutiny: Beyond 'Either/Or' Approaches to Equal Protection." *Yale Law Journal* 129. www.yalelawjournal.org.

Card, David. 2017. *SFFA v. Harvard Court Documents*. 2018. David Card, Report, Page 108 (Dkt. 419–33 at 110). https://projects.iq.harvard.edu.

Carlson, Jennifer. 2019. "Revisiting the Weberian Presumption: Gun Militarism, Gun Populism, and the Racial Politics of Legitimate Violence in Policing." *American Journal of Sociology* 125 (3): 633–82.

Carter, Prudence. 2005. *Keepin' It Real: School Success beyond Black and White*. New York: Oxford University Press.

———. 2006. "Straddling Boundaries: Identity, Culture, and School." *Sociology of Education* 79 (4): 304–28.

Centers for Disease Control and Prevention (CDC). N.d. 1991–2019 High School Youth
    Risk Behavior Survey Data. Available at http://nccd.cdc.gov. Accessed on June 30,
    2021.

The Century Foundation. 2019. "The Benefits of Socioeconomically and Racially Inte-
    grated Schools and Classrooms." Century Foundation, April 29. tcf.org.

Chaidez, Alexandra, and Samuel Zwickel. 2018. "Meet the Class of 2022." *Harvard
    Crimson*. https://features.thecrimson.com.

Chang, Edward H., Katherine L. Milkman, Laura J. Zarrow, Kasandra Brabaw, D.
    M. Gromet, Reb Rebele, Cade Massey, Angela L. Duckworth, and Adam Grant.
    2019. "Does Diversity Training Work the Way It's Supposed To?" *Harvard Business
    Review*, July.

Chao, Eveline. 2021. "The Forgotten Neighborhood: How New York's Chinatown Sur-
    vived 9/11 to Face a New Crisis." *Guardian*, September 15.

"Charter Schools." 2016. *Last Week Tonight with John Oliver*. HBO, August 21.

Cheney-Rice, Zak. 2020. "Why Police Abolition Is a Useful Framework—Even for
    Skeptics." *New York Magazine*, June 15.

Cherng, H. Y. Sebastian, Jessica Calarco, and Grace Kao. 2013. "Along for the Ride: Best
    Friends' Resources and Adolescents' College Completion." *American Educational
    Research Journal* 50 (1): 76–106.

Chiang, Yi-Lin. 2017. "Due Distinction: Elite Student Status Hierarchies in China."
    Publicly Accessible Penn Dissertations, 2806.

Chin, Margaret, M. 2005a. *Sewing Women: Immigrants and the New York City Garment
    Industry*. Reprint 2015. Columbia University Press.

——. 2005b. "Moving On: Chinese Garment Workers after 9/11." In *Wounded City:
    The Social Impact of 9/11 on New York City*, ed. Nancy Foner. New York: Russell
    Sage Foundation.

——. 2012. "In the Factories and on the Streets: Studying Asian and Latino Garment
    Workers in New York City." In *Handbook of Research Methods in Migration*, ed.
    Carlos Vargas-Silva. Cheltenham, UK: Elgar Original Reference.

——. 2017. "Beneath Each Layer of Cloth." In *The Routledge Handbook of Asian
    American Studies*, ed. Cindy I-Fen Cheng. New York: Routledge.

——. 2020a. *Stuck: Why Asian Americans Don't Reach the Top of the Corporate Lad-
    der*. New York: NYU Press.

——. 2020b. "The Back Bone of New York City's Chinatown: Chinese Women and
    the Garment Industry, 1950—2009." In *Our Voices, Our Histories*, ed. Shirley Hune
    and Gail Nomura. New York: NYU Press.

Christ, Lindsey Whitton. 2009. "Principal of PS 20 Arrested for Attacking Teacher."
    InsideSchools, May 22. InsideSchools.com.

Chua, Amy. 2011. *Battle Hymn of the Tiger Mother*. New York: Bloomsbury Publishing.

Citizens Budget Commission. 2021. "Five Fast Facts about the NYPD's Adopted FY
    2022 Budget." Citizen Budget Commission, July 15. cbcny.org.

"Civil Forfeiture." 2014. *Last Week Tonight with John Oliver*. HBO, October 6.

The Civil Rights Project. 2014. "New York Schools Most Segregated in the Nation." Civil Rights Project, March 26. civilrightsproject.ucla.edu.

CNN News. 2015. "Tamir Rice Shooting." *CNN News*, December 12. www.cnn.com.

Corcoran, Sean, and E. Christine Baker-Smith. 2018. "Pathways to an Elite Education: Application, Admission, and Matriculation to New York City's Specialized High Schools." *Education Finance and Policy* 13 (2): 256–79.

Crosnoe, Robert. 2011. *Fitting In, Standing Out: Navigating the Social Challenges of High School to Get an Education*. New York: Cambridge University Press.

Cunningham, Jamein, Donna Feir, and Rob Gillezeau. 2021. "Collective Bargaining Rights, Policing, and Civilian Deaths." IZA Institute of Labor Economics, March.

Dahl, Melissa. 2016. "Don't Believe the Hype about Grit, Pleads the Scientist behind the Concept." *The Cut*, May 9.

Davis, Elizabeth, Anthony Whyde, and Lynn Langton. 2018. "Contacts between Police and the Public, 2015." Bureau of Justice Statistics, October.

DeGregory, Priscilla, and Craig McCarthy. 2021. "Ex-Cop Daniel Pantaleo Loses Bid to Get NYPD Job Back." *New York Post*, March 25.

Delmont, Matthew. 2016. "The Lasting Legacy of the Busing Crisis." *Atlantic*, March 29.

———. 2019. "There's a Generational Shift in the Debate over Busing." *Atlantic*, July 1.

Desmond-Harris, Jenée. 2017. "The Myth about Smart Black Kids and 'Acting White' That Won't Die." *Vox*, January 5. vox.com.

DeVenny, Keecee. 2022. "We Won't Go Back." Legal Defense Fund, November 3. www.naacpldf.org.

Devine, Miranda. 2019. "The 'Pantaleo Effect' Proves the City Can't Afford to Soften the NYPD." *New York Post*, July 28.

Dhingra, Pawan. 2020. *HyperEducation: Why Good Schools, Good Grades, Good Behavior Are Not Enough*. New York: NYU Press.

Dimmock, Stephen, and William Gerken. 2018. "How One Bad Employee Can Corrupt a Whole Team." *Harvard Business Review*, March 5.

Dimmock, Stephen, William Gerken, and Nathaniel Graham. 2018. "Is Fraud Contagious? Coworker Influence on Misconduct by Financial Advisors." *Journal of Finance* 73 (3): 1417–50.

Dingari, Chai, Adam Westbrook, and Brendan Miller. 2021. "'I'm Speechless': We Asked Law Enforcement Officers around the World How American Policing Looks from Abroad." *New York Times*, May 12.

Dixon-Fyle, Sundiatu, Kevin Dolan, Vivian Hunt, and Sara Prince. 2020. "Diversity Wins: How Inclusion Matters." McKinsey & Company.

Dobbie, Will, and Roland Fryer Jr. 2013. "Getting beneath the Veil of Effective Schools: Evidence from New York City." *American Economic Journal: Applied Economics* 5: 28–60.

———. 2014. "The Impact of Attending a School with High-Achieving Peers: Evidence from the New York City Exam Schools." *American Economic Journal: Applied Economics* 6: 58–75.

Dobbin, Frank, and Alexandra Kalev. 2016. "Why Diversity Programs Fail." *Harvard Business Review* 94 (7): 52–60.

———. 2021. "The Civil Rights Revolution at Work: What Went Wrong." *Annual Review of Sociology* 47: 281–303.

———. 2022. *Getting to Diversity: What Works and What Doesn't.* Cambridge, MA: Harvard University Press.

Domina, Thurston, Deven Carlson, James Carter III, Matthew Lenard, Andrew McEachin, and Rachel Perera. 2021. "The Kids on the Bus: The Academic Consequences of Diversity-Driven School Reassignments." *Journal of Policy Analysis and Management* 40 (4): 1197–1229.

Dorn, Sara. 2022. "Eric Adams to Launch 'Modified' Version of NYPD Plainclothes Unit." *City and State New York*, January 24.

Downey, Douglas, and James Ainsworth-Darnell. 2002. "The Search for Oppositional Culture among Black Students." *American Sociological Review* 67 (1): 156–64.

Drug Enforcement Agency. 2004. "Steroid Abuse by Law Enforcement Personnel: A Guide for Understanding the Dangers of Anabolic Steroids." US Department of Justice, March.

Dwyer, Jim. 2018. "Decades Ago, New York Dug a Moat around Its Specialized Schools." *New York Times*, June 8.

Elsen-Rooney, Michael, and Alex Zimmerman. 2022. "NYC Middle Schools Bring Back Selective Admissions, but to Far Fewer Campuses." *Chalkbeat*, October 26. chalkbeat.org.

England, Paula. 2016. "Is a 'Warm Hookup' an Oxymoron?" *Contexts* 15 (4): 58–59.

Engle, Jennifer, and Colleen O'Brien. 2008. "Demography Is Not Destiny: Increasing the Graduation Rates of Low-Income College Students at Large Public Universities." Pell Institute for the Study of Opportunity in Higher Education.

Fantz, Ashley, Steve Almasy, and Catherine Shoichet. 2015. "Tamir Rice Shooting: No Charges for Officers." CNN, December 28.

Featherstone, Steve. 2017. "Professor Carnage." *New Republic*, April 17.

Fields, Rarkimm. 2020. "Police Officers Need Liability Insurance." *Contexts*, June 12. contexts.org.

Finnegan, William. 2020. "How Police Unions Fight Reform." *New Yorker*, July 27.

Fordham, Signithia, and John Ogbu. 1986. "Black Students' School Success: Coping with the 'Burden of Acting White.'" *Urban Review* 18: 176–206.

Freeman, Lance. 2020. "Gentrification Facts and Myths: Let's Deal in Reality, Not Manufactured Fear." *New York Daily News*, November 9.

Fronius, Trevor, Hannah Persson, Sarah Guckenburg, Nancy Hurley, and Anthony Petrosino. 2016. "Restorative Justice in US Schools: A Research Review." WestEd Justice and Prevention Training Center.

Frosch, Dan, and Ben Chapman. 2020. "Black Officers Say Discrimination Abounds, Complicating Reform Efforts." *Wall Street Journal*, June 16.

Fryer, Roland, Jr. 2016. "An Empirical Analysis of Racial Differences in Police Use of Force." National Bureau of Economic Research, July.

Gallup. 2021. "Honesty/Ethics in Professions." Gallup News. news.gallup.com.

Gans, Herbert. 1962. *The Urban Villagers: Groups and Class in the Life of Italian Americans.* New York: Free Press.

GAO (US Government Accountability Office). 2016. "K–12 Education: Better Use of Information Could Help Agencies Identify Disparities and Address Racial Discrimination." US Government Accountability Office, April 21.

German, Mike. 2020. "The FBI Warned for Years That Police Are Cozy with the Far Right: Is No One Listening?" *Guardian,* August 28.

al-Gharbi, Musa. 2020. "Police Punish the 'Good Apples.'" *Atlantic,* July 1.

Ghartey, Saratu. 2018. "We're a Middle-Class Black Family: Here's Why We've Skipped Our Local Schools for Now." *Chalkbeat,* October 17. chalkbeat.org.

Goldenberg, Sally. 2016. "Records Show Increased Earnings for Officer Involved in Garner Death." *Politico,* September 12.

Goldhill, Olivia. 2017. "The World Is Relying on a Flawed Psychological Test to Fight Racism." *Quartz,* December 3. qz.com.

Goldstein, Joseph. 2018. "'Testilying' by Police: A Stubborn Problem." *New York Times,* March 18.

Goldstein, Katherine. 2018. "I Was a Sheryl Sandberg Superfan: Then Her 'Lean In' Advice Failed Me." *Vox,* December 6. vox.com.

Gonen, Yoav. 2018. "Brooklyn President Turns on School Testing Plan after Donor Backlash." *New York Post,* June 18.

Goodman, J. David. 2015. "Officer Who Disclosed Police Misconduct Settles Suit." *New York Times,* September 29.

Gould, Eric, and Todd Kaplan. 2008. "Learning Unethical Practices from a Co-Worker: The Peer Effect of Jose Canseco." IZA Institute of Labor Economics, January. Working Paper No. 3328.

———. 2011. "Learning Unethical Practices from a Co-Worker: The Peer Effect of Jose Canseco." *Labour Economics* 18 (3): 338–48.

Greene, Leonard. 2020. "Repeal of Shield Law Reveals Sordid Past of Cop Whose Chokehold Led to Eric Garner's Death." *New York Daily News,* June 22.

Greenhouse, Steven. 2020. "How Police Unions Enable and Conceal Abuses of Power." *New Yorker,* June 18.

Greenwald, Anthony, Mahzarin Banaji, and Brian Nosek. 2015. "Statistically Small Effects of the Implicit Association Test Can Have Societally Large Effects." *Journal of Personality and Social Psychology* 108 (4): 553–61.

Gregory, Ann, Russi Soffer, Easton Gaines, Aria Hurley, and Neela Karikehalli. 2016. "Implementing Restorative Justice in Schools: Lessons Learned from Restorative Justice Practitioners in Four Brooklyn Schools." Brooklyn Community Foundation, November.

Griffith, David. 2016. "The 2016 Police Presidential Poll." *Police Magazine*, September 2. policemag.com.

Hamilton, Laura. 2016. *Parenting to a Degree: How Family Matters for College Women's Success*. Chicago: University of Chicago Press.

Hancock, LynNell. 2011. "Why Are Finland's Schools Successful?" *Smithsonian Magazine*, September.

Hannah-Jones, Nikole. 2017. "The Resegregation of Jefferson County." *New York Times*, September 6.

Harding, David. 2009. "Violence, Older Peers, and the Socialization of Adolescent Boys in Disadvantaged Neighborhoods." *American Sociological Review* 74 (3): 445–64.

Harris, Judith Rich. 2009. *The Nurture Assumption: Why Children Turn Out the Way They Do*. New York: Simon and Schuster.

Harris, Luke. 2003. "Contesting the Ambivalence and Hostility to Affirmative Action within the Black Community." In *A Companion to African American Philosophy*, edited by Tommy J. Lott and John Pittman. Oxford, UK: Blackwell.

Hayes, Mike. 2021. "New York City Paid an NBA Star Millions after an NYPD Officer Broke His Leg: The Officer Paid Little Price." *ProPublica*, January 12. propublica.org.

Haynie, Dana, and Wayne Osgood. 2005. "Reconsidering Peers and Delinquency: How Do Peers Matter?" *Social Forces* 84 (2): 1109–30.

Hess, Frederick, Mark Schneider, Kevin Carey, and Andrew P. Kelly. 2009. "Diplomas and Dropouts: Which Colleges Actually Graduate Their Students (and Which Don't)." American Enterprise Institute.

Horel, Thibaut, Trevor Campbell, Lorenzo Masoero, Raj Agrawal, Andrew Papachristos, and Daria Roithmayr. 2018. "The Contagiousness of Police Violence." Unpublished ms., University of Chicago Law School. www.law.uchicago.edu.

Hvistendahl, Mara, and Alleen Brown. 2020. "Armed Vigilantes Antagonizing Protestors Have Received a Warm Reception from Police." *Intercept*, June 19. theintercept.com.

Hyland, Shelley, and Elizabeth Davis. 2019. "Local Police Departments, 2016: Personnel." Bureau of Justice Statistics, June.

Illing, Sean. 2019. "How Elite Colleges Fail Half of the Poor Students They Admit." *Vox*, June 17. vox.com.

Jack, Anthony. 2015. "What the Privileged Poor Can Teach Us." *New York Times*, September 13.

———. 2019. *The Privileged Poor: How Elite Colleges Are Failing Disadvantaged Students*. Cambridge, MA: Harvard University Press.

James, Susan Donaldson. 2009. "Police Juice Up on Steroids to Get 'Edge' on Criminals." *ABC News*, February 18.

Jiménez, Tomás, and Adam Horowitz. 2013. "When White Is Just Alright: How Immigrants Redefine Achievement and Reconfigure the Ethnoracial Hierarchy." *American Sociological Review* 78 (5): 849–71.

———. 2015. "Whitewashing Academic Mediocrity." *Contexts* 14 (3): 38–43.

Joffe-Walt, Chana. 2020. "Nice White Parents, Episode Five: We Know It When We See It." *New York Times*, August 20.

Johnson, Jean, and Jon Rochkind. 2009. "With Their Whole Lives Ahead of Them: Myths and Realities about Why So Many Students Fail to Finish College." Bill and Melinda Gates Foundation.

Johnson, Rucker. 2019. *Children of the Dream: Why School Integration Works*. New York: Basic Books.

Joseph, George, and Liam Quigley. 2018. "Plainclothes NYPD Cops Are Involved in a Staggering Number of Killings." *Intercept,* May 9. theintercept.com.

Kaba, Mariame. 2020. "Yes, We Mean Literally Abolish the Police: Because Reform Won't Happen." *New York Times*, June 12.

Kahlenberg, Richard. 2016. "School Integration in Practice: Lessons from Nine Districts." The Century Foundation, October 14.

Kalev, Alexandra, Frank Dobbin, and Erin Kelly. 2006. "Best Practices or Best Guesses? Assessing the Efficacy of Corporate Affirmative Action and Diversity Policies." *American Sociological Review* 71 (4): 589–617.

Kandel, Denise. 1985. "On Processes of Peer Influences in Adolescent Drug Use: A Developmental Perspective." *Advances in Alcohol and Substance Abuse* 4 (3–4): 139–63.

Kao, Grace, Kara Joyner and Kelly Stamper Balistreri. 2019. *The Company We Keep: Interracial Friendships and Romantic Relationships from Adolescence to Adulthood*. New York: Russell Sage Foundation.

Katersky, Aaron. 2015. "NYPD Officer Who Shot Brooklyn Man Indicted by Grand Jury." *ABC News*. February 10. https://abcnews.go.com..

Katznelson, Ira. 2006. *When Affirmative Action Was White: An Untold History of Racial Inequality in Twentieth-Century America*. New York: Norton.

Khan, Shamus. 2011. *Privilege: The Making of an Adolescent Elite at St. Paul's School*. Princeton, NJ: Princeton University Press.

Kim, Michelle MiJung. 2020. "Urgently Looking for Anti-Racism Training for Your Company? Start Here." *Medium*, June 4. medium.com.

King, Geoffrey. 2020. "Vallejo Police Bend Badges to Mark Fatal Shooting." *Open Vallejo*, July 28. openvallejo.org.

Kotwal, Ashwin, Shannon Fuller, Janet Myers, Daniel Hill, Soe Han Tha, Alexander Smith, and Carla Perissinotto. 2021. "A Peer Intervention Reduces Loneliness and Improves Social Well-Being in Low-Income Older Adults: A Mixed-Methods Study." *Journal of the American Geriatrics Society* 69 (12): 3365–76.

Krauth, Olivia, and Mandy McLaren. 2021. "Giving Up on Integration? Why JCPS Is Breaking Its Rules for Diversity in Schools." *Louisville Courier-Journal*, February 10.

Kreager, Derek. 2008. "Guarded Borders: Adolescent Interracial Romance and Peer Trouble at School." *Social Forces* 82 (2): 887–910.

Kruse, Hanno, and Clemens Kroneberg. 2022. "Contextualizing Oppositional Cultures: The Variable Significance of Gender and Ethnic Minority Status across Schools." *Social Networks* 70: 64–76.

Lapin, Tamar. 2020. "NYPD Cop Suspended for Caught-on-Camera Chokehold in Queens." *New York Post*, June 21.

Lareau, Annette. 2003. *Unequal Childhoods: Class, Race, and Family Life.* Berkeley: University of California Press.

Lartey, Jamiles. 2016. "Ex-NYPD officer Peter Liang Spared Jail for Killing Unarmed Man." *Guardian*, April 19. www.theguardian.com..

Lassiter, Matthew. 2021. "How White Americans' Refusal to Accept Busing Has Kept Schools Segregated." *Washington Post*, April 20.

Lawrence, Charles R., III, and Mari J. Matsuda. 1997. *We Won't Go Back: Making the Case for Affirmative Action.* Boston: Houghton Mifflin.

Lee, Erika. 2015. *The Making of Asian America.* New York: Simon and Schuster.

———. 2019. *American for Americans: A History of Xenophobia in the United States.* New York: Basic Books.

Lee, Hyein, and Margaret M. Chin. 2016. "Navigating the Road to Work: Second Generation Asian American Finance Workers." *Asian American Policy Review: A Harvard Kennedy School Student Publication* 26.

Lee, Jasmine C., and Haeyoun Park. 2018. "15 Black Lives Ended in Confrontations with Police: 3 Officers Convicted." *New York Times*, October 5.

Lee, Jennifer, and Min Zhou. 2015. *The Asian American Achievement Paradox.* New York: Russell Sage Foundation.

Lepore, Jill. 2020. "The Invention of the Police: Why Did American Policing Get So Big, So Fast? The Answer, Mainly, Is Slavery." *New Yorker*, July 20.

Levinson, Reade. 2017. "Across the U.S., Police Contracts Shield Officers from Scrutiny and Discipline." *Reuters*, January 13.

Lewin, Tamar. 2005. "Are These Parties for Real?" *New York Times*, June 30.

Lewis, Robert. 2015. "DA Says No Politics in Police Prosecutions." *WNYC News,* February 19. www.nyc.org.

Li, David. 2017. "Eric Garner Chokehold Cop Ties the Knot." *New York Post*, June 19.

Lockhart, P. R. 2018. "Michelle Obama's Story of 'Talking White' Shines a Light on the Complexities of Code-Switching." *Vox*, November 13. vox.com.

Louie, Vivian. 2004. *Compelled to Excel: Immigration, Education, and Opportunity among Chinese American Students.* Stanford, CA: Stanford University Press.

Loveless, Tom. 2013. "Charter School Study: Much Ado about Tiny Differences." Brookings, July 3. brookings.edu.

MacLean, Nancy. 2021. "'School Choice' Developed as a Way to Protect Segregation and Abolish Public Schools." *Washington Post*, September 27.

MacLeod, Jay. 2009. *Ain't No Makin' It: Aspirations and Attainment in a Low-Income Neighborhood.* Boulder, CO: Westview.

Mader, Nicole, Clara Hemphill, and Qasim Abbas. 2018. *The Paradox of Choice: How School Choice Divides New York City Elementary Schools*. New York: Center for New York City Affairs.

Madrigal, Alexis C. 2014. "The Racist Housing Policy That Made Your Neighborhood." *Atlantic*, May.

The Marshall Project. N.d. Police Misconduct Payouts: A Curated Collection of Links. *Marshall Project*. themarshallproject.org.

Massey, Douglas, and Nancy Denton. 1993. *American Apartheid: Segregation and the Making of the Underclass*. Cambridge, MA: Harvard University Press.

McCabe, Janice. 2016. "Friends with Academic Benefits." *Contexts* 15 (3): 22–29.

McCartney, Robert. 2020. "Police Critic Says Officers Need More Money and Less Stress, along with Greater Accountability." *Washington Post*, June 22.

Mervosh, Sarah. 2021. "In Minneapolis Schools, White Families Are Asked to Help Do the Integrating." *New York Times*, November 27.

Meyer, Susan E. 2005. *Stuyvesant High School: The First 100 Years*. New York: Campaign for Stuyvesant/Alumni(ae) & Friends Endowment Fund Inc.

Millheiser, Ian. 2014. "'Brown v. Board of Education' Didn't End Segregation, Big Government Did." *Nation*, May 14.

Milner, Murray, Jr. 1994. *Status and Sacredness: A General Theory of Status Relations and an Analysis of Indian Culture*. New York: Oxford University Press.

———. 2004. *Freaks, Geeks, and Cool Kids: American Teenagers, Schools, and the Culture of Consumption*. New York: Routledge.

———. 2013. "Paradoxical Inequalities: Adolescent Peer Relations in Indian Secondary Schools." *Sociology of Education* 86 (3): 253–67.

Monarrez, Tomas, and Carina Chien. 2021. "Dividing Lines: Racially Unequal School Boundaries in US Public School Systems." Urban Institute.

Monarrez, Tomas, Brian Kisida, and Matthew M. Chingos. 2022. "The Effect of Charter Schools on School Segregation." *American Economic Journal: Economic Policy* 14 (1): 301–40.

Moody, James. 2001. "Race, School Integration, and Friendship Segregation in America." *American Journal of Sociology* 107 (3): 679–716.

Morgan, Hani. 2021. "Restorative Justice and the School-to-Prison Pipeline: A Review of Existing Literature." *Education Sciences* 11 (4): 159–69.

Morin, Rich, Kim Parker, Renee Stepler, and Andrew Mercer. 2017. "Behind the Badge: Inside America's Police Departments." Pew Research Center, January 11.

Mueller, Anna S., and Seth Abrutyn. 2015. "Suicidal Disclosures among Friends: Using Social Network Data to Understand Suicide Contagion." *Journal of Health and Social Behavior* 56 (1): 131–48.

———. 2016. "Adolescents under Pressure: A New Durkheimian Framework for Understanding Adolescent Suicide in a Cohesive Community." *American Sociological Review* 81 (5): 877–99.

Murphy, Alexandra, and Colin Jerolmack. 2016. "Ethnographic Masking in an Era of Data Transparency." *Contexts* 15 (2): 14–17.

Murphy, Francis X. 2019. "Does Increased Exposure to Peers with Adverse Characteristics Reduce Workplace Performance? Evidence from a Natural Experiment in the US Army." *Journal of Labor Economics* 37 (2): 435–66.

Nagel, Joane. 1994. "Constructing Ethnicity: Creating and Recreating Ethnic Identity and Culture." *Social Problems* 41 (1): 152–76.

Nasheed, Jameelah. 2021. "What Is Redlining? How Residential Segregation Shaped U.S. Cities." *Teen Vogue*, February 19.

National Center for Educational Statistics. N.d. "Undergraduate Graduation Rates." nces.ed.gov.

Neely, Megan. 2022. *Hedged Out: Inequality and Insecurity on Wall Street*. Oakland: University of California Press.

New York City Civilian Complaint Review Board (CCRB). 2018. "Annual Report 2018." www.nyc.gov.

———. 2021. "Data Transparency Initiative: Current NYPD Members of Service." www.nyc.gov.

———. 2022. "Data Transparency Initiative: Current NYPD Members of Service." www.nyc.gov.

New York City Department of Education. 2021. "DOE Data at a Glance." www.schools.nyc.gov.

———. 2022. NYC Infohub: Admissions and Enrollment. https://infohub.nyced.org.

New York City Open Data. 2020. "2019–20 Demographic Snapshot—School." September 15. data.cityofnewyork.us.

———. 2022a. "2017–18—2021–22 Demographic Snapshot." data.cityofnewyork.us.

———. 2022b. "2006–2012 School Demographics and Accountability Snapshot." data.cityofnewyork.us.

New York State Bureau of Tobacco Control. 2021. "Milestones in Tobacco Control: Youth Tobacco Use Declines across All Product Types in 2020, Lowest Youth Smoking Rate on Record." *StatShot* 14 (3), September.

Newkirk, Pamela. 2020. *Diversity, Inc.: The Fight for Racial Equality in the Workplace*. New York: Bold Type Books.

Ngai, Mae. 2012. *The Lucky Ones: One Family and the Extraordinary Invention of Chinese America*. Princeton, NJ: Princeton University Press.

Nir, Sarah Maslin. 2016. "Officer Peter Liang Convicted in Fatal Shooting of Akai Gurley in Brooklyn." *New York Times*, February 11.

Nolan, Tom. 2020. "Militarization Has Fostered a Policing Culture That Sets Up Protesters as 'The Enemy.'" *Conversation*, June 2.

Oakes, Jeannie. 2005. *Keeping Track: How Schools Structure Inequality*. New Haven, CT: Yale University Press.

Office of the New York City Comptroller Scott Stringer. 2020. *Claims Report: Fiscal Year 2019*. Office of the New York City Comptroller.

Okihiro, Gary, and Leslie A. Ito. 1999. *Storied Lives: Japanese American Students and World War II*. Seattle: University of Washington Press.

Olivier, Indigo. 2020. "Police Budgets Are Ballooning as Social Programs Crumble." *In These Times*, July 22.

O'Neil, John. 1992. "On Tracking and Individual Differences: A Conversation with Jeannie Oakes." *Educational Leadership* 50 (2): 18–21.

Orfield, Gary, Jongyeon Ee, Erica Frankenberg, and Genevieve Siegel-Hawley. 2016. "Brown at 62: School Segregation by Race, Poverty, and State." Civil Rights Project UCLA, May 16.

Ouimet, Paige, and Geoffrey Tate. 2020. "Learning from Coworkers: Peer Effects on Individual Investment Decisions." *Journal of Finance* 75 (1): 133–72.

Page, Joshua. 2015. "The Shame Game: New York City Cops' Union and Power Politics." *Contexts*, January 8. contexts.org.

Paluck, Elizabeth Levy, and Donald Green. 2009. "Prejudice Reduction: What Works? A Review and Assessment of Research and Practice." *Annual Review of Psychology* 60 (1): 339–67.

Paluck, Elizabeth, Hana Shepherd, and Peter Aronow. 2016. "Changing Climates of Conflict: A Social Network Experiment in 56 Schools." *Proceedings of the National Academy of Sciences* 113 (3): 566–71.

Paoline, Eugene A., III, and Jacinta M. Gau. 2018. "Police Occupational Culture: Testing the Monolithic Model." *Justice Quarterly* 35 (4): 670–98.

Parcel, Toby, Joshua Hendrix, and Andrew Taylor. 2016. "The Challenge of Diverse Public Schools." *Contexts* 15 (1): 42–47.

Parker, B. A., and Sarah Qari. 2020. "No Special Duty." *Radiolab*, October 2. radiolab.org.

Pereira, Sydney. 2020. "NYPD Disbands Plainclothes 'Anti-Crime' Units." *Gothamist*, June 15. gothamist.com.

Pfaelzer, Jean. 2008. *Driven Out: The Forgotten War against Chinese Americans*. Berkeley: University of California Press.

Pinkney, Alphonso, and Roger Woock. 1970. *Poverty and Politics in Harlem*. New York: Rowman and Littlefield.

Pinsker, Joe. 2015. "America Is Even Less Socially Mobile Than Most Economists Thought." *Atlantic*, July 23.

Potter, Halley, and Michelle Burris. 2020. "Here Is What School Integration in America Looks Like Today." The Century Foundation, December 2. tcf.org.

Qiu, Linda. 2022. "Here's What Diversity Means for One Group of Harvard Students." *New York Times*, November 1.

Quillan, Lincoln, and Mary Campbell. 2003. "Beyond Black and White: The Present and Future of Multiracial Friendship Segregation." *American Sociological Review* 68 (4): 540–66.

Quinn, Rand. 2020. *Class Action: Desegregation and Diversity in San Francisco Schools*. Minneapolis: University of Minnesota Press.

Quispe-Torreblanca, Edika, and Neil Stewart. 2019. "Causal Peer Effects in Police Misconduct." *Nature Human Behaviour* 3 (8): 797–807.

Rankin, Kenrya. 2016. "Thousands Protest Ex-NYPD Cop Peter Liang's Conviction." *Colorlines*, February 22. https://colorlines.com.

Ray, Victor. 2019. "A Theory of Racialized Organizations." *American Sociological Review* 84 (1): 26–53.

Rayman, Graham. 2010. "The NYPD Tapes: Inside Bed-Stuy's 81st Precinct." *Village Voice*, May 4. villagevoice.com.

———. 2012. "The NYPD Tapes Confirmed." *Village Voice*, March 7. villagevoice.com.

Renzulli, Linda, and Lorraine Evans. 2005. "School Choice, Charter Schools, and White Flight." *Social Problems* 52 (3): 398–418.

Richtel, Matt. 2021. "Youth Vaping Declined Sharply for Second Year, New Data Show." *New York Times*, September 30.

Rios, Edwin. 2022. "US Students on Why Affirmative Action Is Crucial: 'They Need Our Voices.'" *Guardian*, October 30. www.theguardian.com.

Ripley, Amanda. 2013. *The Smartest Kids in the World: And How They Got That Way.* New York: Simon and Schuster.

Rivera, Lauren. 2012. "Hiring as Cultural Matching: The Case of Elite Professional Service Firms." *American Sociological Review* 77 (6): 999–1022.

Rivlin-Nadler, Max. 2016. "Police Union Turns Its Back on Cop Who Killed Innocent Man in Brooklyn Stairwell." *Gothamist*, January 28. gothamist.com.

Roberts, Sam. 2010. "No Longer Majority Black, Harlem Is in Transition." *New York Times*, January 5.

Robbins, Christopher, George Joseph, Jake Offenhartz, Zach Gottehrer-Cohen, Jacob Dobkin. 2020. "Newly Released Data Shows 1 out of Every 9 NYPD Officers Has a Confirmed Record of Misconduct." *Gothamist*, July 28. gothamist.com.

Rosales, John, and Tim Walker. 2021. "The Racist Beginnings of Standardized Testing." *National Education Association (NEA) News*, March 20. nea.org.

Rosaz, Julie, Robert Slonim, and Marie Claire Villeval. 2016. "Quitting and Peer Effects at Work." *Labour Economics* 39: 55–67.

Rosenberg, Tina. 2011. *Join the Club: How Peer Pressure Can Transform the World.* New York: Norton.

Sacerdote, Bruce. 2001. "Peer Effects with Random Assignment: Results for Dartmouth Roommates." *Quarterly Journal of Economics* (May): 681–704.

———. 2011. "Peer Effects in Education: How Might They Work, How Big Are They, and How Much Do We Know Thus Far?" *Handbook of the Economics of Education*, vol. 3, ed. Eric A. Hanushek, Stephen Machin, and Ludger Woessmann. San Diego, CA: North-Holland.

Sawyer, Nuala. 2014. "A History of Redlining in San Francisco Neighborhoods." *Hoodline*, June 3. https://hoodline.com.

Semuels, Alana. 2015. "The City That Believed in Desegregation." *Atlantic*, March 27.

The Sentencing Project. 2019. "Criminal Justice Facts." Sentencing Project. www.sentencingproject.org.

Sexton, Joe. 2018. "'I Don't Want to Shoot You, Brother: A Shocking Story of Police and Lethal Force: Just Not the One You Might Expect." *ProPublica*, November 29. propublica.org.

Shapiro, Eliza. 2019. "Desegregation Plan: Eliminate All Gifted Programs in New York." *New York Times*, August 26.

Shapiro, Eliza, and K. K. Rebecca Lai. 2019. "How New York's Elite Public Schools Lost Their Black and Hispanic Students." *New York Times*, June 3.

Shapiro, Eliza, and Vivian Wang. 2019. "Amid Racial Divisions, Mayor's Plan to Scrap Elite School Exam Fails." *New York Times*, June 24.

Sierra-Arévalo, Michael. 2019. "The Commemoration of Death, Organizational Memory, and Police Culture." *Criminology* 57 (4): 632–58.

Silver, Nate. 2014. "Most Police Don't Live in the Cities They Serve." *FiveThirtyEight*, August 20. fivethirtyeight.com.

Singal, Jesse. 2017. "Psychology's Favorite Tool for Measuring Racism Isn't Up to the Job." *The Cut*, January 13. thecut.com.

Smith, Mychal Denzel. 2015. "Abolish the Police: Instead, Let's Have Full Social, Economic, and Political Equality." *Nation*, April 15.

Steier, Richard. 2013. "NYPD Unaccountability: Boot the Messenger." *The Chief*, August 12. thechiefleader.com.

Stone, Lyman. 2020. "Above the Law: The Data Are In on Police, Killing, and Race." *Public Discourse*, June 23. thepublicdiscourse.com.

Stumpf, Alie. 2019. "I'm a White Teacher Who Chose a High-Poverty School for My Daughter: Here's Why." *Chalkbeat*, January 11. chalkbeat.org.

Subramaniam, Ram, and Leily Arzy. 2021. "State Policing Reforms since George Floyd's Murder." Brennan Center for Justice, May 21. brennancenter.org.

Taylor, Jonathan. 2015. *Policy Implications of a Predictive Validity Study of the Specialized High School Admissions Test at Three Elite New York City High Schools*. New York: CUNY Academic Works.

Tett, Gillian. 2012. "'An Anthropologist on Wall Street': Theorizing the Contemporary." *Fieldsights*, May 16. culanth.org.

Thompson, Derek. 2020. "Unbundle the Police: American Policing Is a Gnarl of Overlapping Services That Should Be Demilitarized and Disentangled." *Atlantic*, June 11.

Thrasher, Steven. 2010. "Inside a Divided Upper East Side Public School." *Village Voice*, February 23. villagevoice.com.

Treisman, Rachel. 2022. "COVID Was Again the Leading Cause of Death among U.S. Law Enforcement in 2021." National Public Radio, January 12. npr.org.

Tso, Phoenix, 2016. "The Splintered Message of the #Justice4Liang Movement." *GQ Magazine*, February 24. https://gq.com.

Turner, Wallace. 1971. "Many Shun Buses in San Francisco." *New York Times*, September 14.

Tyson, Karolyn, William Darity Jr., and Domini R. Castellino. 2005. "It's Not 'a Black Thing': Understanding the Burden of Acting White and Other Dilemmas of High Achievement." *American Sociological Review* 70 (4): 582–605.

Tyson, Karolyn, and Amanda Lewis. 2021. "The 'Burden' of Oppositional Culture among Black Youth in America." *Annual Review of Sociology* 47: 459–77.

Ueno, Koji. 2005. "The Effects of Friendship Networks on Adolescent Depressive Symptoms." *Social Science Research* 34 (3): 484–510.

Umansky, Eric. 2020. "We're Publishing Thousands of Police Discipline Records That New York Kept Secret for Decades." *ProPublica*, July 26. propublica.org.

Ungar-Sargon, Batya, and Andrew Flowers. 2014. "Reexamining Residency Requirements for Police Officers." *FiveThirtyEight*, October 1. fivethirtyeight.com.

United States Census Bureau. N.d. "Quick Facts: New York City, New York." US Census Bureau. census.gov.

United States Department of Justice. 2017. "Investigation of the Chicago Police Department." US Department of Justice, January 13. justice.gov.

Van Cleve, Nicole, and Somil Trivedi. 2020. "Why Prosecutors Keep Letting Police Get Away with Murder." *Slate*, June 5. slate.com.

Veenstra, René, Jan Kornelis Dijkstra, and Derek Kreager. 2018. "Pathways, Networks, and Norms: A Sociological Perspective on Peer Research." In *Handbook of Peer Interactions, Relationships, and Groups*, 2nd ed., ed. William Bukowski, Brett Laursen, and Kenneth Rubin. New York: Guilford Press.

Viega, Christina. 2018. "Brooklyn Middle Schools Eliminate 'Screening' as New York City Expands Integration Efforts." *Chalkbeat*, September 20. chalkbeat.org.

———. 2021. "Where Is NYC's Plan for 'Gifted & Talented' Admissions?" *Chalkbeat*, October 5. chalkbeat.org.

———. 2022. "These Schools Will Host 'Gifted' Classrooms as NYC Expands Segregated Program." *Chalkbeat*, May 24. chalkbeat.org.

Viega, Christina, and Amy Zimmer. 2019. "A Push to Integrate Brooklyn Middle Schools Is Starting to Show Results, according to New Data." *Chalkbeat*, November 14. chalkbeat.org.

Wade, Lisa. 2017a. *American Hookup: The New Culture of Sex on Campus*. New York: Norton.

———. 2017b. "What's So Cultural about Hookup Culture?" *Contexts* 16 (1): 66–68.

Wade-Leeuwen, Bronwen, Jessica Voyers, and Melissa Silk. 2018. "Explainer: What's the Difference between STEM and STEAM?" *Conversation*, June 10. theconversation.com.

Wall, Patrick. 2016. "Brooklyn's Middle Schools Are Highly Segregated—but They Don't Have to Be: How a Series of Choices Has Deepened the Divide." *Chalkbeat*, July 13. chalkbeat.org.

Warikoo, Natasha. 2022. *Race at the Top: Asian Americans and Whites in the Pursuit of the American Dream in Suburban Schools*. Chicago: University of Chicago Press.

———. 2023. *Is Affirmative Action Fair? The Myth of Equality in College Admissions*. Cambridge, UK: Polity Press.

Waxman, Olivia. 2020. "Nearly Half of New York City's Public-School Students Stayed Home to Protest Segregation in a 1964 Boycott: That Fight Is Still Unfinished." *Time*, September 22.

Weichselbaum, Simone. 2020. "One Roadblock to Police Reform: Veteran Officers Who Train Recruits." *Marshall Project*, July 22. themarshallproject.org.

Weichselbaum, Simone, and Jamile Lartey. 2020. "What Are Cops Really Thinking When Routine Arrests Turn Violent?" *Marshall Project*, June 26. themarshallproject.org.

Welteke, Clara, and Katharina Wrohlich. 2019. "Peer Effects in Parental Leave Decisions." *Labour Economics* 57: 146–63.

Westhill, Devon. 2021. "When Academic Achievement Means 'Acting White.'" *National Review*, March 8. nationalreview.com.

Wihbey, John, and Leighton Kille. 2016. "Excessive or Reasonable Force by Police? Research on Law Enforcement and Racial Conflict." *Journalist's Resource*, July 28. journalistsresource.org.

Wilkerson, Isabel. 2010. *The Warmth of Other Suns: The Epic Story of America's Great Migration*. New York: Random House.

Williams, Christine L. 2021. *Gaslighted: How the Oil and Gas Industry Shortchanges Women Scientists*. Oakland: University of California Press.

Willis, Paul. 1977. *Learning to Labour: How Working-Class Kids Get Working-Class Jobs*. Aldershot, UK: Gower.

Wimmer, Andreas, and Kevin Lewis. 2010. "Beyond and below Racial Homophily: ERG Models of a Friendship Network Documented on Facebook." *American Journal of Sociology* 116 (2): 583–642.

Wingfield, Adia Harvey. 2019. *Flatlining: Race, Work, and Health Care in the New Economy*. Oakland: University of California Press.

Wu, Katherine. 2019. "Study Finds Misconduct Spreads among Police Officers like Contagion." *Nova*, PBS, May 27. pbs.org.

WXYStudio. 2018. *D15 Diversity Plan: Final Report*. wxystudio.com.

Yan, Holly. 2016. "States Require More Training Time to Become a Barber Than a Police Officer." *CNN*, September 28.

Zahneis, Megan. 2020. "Diversity without Dollars." *Chronicle of Higher Education*, September 9.

INDEX